DISSENT EVENTS

Sean Scalmer is a Research Fellow in the Department of Politics, Macquarie University. He has written on topics from the history of the intelligentsia to the rise of the One Nation Party for a series of Australian and international publications, including *Alternatives, Labour History, Theory and Event,* and the *Journal of Political Ideologies.* He is a Sydney editorial correspondent for the literary and cultural magazine *Overland,* to which he is a regular contributor.

DISSENT EVENTS
PROTEST, THE MEDIA AND THE POLITICAL GIMMICK IN AUSTRALIA

Sean Scalmer

A UNSW Press book

Published by
University of New South Wales Press Ltd
University of New South Wales
UNSW Sydney NSW 2052
AUSTRALIA
www.unswpress.com.au

© Sean Scalmer 2002
First published 2002

This book is copyright. Apart from any fair dealing for purposes of private study, research, criticism or review, as permitted under the Copyright Act, no part may be reproduced by any process without written permission. Inquiries should be addressed to the publisher.

Every effort has been made to acknowledge all copyright holders. The author and the publishers would like to apologise for any omissions.

National Library of Australia
Cataloguing-in-Publication entry:

   Scalmer, Sean.
   Dissent events: protest, the media and the political gimmick
   in Australia.

   Includes index.
   ISBN 0 86840 651 1.

   1. Mass media — Political aspects. 2. Mass media — Social aspects. 3. Government and the press — Australia. I. Title.

   302.230994

Printer Griffin Press

CONTENTS

	Acknowledgments	vi
	Abbreviations	ix
	Introduction: What is the 'political gimmick'?	1
1	Translation	11
2	Staging	31
3	Diffusion	76
4	Theory	109
5	Media	137
	Conclusion	175
	Endnotes	178
	Index	212

ACKNOWLEDGMENTS

Anyone who publishes a book in the current intellectual climate is lucky and much assisted. Anyone who publishes a book on Australian political history from a radical perspective should probably buy a lottery ticket and distribute the winnings to a small army of supporters. Before I do that, I should pay public thanks to the many friends, workmates and institutions that have made it possible.

I started work on this book as a Macquarie University Research Fellow. That fellowship was generously supported by Winton Higgins, and introduced me to the comradely corridors of the Department of Politics. All departmental members have attended seminars at one time or another where I presented parts of this work. I thank them for their comments and their interest. Murray Goot has been a particular source of inspiration and assistance — throwing a torrent of articles and newspaper clippings my way, championing funding applications, and diligently reading large slabs of work. It was with Murray's help that I was able to attain a Macquarie University Research Grant and an Australian Research Council Postdoctoral Fellowship, and thereby to finish the work. Thank you also to those institutions for the financial support (i.e. for helping me to keep paying the rent).

Peter Browne of UNSW Press has been a model of friendliness and efficiency. Dennis Altman, Rodney Tiffen and Verity Burgmann all acted as readers for the Press, and without their sympathetic engagement and measured enthusiasm the book would either have failed to reach the light of day or would have been a whole lot worse. Others who read or listened to parts of this work in less official capacities include Ian Syson, Nathan Hollier, Robert Reynolds, Megan Jones,

Ken Wark and members of the Department of Social, Policy, and Curriculum Studies, Sydney University. Thanks to all of them.

Others have generously granted me access to sources. Meaghan Morris granted me access to her papers; (after help from Terry Irving and Beverley Symons) Eric Aarons and the Search Foundation granted me the right to reproduce images from the *Tribune* collection; Peter Browne helped with photographs from the *Australian Society* archives; (after help from Elizabeth Agostino and John Ellis) Melbourne University Archives granted me the right to reproduce images from the John Ellis collection; Patrick Dupont and the Melbourne indymedia group granted me permission to reproduce photos of the S11 protest from the latter's website (www.melbourne.indymedia.org). Librarians in the Manuscripts Room at the National Library of Australia and in the Mitchell Library, Sydney, have provided great assistance over many years. I owe a large debt to all.

I began this research after completing doctoral studies in what was then the Department of Government and Public Administration at the University of Sydney. Terry Irving helped me to learn about politics then, and continues to help and teach me still. Charles Tilly hosted me as a Visiting Fellow at the New School for Social Research, introduced me to the exciting world of social movement study, and continues to frighten me with searching questions and helpfully critical emails. Tim Rowse acted as a marker of my PhD and has since become a sensitive reader of almost everything I write. His rapid and useful comments on the complete manuscript are much appreciated. Stuart Macintyre also marked my PhD thesis. Since that time he has also become a great source of advice, friendly encouragement and intellectual guidance. Without his support I may have given up on writing a book at all.

Friends around the country and around the world have also helped in various ways. Thanks to Karen Burke, Hugh Kennedy, Lachlan Kennedy and Winona Kennedy for delightful accommodation and diversions (including Thomas the Tank Engine) during research trips to Melbourne. Thanks to Monica Dux, Eris Smyth, Ian Syson, Dan Syson, Harry Syson and Nathan Hollier for also helping to make those stays enjoyable.

Kurt Iveson and Nancy Griffiths provided a home away from home in Canberra, filled with fine times, culinary adventures and long chats. Many of the ideas in this book were worked out in conversation and email exchanges with Kurt, and I look forward to many more with this marvellous friend now at Durham University.

The book was finished while staying with Richard Short, Judith Smart and Jon Smart in London. Thanks to them for putting up with shifting moods and crowded lounge rooms, and for sharing the fun of superclubs and early mornings. Judith Smart compiled the index with her customary thoroughness, generosity, and intensity.

Other friends who helped and hindered with fun diversions (and who may want to see their name in print) include Pat Flynn, Buzz Coleman, Luke Chess, Trudy Phelps, Gina Laurie, Jam Dickson, Dave Tomley, Nikki Potent, Trisha Pender, Celia Roberts, Adrian Mackenzie, Robin Flynn, Gill Dempsey and Paul Martin. Gill Dempsey acted as a purposeful and engaged research assistant, and spent many long hours in front of a microfilm reader for the cause. Thanks and sorry for the eye strain. The Valentine family have been a more recent source of support and warmth.

The support of my own family has been invaluable. Joan and Kevin Scalmer were proud to get a son who made it to a university. Their continued pride and interest in the book at a very difficult time, along with that of my sister Simone Scalmer and my grandmother Merle Maloney, is very gratefully acknowledged.

My greatest debt is to kylie valentine. She has listened to long monologues, read every word many times, helped me back from defeats, tempered paranoid fears, and suggested new approaches. She has filled my life with her own love and fire, and made the years I spent working on this book happy ones.

ABBREVIATIONS

ABC	Australian Broadcasting Commission
ACTU	Australian Council of Trade Unions
ALF	Association for Love and Freedom
ALP	Australian Labor Party
ANU	Australian National University
ANNOD	Australian National News of the Day
BLF	Builders Labourers' Federation
CND	Campaign for Nuclear Disarmament
CPA	Communist Party of Australia
FCAATSI	Federal Council for the Advancement of Aborigines and Torres Strait Islanders
MLC	Member of the Legislative Council
NLA	National Library of Australia
NLF	National Liberation Front
ONP	One Nation Party
PKIU	Printing and Kindred Industries Union
SAFA	Student Action for Aborigines
SDS	Students for a Democratic Society
SOS	Save Our Sons
SMH	*Sydney Morning Herald*
SNCC	Student Non-Violent Co-ordinating Committee
UNSW	University of New South Wales
WEF	World Economic Forum

INTRODUCTION: WHAT IS THE 'POLITICAL GIMMICK'?

A MYTHICAL PREHISTORY: 13 NOVEMBER 1934

He jumped.

Comrades stood on the shore. Stickers proclaiming his right to land bedecked the ship. Stewards stood by his side. He had travelled 18 000 miles. He had been forbidden to land by the Attorney-General of the Commonwealth of Australia. The Congress Against War and Fascism, to which he had been sent as an international representative, had already begun.

He was on the lower deck of the *Strathaird*, between 8 ft and 18 ft above Melbourne Port, depending on which newspaper you read, or how foolish you thought he was.

But he jumped: a flabby, 49-year-old novelist, a Czechoslovakian pacifist, journalist, and amateur magician known colloquially as the 'rampaging reporter'. He scrambled over the ship's railing, pushed himself forward, flew, briefly, ingloriously, through the air, and landed with a thud on hard Australian concrete.[1]

The jump for freedom of Egon Erwin Kisch, 13 November 1934, could not be considered an immediate success by even the most ardent of anti-war activists. He sprained his ankle and broke his leg. His foot was stuck unceremoniously in a steel railway cable. He took no more than a few steps before he was surrounded by police and carried, amid severe protestations, back to the *Strathaird*.

The jump had been made for the most practical of reasons: Kisch had believed that once he set foot on Australian land, he would be arrested and detained on Australian soil. Instead, he was borne back to sea, and a series of legal challenges and state responses were set in train. Over the next few months he would be released after appeal to the

High Court; arrested again; face a dictation test in Gaelic; be sentenced to six months' imprisonment; appeal; have his conviction quashed; be sentenced to three months' hard labour; appeal; and begin negotiations for settlement. He would address countless meetings, generate enthusiasm for the growing campaign against war, and dent the political ambitions of the youngish Attorney-General, a certain Robert Gordon Menzies, who fruitlessly pursued this 'Red' for months.[2]

In a certain sense, Kisch's action and those that followed it had important precedents. His jump to shore and the demonstrations that followed in its wake represented a classic form of what sociologists have called 'contentious politics'. In each case, a public, collective claim was asserted that bore on the interests of other parties — a claim that Kisch be allowed to land in Australia, attend a public conference, and spread his anti-war message to interested citizens. In order to assert this claim, the peace movement used a whole range of political tools, from the display of banners to public rallies, from the distribution of leaflets to brave, foolhardy leaps.

In another sense, however, Kisch's action represented an innovative presence in Australian political history. Kisch leaped right onto the front page of major Australian newspapers. His single leap generated enormous publicity within the Australian media. From this point, he was invariably described in theatrical terms: as 'melodramatic', as the actor in a comedy-drama, as the recipient of publicity that rivalled a stage star.[3] For those struggling to oppose militarism in the 1930s, this was a peculiar, disorienting development.

Kisch's ability to generate publicity is made amply clear in Kenneth Slessor's satire of the affair, 'Bertha Blither's Adventures in Czechoslovakia'. In Slessor's imagination, the Kisch saga is reversed, and it is an unlikely Australian heroine, Bertha Blither, who is forbidden from landing 'where the Kischs come from'. This is a strange land, filled with unaccustomed sights. Blither leaps away from 200 Grenadier Guards, lands comically on the points of three bayonets, and converses with the movie star Bela Lugosi. Lugosi claims to be an old friend and admirer of Kisch, and is so impressed by the writer's newly won prominence that he asks if Bertha would collect an autograph from his now famous compatriot. 'He's got a perfect horror of publicity', Bertha deadpans. 'I don't think he'd come at an autograph, but he's a moral cert to let you have a signed photograph of himself on postcard'.[4] Europe and Australia, film and politics are confused; celebrity, photography and 'free speech' are mixed up in a heady brew.

The speech that Kisch had travelled to Australia to deliver at the Congress Against War and Fascism was now printed and distributed to 10 000 people. As A. F. Howells remembered, 'A month before Kisch would have been hardly noticed — now, he was big news'. He travelled up and down the east coast, greeted with rallies, cheers and substantial audiences. The Movement Against War and Fascism, which had previously struggled to get support, was now the subject of persistent interest. West Melbourne Stadium was packed with 8000 people to protest against Kisch's treatment. The Domain in Sydney, where Kisch first appeared to the Australian public, was filled with 20 000, and his short speech was followed by rousing cheers. At the demonstration's end he was surrounded by thousands of men and women — a collective bodyguard that shepherded him to Macquarie Street, shouting, marching and singing the 'Internationale'. The *Sydney Morning Herald* thought this a 'strange happening', the *Workers' Weekly* 'a wonderful, inspiring demonstration of the workers of Sydney against war and fascism'.[5]

Peace activists would later concede that the movement did not fully convert these public successes into organisational or policy victories. But the Kisch jump and its aftermath nonetheless stands as an important point of transition in the history of Australian politics. Public interest was not won through a series of small, local actions but through a spectacular activity and a blaze of subsequent media coverage. Organisation, the traditional tool of the labour movement, was less important than public communication through the conduit of the press. The tools of celebrity and theatre were being used to promote a radical movement. Indeed, if Kisch's ultimate success was a product of commitment by communist activists and courage on his own part, then it still seemed closer to a public performance than a manifestation of class war. Equally, the stage of Australian politics was also changing: it was now being invaded by flying 'foreign' performers and relayed to distant foreign shores.

Opponents of Kisch suggested that his message was irrelevant in Australia, while supporters pointed to his treatment by federal authorities as proof that fascism lurked in the Antipodes. Kisch himself was always attentive to the circulation of his fate from Australia to Europe. He argued persistently that the actions of the state made Australia a laughing-stock in the wider world. His racy account of Australian experiences, *Australian Landfall*, traces the newspaper reports that were cabled to London and Germany, and documents how European reactions to such reports shaped Australian politics. An endorsement of Menzies' actions by the German Government strengthened the Australian Government's resolve; British criticism eroded public support for the action; British reports on Kisch's writerly reputation reassured Australians that he was not simply a 'trouble-maker'.[6]

This passage of news reports from Australia to Europe continued to shape the reputation of the Czechoslovakian. When Kisch returned to Paris in 1935, he was welcomed by 1500 at a banquet in his honour. But this was not reported in the regular Australian press, and Australian supporters lamented their distance from 'the busy stream of world communication which lies near the pumping heart of humanity'.

When Kisch's book was reprinted, nearly half a century later, one Australian writer worried that this apparently 'malicious' picture of Australia would be 'circulating anew in Europe'.[7]

Kisch's landfall, then, gestured at what seemed to many Australians a new form of politics — powerful, theatrical, media-enhanced, internationally attuned. It promised new resources and techniques for those who wanted to make public claims and to contend for power. It suggested that rapid political mobilisation may be more successfully achieved working *through* rather than against the burgeoning media. It promised a cosmopolitan, worldly form of politics in the Antipodes — a politics that connected Australia with the world rather than retreated from it.

Indeed, it is tempting today to read Kisch's jump as metaphor: the soaring, liberating entry of a 'foreign' form of political activity onto Australian soil; an exotic foreign species that would attempt to thrive in the very different Australian environment. But how would this form of politics operate in Australia? To what ends would it be put? Did Australian citizens, with their trade unions and Labor parties, committed Communists and Catholic reformists, have any need of it at all?

Certainly, as the next two decades passed, it would have seemed not. As Depression, World and then Cold War rapidly followed, there were few signs of local political activity that resembled Kisch's exhilarating leap. The electoral rally outranked the publicity stunt, the collective strike the theatrical demonstration, the numbers game the flying leap. It was not until nearly a quarter of a century had passed, in February 1966, that the roving historian's eye notices a similar event that embraced and even extended Kisch's astonishing legacy.

A MYTH OF AUSTRALIAN DISCOVERY: THE PROCLAMATION OF THE 'POLITICAL GIMMICK', 2 FEBRUARY 1966

On 2 February 1966, something interesting happened during the early evening in Belmore Park, Sydney. Three men, all in their late teens or early twenties, burnt their national service registration papers in front of an audience of approximately 200 people. 'This is a political gimmick, and I refuse to go to Vietnam', Wayne Haylen was reported to have said as he stood atop a large box, brandishing a folded square of blazing paper for the photographers of the major Australian newspapers. He was succeeded by Barry Robinson and Greg Barker, both of whom echoed his opposition to fighting as a conscript in Vietnam, as the crowd cheered and sang 'For He's a Jolly Good Fellow'.[8]

This was the first documented case of 'draft card burning' in Australia. It came at the end of a day of disorganised and frustrating anti-conscription protest. Earlier on, members of the Youth Campaign

Against Conscription and the Save Our Sons (SOS) movement had assembled at Central Railway Station, planning to demonstrate as a contingent of conscripted national servicemen left for army training camp at Singleton. The departure of national servicemen had already provided a platform for protest activity in July and September 1965. On both these prior occasions, demonstrators had gained useful publicity when they had swarmed onto the station concourse, battled with police, struggled to hold up anti-conscription placards, and then bowed their heads as the trains pulled away. A similar protest was planned.

But this time the army wrongfooted opponents by secretly moving the conscripts out of Sydney by bus and plane on the previous day. As a result, on 2 February the anti-conscription demonstrators seemingly 'had nothing to demonstrate against', as one newspaper put it unkindly.[9] They milled about the railway station aimlessly, attempting to come to grips with the ruse, even claiming symbolic victory, until an impromptu speech urged those attendant to march down to Belmore Park for a protest meeting. It was here that the unprecedented burning of draft cards occurred, and front-page newspaper coverage was secured by an apparently spontaneous, theatrical, novel political event.

It was the beginning of a wave of similar actions. Over the next few months draft cards would be burnt publicly by a nervous Robin Melrose at Sydney University, by twelve protesters in Hyde Park, Sydney, by John Marchant of the Eureka Youth League, by demonstrators in Perth and outside the US Consulate in Adelaide. Fire became a potent political symbol, summoning up the self-immolation of Buddhist monks in South Vietnam, and drawing more direct inspiration from the draft card burnings of American peace protesters.[10] Draft card burner and leader of the Youth Campaign Against Conscription, Barry Robinson, argued that such actions would continue:

> Draft card burning will go on.
>
> More cards will be destroyed at the [approaching] demonstration. But this is an ongoing campaign.
>
> Some people will burn their cards as they receive them.

While angry correspondents mocked the childishness of the young protesters, the anti-conscription movement gained generous media coverage. Indeed, the prospect of draft card burnings was even used to promote forthcoming demonstrations.[11]

Clearly, a new form of public claim-making was developing. If the Kisch affair gestured at the power of the theatrical action, then the draft card burning demonstrated that activists now clearly understood such power. If Kisch's quite practically minded jump became a kind of political symbol, then the actions of the Sydney anti-conscriptionists were almost purely symbolic in nature. Their direct impact on the system of conscription was negligible, their ability to dramatise and foment opposition to that system, considerable.

Critics of draft card burning thought that it was infantile and self-important — 'a chance to get one's name in the paper'. Strikingly, the adherents of this strange new performance did not deny such an aim. They felt, nonetheless, that the theatrical action communicated a powerful message to television watchers and newspaper readers alike — a sense of political seriousness and absolute opposition to conscription; a newly won illegal status that demonstrated a dedication to 'the movement'; a desire to bring those wavering onto the side of anti-conscription through sincere, if disruptive display. Others still attempted to indigenise the action, constructing an imaginary link between the anti-conscriptionists of the 1960s and the Eureka miners of 1854:

> We being opposed to the National Service Act and the Vietnam War are also revolting against unjust Government. The miners in 1854 burnt their mining licenses; twenty-year olds today are burning their call-up papers ... Both acts being illegal they serve to illustrate the sincerity with which the opposition to unjust rule is held by the people concerned.[12]

But despite the resonances with Eureka, this action still seemed different, unfamiliar, almost 'unpolitical' in its recourse to theatre and symbolism. If the 'political gimmick' drew from a stock of quite established actions — demonstrations, ritual burnings, leaps, rallies and petitions — it used and modified them in quite unaccustomed ways. Whereas members of political movements had traditionally attempted to present their collective cause as worthy, unified, numerous and committed, the actions associated with the 'political gimmick' had no such intention. Its uses seemed more varied and sometimes doubtful. It was often scandalous, outrageous, or reliant on very small numbers. Although it sometimes involved law-breaking, it could also include the urge to escape rather than accept the state's penalty. It was faintly disreputable, tarnished — a 'gimmick'.[13]

For those interested in the history of grand debates and public policies, the 'political gimmick' has usually appeared as an eruption, an intrusion. It is not 'rational', but theatrical; it does not establish an argument, but a claim to public attention. Its aim is 'publicity' — entry into the public realm, not the subtle massaging or robust chiselling of 'public opinion'. Its methods are 'shocking' rather than uplifting — the cream pie delivered to the face; the surfboard paddled at the front of the warship. Its impacts are sometimes counterproductive — the demonstration marked by smashed windows; the blocked traffic that alienates the cab-driver. It is no coincidence that the biography of 'the great demonstrator' is rarely written. Indeed, for many it would appear to be a contradiction in terms. 'Great' historical figures may occasionally attend demonstrations, but they are rarely identified with them;

they may participate in political gimmicks, but they are almost never defined by them.

Equally, for those most interested in social change, the 'political gimmick' has also failed to elicit much enthusiasm or interest. Burning a draft card does not make a revolution. Regimes have seldom been overturned by creative and theatrical political performances. Large-scale change is usually understood to require numbers, organisation, and sometimes arms. Alongside such heroic actions, the political gimmick seems to pale. Like a firecracker on bonfire night, its very use is most often understood to constitute its exhaustion. It is disposable rather than enduring, diverting rather than typically inspiring.

It is true that as protesters burned their draft cards in February 1966, their aspirations seemed more limited than grand, more symbolic than discursive. They aimed to perform self-consciously theatrical gestures, to attain 'newsworthiness', and therefore draw the attention of television and print journalists. That is, they aimed to produce 'publicity' by their own actions, and thereby to advance their own political cause.

Thought of in this way, the events in Belmore Park can serve as a kind of (imperfect) historical marker. Clearly, political actors were beginning to understand the mass media's appetite for startling theatrical images and to adjust their behaviour accordingly. A new dynamic was at play. Indeed, alongside the burning of draft cards, other forms of theatrical political activity were also being adopted: sit-ins, teach-ins, picketing, paint-throwing. The repertoire of 'expressive' political activity that academics would come to associate with the New Left and the new social movements was being taken up in a period of extensive political ferment.

The age of the political gimmick, when thousands of citizens would take up and extend the actions of Kisch, Haylen, Robinson and Barker, was dawning. But what was this age, and what were the rules governing this new moment? The era of the political gimmick can be defined on the basis of a relationship, an aim, a method, a dynamic, and a dilemma.

- *The relationship*: between political actors and the contemporary media.
- *The aim*: publicity.
- *The method*: theatrical performances that symbolise demands.
- *The dynamic*: as new theatrical performances become more acceptable and routine, they become increasingly less appealing to the media and therefore less able to achieve publicity; hence there is a dynamic of constant invention.
- *The dilemma*: if the disruptive elements of theatrical performance become too great, they become counterproductive; hence there is a danger that if performances are too routine they will not achieve publicity, yet if they are too challenging they will bring only infamy.

In different ways, a number of scholars have recognised all or part of these conditions. A cluster of sociologists have emphasised the importance of drama to the operation of contemporary social movements.[14] Others have recognised that the presence of the media shapes the strategy, tactics and organisational activities of contemporary challengers.[15] In an environment saturated by communications media, it has increasingly been understood that political protesters will explicitly aim to draw the attention of reporters, generate publicity, and thereby reach their fellow consumers of the mass media (who are also their fellow citizens). More than that, a number of studies have argued that political activists attempt to take account of which protests are reported by the media, and to shape their behaviour accordingly — they are involved in 'mediatised' politics (see Chapter 5).[16]

For a large number of observers, this close relationship between the media and movements has been understood as self-defeating. The tendency for contentious politics to be labelled as deviance or appropriated as spectacular entertainment by the commercial media has been emphasised. A growing number of studies have chronicled the way in which the media have marginalised the aims of activists or encouraged more dramatic and violent forms of political behaviour.[17] The message has been clear: for those dedicated to political change, the media are not reliable friends.

But if the existence of these relations, aims and dilemmas has been well documented, the history of this moment still seems sketchy, vague, only imperfectly grasped. If the media are not 'reliable friends', must they always turn upon the activist? If the political gimmick is beset by persistent dilemmas, can these ever be negotiated? If there is a constant dynamic of invention, what are the precise fruits of political improvisation? If the political gimmick is aimed at the contemporary media, how does the emergence of the Internet change its form and likely impact? Few of these questions have been consistently posed. Perhaps because the political gimmick has appeared as so minor and ineffectual, such a fleeting example of performance, its history has not seemed worth writing. As a result, we lack a clear, serious account of how political activists have interacted with the media over the last forty years. The history of the political gimmick remains unwritten.

THE AIMS OF THIS BOOK

This book is conceived as a response to such lacunae. It offers a history of the era of the political gimmick in Australia over the last four decades. Clearly, this is a discontinuous, thematic history, as much detective work as sober historical narrative. It will be incomplete, interpretive, analytical. Writing the history of a political relationship is not like writing the history of an institution or a work of biography. It does not fall into easy sequential slices. It is not punctuated by obvious chronology and regular signs of achievement.

In fact the question of the 'origin' of the political gimmick is itself beset by controversy. Many historians would be keen to emphasise the time-honoured, venerable nature of the political performances that are discussed in this book. The Situationist International had already combined art and politics in the 1950s, performing dadaist stunts and anti-capitalist resistance. The Industrial Workers of the World adopted direct action and theatrical display on the streets of Sydney and Melbourne almost ninety years ago. The suffragettes scandalised respectable London with marches, 'raids' on Parliament, stone-throwing and hunger strikes a few years earlier. American protesters were already making creative use of street theatre, skits, effigies, dumb shows and stylised symbolic behaviour in the latter part of the eighteenth century. Indeed, the history of non-violent collective action has even been traced back to the plebeians of ancient Rome.[18]

In this sense, searching for the origin of particular forms of political behaviour would seem to be a labyrinthine, ultimately ineffectual quest. *Dissent Events* does not attempt to offer a complete history of the birth and life cycle of specific political actions or movements. Instead it offers a more humble, limited history of the changing political relations between collective action and the media over the last four decades. The origins of the political gimmick in Australia are deliberately mythical — moments of self-consciousness, proclamation and (re)invention rather than any objective founding. This is a history of circulations, connections and transformations, not obvious beginnings and neat delineations.

More specifically, this book examines the changing connections between collective action and the media in terms of five processes: *translation; staging; diffusion; theory,* and *direct engagement with the media.* The book's five chapters take up each of these processes in turn. While all of the processes are evident across the period there is, nonetheless, a broad historical movement over the course of the text from the importation of the political gimmick to its sustained production, diffusion, interpretation and eventual extension. That is, if the history of the political gimmick does not unfold like a simple biography, there remains a clear historical logic to its impact and development. This is a history still very much in formation, as political improvisations continue apace, and combinations of the 'new' electronic media and older theatrical performance result in still uncertain political changes. The final chapter addresses this contemporary change. It includes a detailed investigation of the impact of the Internet and an analysis of how new movements of the Right and Left have sought to enhance the scope and force of theatrical political behaviour. The book moves from the invention of the political gimmick to the very recent invention of the 'cyberbattle'.

Ephemeral, apparently trivial, perpetually in danger of incorporation, the political gimmick also emerges as an important political resource, a previously hidden contributor to contemporary social history, and a dynamic that has helped to reshape Australian politics, society and knowledge.

1
TRANSLATION

translate: express the sense of (a word, sentence, speech, book, etc.) in another language; express (an idea, book, etc.) in another, esp. simpler, form; interpret the significance of; infer as (*translated his silence as dissent*); move or change, esp. from one person, place, or condition, to another (*was translated by joy*).

— *Concise Oxford Dictionary*

As Egon Kisch leapt onto the concrete at Melbourne Port in 1934, this was, quite literally, a foreign invasion. His theatrical presence was alien, unaccustomed, his political methods unfamiliar. For Australian conservatives he was illegitimate and un-Australian; for Australian radicals he was admirable and inspiring. But for all his persistent publicity, Kisch had few direct Australian successors. Theatrical forms of political performance by admiring local citizens did not begin immediately. The confident proclamation of the political gimmick would not be for another two decades.

Why did this happen? Why is it that the draft card burning of American activists was so eagerly restaged in Belmore Park, while the actions of Kisch seemed so alien and unrepeatable? To put the question more abstractly, how is it that some forms of political performance are *translated*, while others are understood to be 'foreign', un-Australian and irrelevant to the local context?

This is a rather obvious question, yet it is one that students of social movements have failed to answer. For the most part, existing scholarship has concentrated on identifying the emergence of collective action, not its transmission. The most influential studies have been those that have identified the development of 'modular' (that is, transportable) actions in the eighteenth century — the demonstration, the strike and the petition — not those that have traced the process of subsequent transport. Indeed, as recent critics like Doug McAdam and Sean Chabot have argued, even the most respected scholars seem to assume that such transmission is automatic, unchanging and unworthy of analysis. To quote the work of Sidney Tarrow, for example, 'when a new form [of collective action] is 'discovered', its appropriateness to a new situation is immediately obvious, and it is widely taken up, spreads rapidly, and gives the impression of a dramatic breakthrough'.[1]

On first impression, this may seem broadly plausible. After all, when American activists began burning their draft cards, this did seem particularly appropriate to their political campaign, it did spread quickly to Australian activists, and it did give the impression of rapid, powerful political advance. But a closer analysis of the history of the political gimmick in Australia unveils a far more jagged, uneven and enculturated process at play. In fact it was only a complex combination of history, media and political events that stimulated Australian students to attempt to restage the draft card burning. It was only after a labyrinthine process of translation that a range of younger Australians began to take up theatrical forms of political performance.

This chapter proceeds with a detailed historical analysis of the process by which Australian students 'translated' the political gimmick. It aims not only to deepen our knowledge of the political gimmick in Australia, but also to develop a more subtle and useful model of 'translation' in other political contexts.

HOW STUDENTS TRANSLATED THE POLITICAL GIMMICK

Famously, in the early 1960s university students began to act with a new political confidence, mobilising throughout the western world as players in the 'vanguard of liberal opinion'.[2] In the United States, new organisations like Students for a Democratic Society enlivened even the most respectable campuses, and causes as diverse as foreign policy, free speech and race relations began to inspire activity. In Britain, students made the Aldermaston marches associated with the Campaign for Nuclear Disarmament (CND) a stunning success from Easter 1958, and gave birth to a distinctive 'New' Left. During the early 1960s, they participated vigorously in the active civil disobedience movement organised by Bertrand Russell around the Committee of 100.[3]

Australian students welcomed these developments. Writing in *Honi Soit*, the University of Sydney's student newspaper, Bob McDonald embraced that fact that 'broad trends can spread throughout the whole student world' as a harbinger of future radical activity on his own campus. Similarly, student leader Peter Wilenski highlighted the need for

Australian students to follow the lead of their fellows overseas and join the battle against apartheid and for human dignity. Mike Leyden showed the influence of British developments when he heartily endorsed Bertrand Russell's dictum concerning the ability of the 'active 5 per cent' to pioneer social change, and when he searched Australia's surfies, folk singers and libertarians for this magical, transformative stratum.[4]

However, the dream of Australian student leaders for a local version of militant British protests was slow in arriving. There was no rapid translation on this occasion. Despite the activity of a university branch of the Campaign for Nuclear Disarmament, only twenty-two Sydney students attended the Hiroshima Commemoration walk for peace in 1963. There were to be no colourful marches or sustained campaigns of civil disobedience on the model of the British peace movement. Radical students in Sydney during 1963 could only recall three 'spectacular' demonstrations over the last decade: for road safety in 1955, in condemnation of the Sharpeville massacre in 1960, and in opposition to the death penalty in 1962. None of these spectacular eruptions was to energise the student population or stimulate ongoing activity.[5]

Typical examples of student political mobilisation in the early 1960s were neither dramatic nor domestically attuned nor particularly effective. Indeed, student actions tended to adhere to four primary characteristics: to be moral in their inspiration, international in their object, restrained in their form, and limited in their numbers. Protest activity was moral: it was based securely on respect for human rights — the rights of lepers in India, of Africans and Indians under apartheid. It was international in object, taking overseas governments as its target, particularly those of less developed countries. It was restrained in form, with typical protest activities including the convening of meetings, the sending of protest letters, the passing of official motions. Even demonstrations were limited in scope. When the South African cricket team arrived for an Australian tour in November 1963, eighty students staged a rare formal protest at a Melbourne airport. But this was the antithesis of the colourful, dramatic, media-attuned displays that would generate publicity later in the decade. One of the participants was to claim proudly in a Christian student publication that 'the protest was a collar-and-tie affair, law-abiding and deeply serious'.[6]

Finally, and most importantly, protest activities were limited in their numbers. Indeed, it was not until 1964 that the pace of student political activity began to pick up. Despite the fact that British activists in the peace movement had deployed dramatic, challenging strategies in the early 1960s, which generated substantial media coverage, these were not taken up as models by young Australians. When dramatic student political activity did arise, the models and inspirations were American rather than British in origin.

THE CULTURAL PRECONDITIONS OF POLITICAL TRANSLATION

AMERICA AS INSPIRATION

For Australian students, it was the political and cultural activity of Americans that loomed largest in their collective imagination. American mass culture was a dominant influence and inspiration for Australian youth. Comics, film, television and music from the United States had provided the staple of popular culture for Australian teens. For university students of the early 1960s, the pranks and stunts of American students were praised and held up for emulation. For connoisseurs of music, it was the novel folk music produced in and around the American civil rights movement that seemed most popular and 'with it'. The tour of American folk singer Pete Seeger in 1963 was greeted with acclaim, and Sydney university students frequently sang American folk songs on public occasions.[7]

The civil rights struggle of which Seeger sang also began to engage the sympathy and admiration of Australian students. The evils of racial segregation in the United States were a frequent subject of comment within the student press. The heroism that African-Americans displayed in the integration of the bus system was acknowledged in first-person accounts. The quest for voter registration in the south of America was relayed courtesy of reports taken from the Forum news service. The memory of four college freshmen who had staged the first sit-ins in the Woolworth's store of Greensborough, North Carolina, in 1960, still lingered as an inspiration for Australian anti-racists, four years later. The 'freedom summer' of 1964, when students from northern American campuses travelled in buses to work for civil rights in southern states, was also a subject of discussion and inspiration. When Australian students participated in traditional, anti-authoritarian processions through city streets, they paid tribute to the civil rights movement with mocked-up 'freedom rides' of their own.[8]

Clearly, the development of a global market for youth culture established the preconditions for the reception, identification and adaptation of American cultural forms by Australian young people. The hegemonic position of American youth in the cultural imagination of Australians helped to establish a practical, ongoing process of cultural translation. New American trends in music and fashion were followed, and adapted by young Australians throughout the 1960s. Australian producers developed local versions of rock'n'roll, local stars, dance crazes, social mannerisms. This process extended from *musical forms*, such as rock'n'roll and folk music, to *dance crazes*, such as the stomp, and to *subcultural groupings*, such as surfies and beatniks.[9]

This process of cultural translation was to have political implications.

Indeed, it provided a direct social model for the translation of the political gimmick later in the decade. When a segment of American youth became connected to the civil rights struggle of African-Americans, then this also loomed as a possible example to be emulated by young Australians. In the same way that folk singing, 'the stomp' or jazz music had motivated Australian youth, so 'the sit-in' or the 'freedom ride' could be taken up and adapted to local situations.

These were not strictly technical, political processes. Culture and politics were indissoluble. Cultural transmissions established the frequency through which political transmissions could later be broadcast; the translating of cultural forms provided the opening through which political forms would also be translated. If this has been lost in the later analyses of political scientists, it was certainly clear to Australian students of the time. When they dreamt wistfully of dramatic student activity reaching Australian shores, student activists like Bob McDonald reached for metaphors that summoned up the migration of American culture:

> broad trends can spread throughout the whole student world, and this, for me, is the really thrilling part of student politics ...
>
> It is exactly the same kind of feeling I get from listening to Pete Seeger sing such songs as the following, which was sung by students protesting against racial discrimination in the USA ...[10]

In early 1964, the moral and political activism of Australian students settled on the United States itself. The US Civil Rights Bill was being introduced into the Senate at this time, and students at Sydney University planned to express their disapproval of the Senate's failure to pass the Bill. The Student's Representative Council passed a motion officially supporting a student demonstration outside the office of the US Consul. But this demonstration would take a strikingly different form from any other protest in the memory of students. Although it was moral in inspiration and international in its target, the protest would be anything but a 'collar-and-tie' affair.

THE TRADITION OF THEATRICAL, PUBLIC ACTIVITY BY AUSTRALIAN STUDENTS

Through an unlikely historical coincidence, the passage of the US Civil Rights Bill to the US Senate coincided with Sydney University's traditional Commemoration Day celebrations. Since 1913, students had used the official celebration of the university's establishment as the opportunity to launch their own, more informal celebrations that irreverently parodied the serious concerns of their elders. The day was traditionally marked by flamboyant stunts, hoaxes, singing, dancing, sports, and by a procession of floats through Sydney's streets.

Although at times barely tolerated by academic and police authorities, such processions became a prized custom among students. The official history of the University of Sydney chronicles a typically raucous 'Commem' procession in 1946:

> Despite a police ban, on 21 May the students managed to manoeuvre floats through the cordon and into Martin Place. Others marched to the Town Hall and showered the police with flour. With the procession returning along City Road smoke bombs were thrown. The following evening large groups of students marched into the city, burning effigies of the police, throwing eggs and flour and raiding the offices of the press. There were no arrests.[11]

Such outrageous, celebratory and theatrical behaviour among students continued into the 1960s. One contemporary student publication advised students that 'anyone who can't tell about the stunt he was in afterwards isn't worth a peanut', and suggested that no stunts would be condemned 'unless they block traffic or cause bodily harm or vandalise'.[12] This was a 'liminal' moment for university students — a term developed by anthropologist Victor Turner to describe those periods when social life is characterised by the suspension of usual norms and social roles, and by an overflowing sense of 'communitas' or collective camaraderie.[13] It provided a socially sanctioned forum in which students possessed a licence to behave in public space in a way not usually granted them.

Commemoration Day proceedings typically lacked political engagement. They were moments of privileged loutishness rather than disciplined political commitment. However, because the US Senate's sitting coincided with 'Commem' Day in 1964, the civil rights protest was effectively integrated into a stream of theatrical Commem Day happenings.[14]

The implications of this historical coincidence were substantial. Both the scope and the character of the action were reshaped to fit the pre-existing norms of student Commem activities. First, because the civil rights demonstration was now a part of Commem Day proceedings, it was able to call on hundreds of Sydney University students who had never before mobilised for a political cause. Second, the form of the protest adhered to typical Commem Day practice, so it possessed a more flamboyant and theatrical character than any previous student political activity. It was staged amid gaudy floats, liminal student activities, vandalism of the Cenotaph war memorial, hijinks on a ferry at South Steyne, and so on. A number of protesting students had dressed up in the robes of the Ku Klux Klan to dramatise the racism of the US Senate. A cross was burnt in Wynyard Park. There was violence and confusion. *Honi Soit* reported events breathlessly as previously 'historic', 'inspiring' American political events seemed suddenly to be enacted in a familiar Australian setting: '1500 students clashed with all available police. It was marked by sporadic sitdowns and isolated folk singing and the unanimous chanting of "civil rights now". Police, taunted and enraged beyond belief, arrested dozens of students and manhandled bystanders'.[15]

Clearly, protesters had not adapted the political techniques of their overseas counterparts in any mechanistic fashion. On the contrary, the political choices of students were thoroughly 'enculturated'. Students reached for American political slogans and actions because this conformed to a practice of ongoing cultural importation from America. Students made the step to become involved in a dramatic protest because the practice of Commem Day had traditionally extended to them a practical licence to behave in a youthful, anti-authoritarian and challenging manner. It was the union of these cultural practices that generated the novel, striking protest of May 1964.

THE PUBLIC CIRCULATIONS OF PROTEST AND THE PROCESS OF IDENTIFICATION

The Commemoration Day protest was to have important consequences. In Sydney, elite members of the community such as the head of the Returned Servicemen's League, the Vice-Chancellor of Sydney University, the head of the Chamber of Commerce and leading conservative aldermen were damning in their criticism. Although some media outlets were critical of police behaviour, most restricted themselves to attacks on student irresponsibility.[16] Struggling with mass arrests, conscious, perhaps for the first time, of the police as a threatening social force, Australian students identified themselves even more strongly with the culture and politics of the American environment. Alongside their concern with the civil rights of African-Americans, they articulated their own assailed right to assemble and demonstrate: 'Ultimately, the original motivation was overwhelmed as police methods and intentions became more obvious and more violent. Now, how many civil rights did students have in their inevitable clashes with police?'[17]

Australian politics, it seemed, was becoming 'Americanised'. In a letter of protest to major Sydney newspapers, J. S. Baker, the public relations officer of the Australian Council of Salaried and Professional Associations, explicitly connected the fate of local protesters with those of civil rights workers in Nashville and Birmingham. For Baker, both situations involved committed students (often from Christian student organisations) facing brutal treatment and imprisonment by authorities. Protesters from Sydney University were to be compared with 'the students conducting their protests in the Southern States of America', as both appeared to receive the same treatment from police.[18] Clearly, in the aftermath of the Commem Day protest the appropriateness of American actions, languages and political techniques to the Australian context was increasingly obvious to both students and observers. Civil rights were now not only a part of American struggles and events but also a frame of reference of direct usefulness for Australian struggles.

At the same time, the place of civil rights in the Australian context was complicated by the circulation of the Commem Day protest to the United States. The protest did not remain within the autarkic realms of Australian life but was both reported and commented on by leading US media outlets. The response from the American media was generally one of defence rather than acclamation. In a typical move that would have a profound impact on Australian students, a CBS news commentator launched a critical riposte to actions in the Antipodes by turning the spotlight on Australian racism and discrimination:

> Their demonstration, although displaying surprising fervor, served only to emphasise that discrimination in one form or another is neither new nor isolated. The Australian students, for example, said not a word about their own immigration policies, which are intended to keep Australia predominantly white. And within Australia, the native aborigines might be said to correspond to our own American Indians ... they have suffered a similar fate.[19]

Similarly, the national US magazine *Life* also pointed to the hypocrisy and cant of the Australian student protesters: 'Students in Sydney have rioted against racial prejudice in the US! Conveniently overlooking the fact that Australia herself possesses some of the most stringent racial exclusion laws in the world'.[20]

The views of American broadcasters were reprinted in *Honi Soit* for the benefit of student readers. At the same time, another American response to the Commem Day action was also reprinted in the student publication. This time it was a letter from an African-American correspondent in San Francisco. Charlie Pyat II was sincere in his thanks for Australian students: 'News of your sympathy demonstrations reaching our shores caused America to look with silent embarrassment', he assured students. He was, however, also concerned with the reports of discrimination within Australia itself. He posed a sympathetic challenge for recent protesters:

> If you cannot deny this [racial discrimination], and if your concern [with civil rights for African-Americans] was sincere, profound, and genuine; I ask you most humbly, most appreciatively, can you find the sympathy in your hearts and consciences to conduct PEACEFUL demonstrations against these laws in your own country?[21]

The international reaction to the Commem protest forced students at Sydney University to re-examine their own conditions and environment. In the following weeks, *Honi Soit* would uncover previously unacknowledged racist dimensions of campus life, such as the use of the term 'black bastard' to describe African students.[22] It would also begin to pay increasing attention to the conditions of life of Australia's indigenous people. The appalling conditions faced by Aboriginal people on Cape Barren Island would be reported; the damage racial prejudice caused to the north of Australia would be discussed; the ongoing ill treatment and underprivilege of Aboriginal people would be broached; the history of 'incidental genocide' by Europeans would be accepted (though not deliberate attempts to destroy Aboriginal people and culture).[23]

Clearly, this new interest in the rights of Aboriginal people was a product of the criticism and prodding that emanated from the United States. Students like Gillian Harrison were quite open that maintaining 'humane', internationalist credentials was an important motive in any engagement with their own country's racial problems: 'Those Australians who speak against racialism in South Africa or the U.S. will never be heard seriously while Aborigines remain underprivileged. Here is another reason to assure [*sic*] that their [Aboriginal people's] future differs from the past'.[24]

Nonetheless, that engagement was sincere and deeply felt. The privileged position of white Australian students was brought to the surface for the first time. Writing in *Crux*, the journal of the Australian Student Christian Movement, Lin Morison was forced to admit that she stood with the American white rather than with the struggling African-American. Reviewing James Baldwin's *The Fire Next Time*, she praised that writer's artistry and passion: 'His words are the more telling since I would want to feel identified with the Negro in his struggle for real liberation, but I am forced to identify myself with the American white, recognising in his ill-founded beliefs and attitudes so many of my own'.[25]

On the basis of such personal realisations, such painful readjustments, Australian students began to reorient themselves from international to domestic issues of protest, and the decades-long Australian movement of dissent, led so often by students, was begun. The framework of civil rights, effectively translated from the actions of protesters in the United States, was now brought to bear on the problems faced by indigenous Australians. A series of student protests were planned for 8 July 1964, to 'give publicity to some alleged injustices, both social and legal, which the Aboriginal suffers in Australia today'.[26]

Coordinated protests were held in Melbourne, Brisbane and Sydney. About 500 students from Sydney University attended a rally in Hyde Park and a later demonstration outside State Parliament. The need to combat 'legal and social discriminations' was emphasised by student organisers, though Aboriginal speakers at the rally tended to emphasise other issues, such as the maintenance of their culture, improved education, housing and employment.

The status of the demonstration as a self-conscious importation of American actions was obvious to observers. Highlighting the importance of America as a cultural and political inspiration, local folk singer Gary Shearston sang a number of 'freedom songs from America', alongside compositions by Aboriginal poet Oodgeroo Noonuccal (then known as Kath Walker). The conceptualisation of the protest as a response to international criticism was also obvious. Delegates attending an International Student Seminar at the University of New South Wales from Malaysia, the United Arab Emirates, Israel, Hong Kong and India expressed their approval for the protest action, and this was emphasised in the student press.[27]

Nonetheless, the demonstration represented a new moment in the translation of theatrical political protest to Australia. Formerly, cultural tools, frames, actions and targets had all been passed to Australian youth from the United States. Because of the power of American images in the Australian media, the tools of folk singing became available for young Australian musicians; the frame of civil rights became available for Australians thinking about privilege and injustice; the tools of the 'sit-in' and the 'freedom ride' became available for emulation; the existence of racism in the United States was opened up as a possible target for young politically engaged Australians. To begin with, those tools were applied by Australians to American problems, as in the Commem protest. Such early experiments expressed what could be thought of as the 'first moment' in the overall process of translation — a moment when replication is cautious and imitative. Like the novice in a novel linguistic situation, who slowly repeats the words mouthed to her, so Australian students directly copied the phrases, techniques, ideas and targets of young American protesters. The actions of US protesters were still mostly unfamiliar and unnatural.

However, once the Commem protest had circulated in the international mass media, Australian students were forced to apply this American legacy to the Australian environment. Now those imported tools were being used to address specific Australian problems, such as the civil rights of Australian Aboriginal people. Certainly, these tools were still unfamiliar, and they seemed 'American' to participants, strange, unlikely; equally, they had been imported as a cultural package, and they were difficult to disentangle at first. In those early days, it would have been impossible to imagine a protest concerned with racism that did not use the frame of 'civil rights'; impossible to imagine a peaceful assembly without the folk singing, the freedom songs; impossible to have political activity by Australian students without the references to American students and international opinion. In fact Australian students were not simply using a 'modular' political technique, an abstract political tool. They were reading a complex cultural script and then translating it to a very different political and social environment — a stage on which it had never before been performed. At this moment, Australian students had entered a second moment in the overall process of the translation of the political gimmick. Now they were self-consciously comparing and contrasting the American model of political action with their own. Like the developing language student, who constantly translates still unfamiliar words back to her 'native' tongue, so the Australian students searched for parallels, focusing now on the new, now on the old. In this way, the tools of participants in the American civil rights struggle began to be adapted to the Australian situation.

In September 1964, that process of adaptation began to accelerate, as Sydney student Jim Spigelman publicised a new organisation, to be explicitly based on the American Student Non-Violent Co-ordinating Committee (SNCC). The new body was known as Student Action For Aborigines, or SAFA, and, according to Spigelman, its first action was already planned. During university vacation in February, a 'freedom ride' through New South Wales and Queensland country towns would be held to investigate and publicise the living conditions of rural Aboriginal people. The methods to be used would draw on the experience of civil rights protesters in gaining media attention through dramatic, organised public activity. As Spigelman put it:

> The principle [sic] aim of SAFA is to arouse public attention to the more fundamental problems of housing, wages, education, etc. The somewhat dramatic action of a 'freedom ride' is the type of sensationalism the press will report. Through this we hope to press upon the public a general belief that all is not well.[28]

TRANSLATING THE FREEDOM RIDE

The story of the Freedom Ride is now well known, and it will not be rehearsed at length.[29] For our purposes, the precise unfolding of events is less important than the Freedom Ride's status as a pivotal moment in the translation of theatrical political performance to Australia. Indeed, it was a translation in at least three senses: a translation of political methods, a translation of political frameworks, and a translation of media reporting practices. The following section examines each of these elements.

In the first place, the Freedom Ride represented a translation of political methods. Historians of the movement have been quick to admit its indebtedness to American civil rights models — its use of a bus tour, of peaceful prayer at the point of departure, its reliance on forms of non-violent direct action.[30] Organisers of the tour understood these American methods as 'passive resistance'. They declared their willingness to 'adopt appropriate methods of passive resistance, depending on the particular instance of discrimination at hand'.[31]

The points of reference for SAFA members were almost exclusively American. Bill Ford and Sondra Silverman, two participants in the American 'freedom summer', functioned as expert counsel to the students. As early as December 1964, the two were already singled out for explicit acknowledgement: 'Their knowledge of techniques to be used and the American publications they have collected should prove most helpful'.[32] Bill Ford, in particular, emphasised the usefulness of 'passive resistance' for 'students and Negroes in the Deep South', as well as the broad similarities of the US and Australian situations. He addressed students before their departure for country New South Wales in February 1965.[33]

More broadly, passive resistance was understood as an outgrowth of the civil rights struggles of African-Americans, rather than traced back to earlier historical antecedents. The writings of Martin Luther King Jr were suggested as a source of inspiration and argument for participants in the Freedom Ride. A leaflet containing excerpts from his writings was distributed by SAFA members at demonstrations, and both his critique of cautious white moderates and his praise for the liberating power of 'creative tension' were particularly highlighted by nervous protesters.[34]

However, if Martin Luther King Jr was used as a point of spiritual reference, Australian students, not surprisingly, tended to have more in common with North American college students. Like participants in the American freedom summer, they understood passive resistance primarily as a tactical rather than ethical imperative.[35] Bill Ford suggested that passive resistance was likely to work in some situations and not in others. Its primary use was in the creation of sympathetic media images:

> if you go into a segregated bar and someone pushes someone else aside and a brawl starts — well, you've lost everything ... Pick out one or two key centres and make sure you've got the camera on you. Remember, a passive demonstration is the most effective. Any violence and you've defeated your own purpose.[36]

Clearly, American tools of political action were being self-consciously grasped as local mechanisms of publicity creation. The aim of the 'translated trip' was to gain the attention of the media, and thereby to crystallise the sympathetic attention of the Australian public. As Jim Spigelman put it directly, 'through the demonstrations we hope to dramatise the problems of aborigines'. In the early planning of the ride, Charles Perkins, SAFA president and path-breaking Aboriginal student, exploited media interest with a series of interviews and an advance trip to country towns with journalists from the *Australian* newspaper.[37] As the Freedom Ride itself unfolded, and violence threatened in Moree, student leaders showed a keen awareness of the power of the dramatic spectacle to reach well-disposed city audiences. Spigelman's tactical arguments to students were pitched at precisely this level:

> I think we should go for something like a twelve hour picket or a twenty-four hour picket of the pool. I think we're going to find a lot of hostility on the part of the white people, we're going to find ourselves more and more in this town, aligned mainly and largely and almost completely with the Aboriginal people. And secondly, as Charlie [Perkins] has just come back from a press conference [an appearance on ABC Four Corners television program with the mayor of Moree], the whole of the national press is queued up on this one incident, and as Charlie's said, if we break through here it doesn't matter if it's only one place, it's signalled, it's an example.[38]

If the Freedom Ride represented the translation of new political methods to the Australian context, it also represented the translation of new political frameworks. When SAFA members used the techniques of 'passive resistance', they used them to highlight examples of racial segregation. The framework of civil rights that had dominated the efforts of the movement for African-American racial equality was intently applied to Australian social problems. Systematic examples of discrimination against Aboriginal people that mirrored the discrimination against African-Americans were surveyed and protested. For the first time, the racial segregation of public spaces in country New South Wales — everything from swimming pools to hotels to picture theatres to clothing retailers — received major publicity. The social and legal discrimination Aboriginal people faced was highlighted by boycotts, pickets and demonstrations at the sites of segregated council pools, returned servicemen's clubs, public bars and country cinemas. More broadly, the appalling living conditions of indigenous people on reserves such as those surrounding Boggabilla were dramatised for ignorant city audiences through the activities of the SAFA students.[39]

However, if the actions of students were important and courageous, their almost exclusive concern with civil rights was undeniably novel. This was an explicit importation of American political frameworks. Certainly, Aboriginal people had demanded liberty, full equality, representation in Federal Parliament, equal access to education, equal wages, the right to live in town, and a range of other political and civil rights during the twentieth century. But as Heather Goodall has shown, this was generally subordinated to the quest for the right to stolen land. Indeed, the aspiration for land remained at the centre of much Aboriginal political activity up to the early months of 1964. Even sympathetic whites conceded that the 'land question' was an 'important' and 'current' issue at the time. As a result, when the framework of civil rights and legislative change was strongly emphasised by students, this was only a highly selective, particular strand of current and historical Aboriginal demands.[40] Because the political action of students was an explicit translation of American models, they were unable to grasp this. The very action of translation that gave students the confidence and the ability to agitate also robbed them of the ability to see Aboriginal aspirations in their entirety. When SAFA campaigned for policies to address Aboriginal disadvantage at the New South Wales state elections in 1965, they focused on the need for increased expenditure, for the implementation of civil rights clauses in legislation, for the ceding of state powers to a more activist federal government. They did not refer to the issue of land rights at all.[41]

The translation pioneered by students was also shared by media organisations. Reporters constantly framed Australian developments in American terms, heightening both the comparability of US and Australian situations and the sense that an 'American' event was happening in an Australian environment. Reporters used three techniques that created such effects: explicit comparisons, translated terms, and translated frames.

The Australian and American campaigns were explicitly compared. For local journalists, this was a freedom ride 'on the American pattern', using the tactics of 'Birmingham, Jackson and Tuscaloosa'. Its participants were to be compared with college activists in the Deep South. Its targets were analogous to the white strongholds of the US South and South Africa. Its unquestioned leader, president of SAFA and Aboriginal student Charles Perkins, was to be compared with Martin Luther King Jr.[42]

The framing of the SAFA tour in US terms also extended to the translation of terms and discourses associated with the US civil rights movement. The label of 'Freedom Ride' was the most obvious example of this technique. The term was initially used by the students themselves, but was later rejected by them as a 'mistaken analogy' — one that had been wrongly employed by inaccurate journalists. Such transpositions of vocabulary extended to other terms. Racial segregation was persistently referred to as a 'color bar', with the unfamiliar American spelling both ubiquitous and unexplained. In the same way, racist country dwellers were labelled as 'poor whites', and Aboriginal people who acquiesced in racial discrimination were called 'Uncle Toms'.[43] The constant use of a typically American vocabulary to narrate the progress of Australian protesters helped to emphasise the transplanted, novel nature of the SAFA tour.

The 'media frames' that had organised reporting of the US civil rights struggle were also applied to Australian reporting of SAFA activities. Doug McAdam has noted that the northern media in the United

States treated the struggles of Martin Luther King Jr sympathetically, framing racial discrimination and inequality as a strictly 'southern problem'. In the same way, a sympathetic city media in Australia framed segregation and Aboriginal underprivilege as a strictly rural phenomenon. While the 'squalor of country towns' was emphasised, it was contrasted with the 'new life' offered for Aboriginal people in the cities. The activities of SAFA were praised for their ability to bring a vexed social problem to the attention of benevolent city folk. The slums in which many urban Aboriginal people dwelt were not addressed in a similar fashion.[44]

Other frames were also imported from the reporting of American racial politics. When SAFA members made a second visit to a segregated swimming pool in Moree, Australian journalists quickly slipped into the 'dramatic' frames that had been used to report violence in Alabama and elsewhere. Moree was described as the site of a 'fast-developing racial crisis', when the only planned action was a protest by almost exclusively white students against a practice instituted by local white councillors. In a similar move, the demonstration, which resulted in harassment, fruit-throwing and assault against a number of SAFA members by local whites, was described with much hyperbole as an outbreak of 'racial violence'.[45]

The temptation of contemporary historians may be to correct such misapprehensions — to emphasise the singularity of the Australian experience, its local colour and regional repercussions; to insist on its overwhelmingly 'Australian' character. While such a quest beckons the historian of the Freedom Ride, it is not so tempting for the historian of 'translation'. Highlighting the constant reference to American parallels, discourses, frames, actions and frameworks serves an important intellectual purpose. It reinstalls the novelty of these Australian events, their precarious footing in the Antipodes, their vulnerable status as recent importations. The Freedom Ride extended the messy process that had begun in 1964, as Australian students began to experiment with American political techniques. But it took that process further than ever before. Now the tools of the political gimmick were being applied in a systematic, deliberate and ongoing fashion. Now, for the first time, they were beginning to deliver significant gains for local activists.

CONSEQUENCES OF THE FREEDOM RIDE

IMMEDIATE POLITICAL GAINS

Whatever the status of the Freedom Ride as a translated political form, its local successes cannot be denied. Charles Perkins believed that the pride, unity and dignity of Aboriginal people had been measurably improved. Local Aboriginal residents were inspired by Perkins' brave and articulate leadership, and the barriers to Aboriginal self-organisation were now considerably reduced. Today the ride is recalled by many Aboriginal people in New South Wales as a major event — a turning point in the history of race relations.[46]

If the Aboriginal population who directly witnessed the collective action of students was inspired, then those who experienced the Freedom Ride through the media were also undeniably influenced by SAFA actions. As a source of 'self-produced publicity', the ride was a triumph. Benefiting from elite support, SAFA activists focused white public attention on the inequalities of Aboriginal life. Sympathetic observers within the media were united in the belief that the Freedom Ride had punctured a 'genteel silence', penetrated beyond a previous 'complacency and lazy indifference' on the part of whites.[47]

The dramatic actions of the SAFA tour forced many white Australians to begin the same process of self-examination that had been thrust on the students after the Commemoration Day protest of 1964. For this larger white audience the fear of international condemnation was again dominant. The presence of BBC television cameras at the SAFA Moree demonstration was noted fearfully in the pages of the *Australian*. An editorial fretted that the position of Aboriginal people was 'increasingly well-known and discussed around the world'. Correspondents warned that the Moree events would be treated with 'exaggerated interest' in Africa and South-East Asia. Others urged action to address the 'Aboriginal problem' in order to protect Australia's 'international rating'. The self-interest of much of this concern was obvious. The *Australian* addressed the position of the embarrassed Australian abroad — the 'sensitive traveller'. Racial inequalities were to be addressed for the sake of national prestige rather than because of the inherent rightness of such action. The position of white Australians rather than that of Aboriginal Australians was to retain political primacy.[48]

Despite the self-interest that motivated much of this white public engagement with the Freedom Ride, there was limited evidence of a minor attitudinal shift. For the first time in many years, polling organisations began to test public attitudes to Aboriginal conditions and to government responses. In the aftermath of the SAFA tour, Australian Public Opinion Polls asked 15–19-year-olds whether funding for Aboriginal education and housing should be increased. Sixty-two per cent of respondents thought a lot more should be spent, and 17 per cent a little more. This compared favourably with an earlier poll of adult Australians, in which 56 per cent agreed that a lot more should be spent. It also compared favourably with polls in other states, which showed lingering support for segregation in both city and country Western Australia. In this sense, the Freedom Ride may have helped (very) marginally to shift public attitudes, as well as substantially increase public knowledge of the persistent discriminations and inequalities of life for Aboriginal Australians.[49]

THE DIFFUSION OF DRAMATIC PROTEST

The favourable reception of the Freedom Ride had important consequences for the history of contentious politics in Australia. It demonstrated to local activists that dramatic actions used overseas — sit-ins, pickets, bus rides, colourful protests — could be equally successful when applied to local problems. It thereby created the conditions for the widespread deployment of the political gimmick by a variety of Australian actors. In the aftermath of the SAFA tour, other actors began to take up these new, now less unfamiliar, political techniques.

The process was astonishing in its rapidity. On 16 February 1965, apparently encouraged by the actions of students and rural Aboriginal people in the flouting of racial discrimination, four Aboriginal men in Sydney directly challenged the widespread segregation practised in Sydney hotels. They entered the Prince of Wales Hotel, asked for service, and after facing rejection, launched 'a successful sit-in demonstration'. After an hour, they were eventually served, and their activities were reported in the Australian press.[50]

Others were to follow suit. Aboriginal people conducted another sit-in Sydney's Burlington Hotel in March 1965. Women, too, began to use these techniques to challenge their own segregation in public hotels. Less than two weeks after the Aboriginal sit-in at the Burlington, two women chained themselves to the public bar at the Regatta Hotel in Brisbane, demanding an end to sexual discrimination. Again, publicity was widespread, and an editorial in the Brisbane's conservative daily newspaper, the *Courier-Mail*, supported the women's cause. A Brisbane Licensing Squad was unimpressed. 'It was obviously a publicity stunt', he noted critically (and correctly). The sit-in was proving its value as a media-attuned protest form. Publicity stunts were now being practised by a range of Australians to make public claims. Everywhere they seemed to be erupting, attracting attention through dramatic display, challenging discrimination and injustice.[51]

Students active in the peace movement also began to take up the tools of dramatic protest used with such flair by the members of SAFA. On 3 May 1965, 250 peace protesters paraded outside the US Consulate in Wynyard Street, Sydney, and a number of participants escalated the demonstration by sitting down in Martin Place. This was an unorthodox action at the time, one that symbolised the new theatrical tactics being developed by younger political activists. When arrests were made, protests followed the next day in Canberra, Sydney and Melbourne, and were given front-page treatment by major broadsheet newspapers. A further protest occurred on the following day — 5 May, as 500 students sat down again, this time outside the US

Consulate. Again, the dramatic actions of protesters gained public attention, as photographs and a story adorned the front page of next day's issue of the *Sydney Morning Herald*. Twenty days later, sixteen students conducted a further sit-down protest in the Civic Shopping Centre, Canberra, with similar publicity collected. Draft card burning would soon follow.[52]

The translation of the political gimmick had entered a new phase. No longer a halting, imitative action or a cautious, self-conscious translation of American tools to address Australian problems, actions like the sit-in were now being used confidently by a range of local actors. In August 1965, students conducted another sit-in, this time on Sydney's Anzac Parade, in an effort to gain transport concessions. Employees began to adopt sit-ins as a part of industrial campaigns. Sixty motorcyclists, members of the Lambretta Club of New South Wales, conducted a 'park-in' in April 1965 as part of their demands for increased motorcycle parking. In June 1965, notoriously conservative restaurant and milkbar owners planned their own 'sit-ins' in an effort to influence the NSW Government. 'It seems to be the modern way to protest and it's very effective', the secretary of the Restaurant and Milkbar Association, Mr V. Mathias, assured an enquiring journalist.[53]

Australians now spoke the language of theatrical political performance in a fluent, flexible manner. They did not need to justify their use of these methods: they were now natural, self-evident political tools. The process of translation had reached its third stage, when once novel actions were smoothly integrated into the repertoire of domestic actors and could be adapted to a variety of purposes without intensive intellectual justification. The 'American' had become the 'Australian'. The modular, transportable tools of the 'sit-in', the challenging, non-violent picket, and the colourful demonstration were now as at home in Melbourne and Brisbane as they were in Birmingham, Chicago or Berkeley.

CONCLUSION

The process of translation was not automatic, self-evident, or acultural. It relied on specific historical processes: on the existence of an historically recent practice of cultural importation from the United States; on a history of theatrical public activity by students which could be turned to political ends; on a developed international media that allowed for rapid transcontinental reporting and commentary. It had been a process saturated in culture: in the cultural dominance of American youth in the Australian imagination; in the indissolubility of the 'new' folk music, the new framework of civil rights, and the new tools of dramatic political challenge; in the central example of Martin Luther King Jr, and an understanding of his methods as embodying the inspiring techniques of 'passive resistance'.

This act of translation was a complex, uneven process. New political methods were not immediately taken up. Their use was initially halting and directly connected to overseas issues and applications. It was only after a period of sustained experimentation and local adaptation that a range of Australian actors began to take up actions like the sit-in, and use them to publicise a range of public and social issues. It was only after the translation performed by students over 1964 and 1965 that peace activists and motorcyclists, milkbar owners and others felt willing and capable of using these new, dramaturgical forms of political action.

This suggests a very different account of 'translation' than the somewhat simplistic view that was presented at the beginning of the chapter, and which tends to dominate the study of social movements. Indeed, translation appears to be neither automatic and immediate nor obvious and acultural. In the conception developed here, the process of 'translation' involves at least three analytically distinct moments:

1 Newly improvised modular collective action reaches a new audience. It is tested in a halting, piecemeal fashion by local actors. This moment may be compared with the time when an unfamiliar language first reaches new ears, and is repeated in an experimental, cautious, repetitive manner. It occurred in the Australia of the mid-1960s when students first learnt of civil rights campaigns in the United States, and when they staged the first Commem Day demonstration.

2 The audience self-consciously receives this new action, and begins to compare the context and dimensions of the act with the audience's own. On the basis of such comparisons, sustained experiment with the new action takes place. This moment may be compared with a speaker learning to use a new language, searching for parallel words, meanings, explicitly, intensively comparing the new with the old. It occurred in the Australia of the mid-1960s when the first demonstrations for Aboriginal rights were organised by young Australians, and when the plan for the Freedom Ride was hatched.

3 On the basis of debate and experiment within the audience's public sphere, the action is integrated into a new, expanded repertoire. This moment may be compared with the achievement of fluency in the speaking of a new language, when complex phrases can be used, adapted and reviewed, without constant reference to the speaker's past language. This is the moment of complete translation. It was only when the translation of theatrical political performance was complete that a range of actors (such as the draft card burners of 1966) would eagerly and confidently experiment with complex forms of political staging.

By 1965, the 'third moment' of translation had been reached. The political gimmick had definitively arrived in Australia. Ordinary Australians had begun to test the application of spectacular actions and publicity stunts to their specific causes and concerns. A new sense of challenge was evident in civil society.

In the next chapter, we follow the story of that challenge, tracing the uses that Australians found for these new techniques over the next decade or so. This is a story at least as complex and important as the story of translation. It orients us to a moment of sustained mobilisation, change and improvisation.

2
STAGING

> I can take any space and call it a bare stage.
>
> Peter Brook, 1968

> The issues dealt with by stagecraft and stage management are sometimes trivial but they are quite general; they seem to occur everywhere in social life, providing a clear-cut dimension for formal sociological analysis.
>
> Erving Goffman, 1959

Nadine Jensen, a 21-year-old secretary, wears a fine dress to the ceremonial military march of 1st Battalion troops through the city's streets. It is cold — early June 1966, outside the Sydney Town Hall. Abruptly, she drenches herself in a mixture of kerosene, turpentine and red paint, pushes through the crowd, and locks Lt-Col. Preece, the commanding officer, in a long embrace. She later claims that the paint is symbolic of the shedding of blood in Vietnam, and urges other Australians to develop moral as well as physical courage. When she faces court two days later, the magistrate ponders whether to subject her to psychiatric testing, but decides eventually on a simple fine.

As the Australian Women's Swimming Championship in the 200 metres butterfly is contested, four large bags of black dye are flung into the pool. The meeting is disrupted and the water is now discoloured. The championship continues, however. There is a national team to select for the upcoming tour of South Africa, 1970.

On Good Friday 1969, the Morning Prayer and Litany at St Andrew's Church, Sydney, witnesses an odd divergence from ritual. Seven young men and three young women advance respectfully to the marble steps in front of the pulpit. Some of them are carrying placards: 'Christians crucify Christ in Vietnam' and 'Silence is a potent political weapon of oppression'. Church warders tear up the placards and remove one man. The police arrive but are waved away by the Archbishop of Sydney, Reverend M. L. Loane.

The traditional Miss Fresher contest at Adelaide University Orientation Week is challenged in 1970, when a contingent of sixty women and men file onto the catwalk and sit down. The group declare their commitment to the ideals of Women's Liberation.

Around ten radical students at the University of New England return home after watching *Z*, a film about the resistance to military dictatorship in Greece. It is 1973. Amid feverish discussion, the students increasingly identify as peasants, locked in a feudal relationship with their own professors. The next day an anti-exam march is publicised as a 'Peasants Revolt'. As the students march through the provincial streets of Armidale they are led by a pipe and flute band, replete with fiddlers and demonstrators in peasant garb.

Marcia Langton, a first year student at Queensland University, and an Aboriginal, uses four pegs and some rope to stake out 100 square feet of land and to take out a miner's right. This will become her land, privately owned. She is in a park, directly opposite the Brisbane Commonwealth Offices, and it is 1969.

A group of hippies march from Kings Cross to Hyde Park in Sydney. Ostensibly, they are part of an organisation: Tolerance for Cannabis. But once they arrive in Hyde Park, the demonstration takes a surprising turn. A baby is baptised in the fountain. A dozen or so decide to swim in the Pool of Remembrance, established to commemorate the loss of members of the Australian Services in wartime. It is a hot January day in 1970, and a bystander takes vehement offence: 'It looks like the last war was all for nothing'.[1]

There is something obviously theatrical about all of these actions. Each of the participants seem, somewhat self-consciously, to inhabit a role. They are insurgent Women's Libbers, literally seizing the stage and demanding redress; transgressive hippies, communing with simple water, unencumbered by militaristic ceremony; sincere Christians, heads bowed in piety and peaceful love. They all present themselves as if on stage, keen that we will comprehend not only their actions but their beliefs, motives, identities. We do not merely learn that they oppose the Vietnam War or support Aboriginal land rights, we also know why that may be so, and what may motivate them. You are 'a hippy', that is why you support the legalisation of cannabis. Your land has been claimed as if you did not exist; this is why you demand land rights from the government today.

Props and preparation are used in order to make the performance more convincing: flutes and fiddles are discovered; the appropriate slogans are composed for the placards; the pegs and rope of a miner are procured. This has been weighed, calculated in advance for its effect. There is, equally, a concern with symbolism: red paint stands for the blood spilt in Vietnam; black dye for the race that will not compete in South Africa; and peasant clothes for the subordinate position of students. This is, in short, the staging of a political performance. Upon the stage of the public park, the swimming pool, the church, the street, the campus, politics suddenly appears.

In some ways, the self-conscious performance involved in each of these actions should not be surprising. For the radicals of the 1960s, theatre had an especially strong political resonance. Street theatre and guerrilla theatre loomed as new political tools. Students held mock trials and brief plays to portray grand conflicts, like John Romeril's 1969 play of the battle between student leader Albert Langer and the Monash University authorities. Students in Sydney, too, seemed convinced of the power of theatrical performance. Members of Students for a Democratic Society (SDS) roamed around the city, dramatising apparent massacres in Vietnam for an audience of office workers, fleeing from police, leaving the Town Hall steps and reappearing in Wynyard Park, hoping that their interventions would communicate and convince.[2]

Some students even had an explanation for the rise of theatre, the apparent ubiquity of role-playing. Ian Channel at the University of New South Waves helped to create the Association for Love and Freedom (ALF). He praised living theatre, 'living as a show all the time', believing that this would break down the distinction between art and life, contemplation and involvement. For Channel, the growth of living theatre was part of the development of a 'new character'. Drawing from Marshall McLuhan, David Riesman and Herbert Marcuse, he postulated a grand theory of performance and personality, in which the rise of the new medium of television was in the process of remaking subjectivity: 'Constant exposure to instantaneous mozaic [*sic*] patterns of electromagnetic communications and greater interpersonal mobility has turned him [the contemporary person] into a self-conscious hedonist concerned more with his relationship to the means of consumption than to the means of production'.[3]

In 1968, the University of New South Wales hosted a myriad of such apocalyptic theories and astonishing performances. A new group, to be known as the Black Guards, declared their establishment, organising a 'mini-lecture, fun-politics, inner-space searching activity'. Following Mao, the Black Guards promised to collect thoughts; following 'the Black Muslims', they claimed to be 'the antithesis and enemy of white'. Under their leadership, art would explode forth, and the 'Puritan era' would be challenged. Their weapons were all around. Poems needed to be written on blackboards and footpaths; the sacred texts of Eric Fromm (*Fear of Freedom*), David Riesman (*The Lonely*

Crowd) and Marshall McLuhan (*Understanding Media*) needed to be read and acted on. Cleanliness, apparent affluence and consumer culture were the enemy, symbolised by products like Omo washing powder and Ajax cleaner. In a parodic manifesto, the Guards articulated their complaints:

> Too long have we lived in an Ajaxed, puritan world where Omo Sapiens reign as the master white race, and people brush their bright gleaming white teeth after every meal ... Faced with this deplorably bright future, men — and women must band together and fight this white peril ... before society as a real and visible entity becomes washed out.[4]

This is not a frequently celebrated political tradition. ALF and the Black Guards are not remembered fondly as the zenith of 1960s radicalism. Ian Channel became a counterweight to the emergence of 'serious' political radicalism on campus. From 1969, he was financially supported by the Vice-Chancellor of the University of New South Wales as a 'university wizard', and he later emerged as the 'Wizard of Christchurch' in New Zealand, ringing bells and delivering mock speeches at civic events, even posing for photographs with laughing tourists. The theories of imminent transformation that Channel propounded are now equally out of fashion. Social theorists no longer think of television as part of the 'new media' that is in the process of changing subjectivity; they now reserve such grand claims for the Internet. If consumption is still seen as an important marker of social identity, its impact is now seen to be less disruptive or transformative. Students celebrate its hedonism and typically embrace the carefully calibrated diversity of the market rather than mock its supposed puritanism or plot escape to an alternative culture. The prophets of the living theatre and the transformative power of electromagnetic communications would now seem quaint, discredited prophets of a far-off time.

Nonetheless, these confused, laughably bold, self-evidently wrong pronouncements *do* suggest that something was changing in Australia in the late 1960s. Channel and the Black Guards expressed a strong connection with consumer culture, and an early, if exaggerated, awareness of its impacts. They expressed too, an awareness of the mass media, and an expectation that it was changing subjectivity — increasing the importance of display, opening up opportunities for 'theatrical' behaviour in everyday life. Finally, their jointly confronting, seemingly irrational style offered a new contrast to the reasoned, sober face of both representative democracy, and 'legitimate' dissent. Like the Yippies and Diggers of the United States, they offered what Julie Stephens has recently called an 'anti-disciplinary' politics, shot through with satire, irony and fun. Their performances broke down the distinction between politics and art, and thereby opened up new forms of participation in political life.[5]

Indeed, while we may mock the stridency of Channel's prophecies, it is true that dramatic performance did become an increasingly important tool of political action over the course of the 1960s. In this chapter, we will draw on the methods of social science to document and to explain this transformation.

PERFORMING POLITICS: DEBATE, REPRESENTATION, STAGING

As Erving Goffman famously argued in *The Presentation of Self in Everyday Life*, it is possible to understand all forms of social interaction as performance and drama. When they are in the presence of others, individuals project a particular definition of the situation. They make an implicit or explicit claim to be a person of a particular kind, and they perform such roles through the modulation of appearance, manner, and so on. This is not only true of 'the hippy' or the paint-spattered peace protester, but also of the 'Commanding Officer', the 'responsible citizen', the 'son' and the 'Archbishop'. In short, all individuals play a series of parts, drawing on and remaking a range of well-established repertoires depending on the situation.

For Goffman, this opened up several fruitful avenues of enquiry. It became possible to analyse the tensions between the performance of a role (*front stage* behaviour) and actions occurring outside that role and its target audience (*back stage* behaviour). The tensions within a 'team' performance were also opened up for examination, as were the processes through which particular performances broke down, or were 'saved' by the interaction of audience and actors. A whole new mode of sociological analysis thereby became available, and it has since been applied to social institutions as diverse as the asylum and the town plan.[6]

Drawing inspiration from Goffman, it is also possible to understand *political interaction* in terms of performance. Indeed, the vocabulary of political analysis is often shot through with dramaturgical connotations. Nancy Fraser, for example, makes the point that even the most rational debate may be apprehended as a performance of a certain kind. She describes the 'public sphere' as 'a theater in modern societies in which political participation is enacted through the medium of talk'.[7] In this sense, the marshalling of evidence and the reliance on proof is a performance of 'rationality'. The process of talking and listening, reworking and responding to the contributions of others is the 'performance of debate'. Political figures play the role of reasonable women and men, perform their passionate attachment to values, modulate their voices to demonstrate their liberalism or conservatism.

In this sense, too, we can begin to analyse collective action as a political performance of a certain kind. When individuals join together to make collective claims, they perform in certain ways: they 'demonstrate' their beliefs for an audience, 'protest' their opposition, and so on. This is obviously true of colourful actions such as the seizing of a stage by Women's Liberationists in 1970. However, as political anthropologists like David Kertzer, Don Handelman and Eric Rothenbuhler have recognised, it is equally true of a small group who hold a public meeting in the local church hall, of worried citizens who sign a petition, or of workers who decide, after meeting and voting, that they will go out on strike.[8]

Of course, simply acknowledging that collective action is a performance does not advance our understanding very far. Social movement scholars have long referred to contention, or collective claim-making, with dramaturgical metaphors ('scripts', 'actors' and 'staging areas', for example), but this has seldom ventured beyond the descriptive. The study of collective action as performance can only gain intellectual purchase and genuinely illuminate our understanding when we move from description to analysis. Is this possible? Can the vast range of collective claim-making be broken down into more discrete categories? Can we specify and analyse particular clusters of roles, particular 'repertoires of collective performance'?

In this chapter I argue that this *is* possible, and I analytically specify three broad forms of 'collective performance':

1   *A repertoire of industrial action:* the refusal to perform labour, for example strikes, work-to-regulations, black bans, stopwork meetings. This is a performance of worker power and autonomy. In refusing to obey the role specified in the employment contract, employees perform both their own centrality to production and their ability to control their own capacities, thereby posing a direct challenge to the employers of labour.

2   *A repertoire of representation:* the performance of actions that involve the use of some institutional structure or media to signify the representation of a broader population, for example conventions, conferences, petitions, the formation of organisations, open letters and telegrams, deputations. This is a performance in which the action of a limited number of individuals and organisations attempts to 'stand' for a larger group of individuals. This larger group is not present but is represented in some way: personally through delegates who have been voted for, scripturally, through the signatures that have been entered onto a petition, and so on.

3   *A repertoire of staging:* the production of a public stage through the joint performance of claim-making by actors present in a particular place, for example public meetings, demonstrations, pickets, paint-throwing, sit-ins, vigils, graffiti, marches, destruction of property. This is a performance that attempts to create a public

forum through the very process of claim-making. In that sense, it involves the performance of a kind of direct democracy: individuals and 'teams' directly declare how the state should be run and how the good life should be pursued. Of course this staging often occurs in places associated with past political performances: town halls, speakers' corners, and so on. But it may also erupt suddenly on a city street, amid a military parade, at a swimming pool, even in apparently 'private' spaces such as offices or homes. Through the performance of staging, these places become 'public'. They become, briefly, stages on which actors make claims on others.

It is the production of a public stage in a particular place that unites actions as moderate as a 'gathering' with actions as radical as violent confrontation; actions as individualistic as daubing graffiti with actions as collective as the 100 000-strong Moratorium march in Melbourne. While it would be contrary to ignore the differences between such performances (these will be explored later on), they nonetheless remain actions of the same family, analytically distinguishable from industrial action and representation.

CHANGING RELATIONS AMONG THE REPERTOIRES: CHARTING THE RISE OF STAGING, 1965–71

The collective performances that I have labelled 'industrial action', 'representation' and 'staging' all have a venerable history. With a few exceptions, all of them can be traced back at least to the eighteenth century. As Charles Tilly has shown, the tools of collective action were largely remade in this period in Britain. The dual challenges of state-making and proletarianisation placed an incredibly arduous burden on ordinary citizens at this time. It was in this context that a new repertoire of collective action emerged. It was cosmopolitan rather than parochial, modular rather than locally bound, and autonomous rather than reliant on the actions of others. Central to this new repertoire were actions such as demonstrations, strikes, rallies and petitions, and these new improvisations ultimately came to supersede the traditional actions of the period, such as grain seizures, festivals and field invasions.[9]

Clearly, the 1960s therefore saw reinvention, reuse and modification of earlier traditions rather than the wholesale creation of new forms of collective action; demonstrations, rallies and occupations of space were energised and remade rather than invented from scratch. Even accepting these limitations, however, the period looms as one of sustained experimentation, advance and change. It was, indeed, a period in which relations among repertoires were reformulated. Central to this change was the rise of staging: over the 1960s, collective performances that drew on what I have called a 'repertoire of staging' increased in both absolute and relative terms. As a result, the means of popular claim-making underwent genuine transformation.

Drawing on the methods of social science, this chapter attempts to document and to explain the rise of staging in Australia between 1965 and 1971. Its arguments are based on a carefully constructed record of collective action. Using the *Sydney Morning Herald* as a source, researchers located, catalogued and coded nearly 3500 reports of collective claim-making in Australia, 1965–71 inclusive. Newspaper sources were consulted for eight different sorts of information about each incident of collective action: the actors involved; institutions; numbers; forms of action; time; space; demands made; and the objects of any claims. I use these data to ground my analysis of collective action in this chapter. I do not, however, attempt to analyse the dynamics of industrial action, sticking instead to the repertoires of representation and staging.

Undoubtedly, the reliance on the *Sydney Morning Herald* will skew the data in certain ways. We can expect it to overrepresent actions within major cities in general and within Sydney in particular. We can expect it to overrepresent actions involving or concerning its readership: the urban middle class. Finally, we can expect it to overrepresent the disruptive actions perpetrated by demonstrators, and to underrepresent those by police and state authorities. The chances of a member of the urban middle class openly smashing the window of a police station and this action 'slipping through the cracks' are very low. The chances that a peaceful protest, organised by a member of the rural proletariat in Bourke and resulting in police violence, will fail to attract coverage are comparatively great.

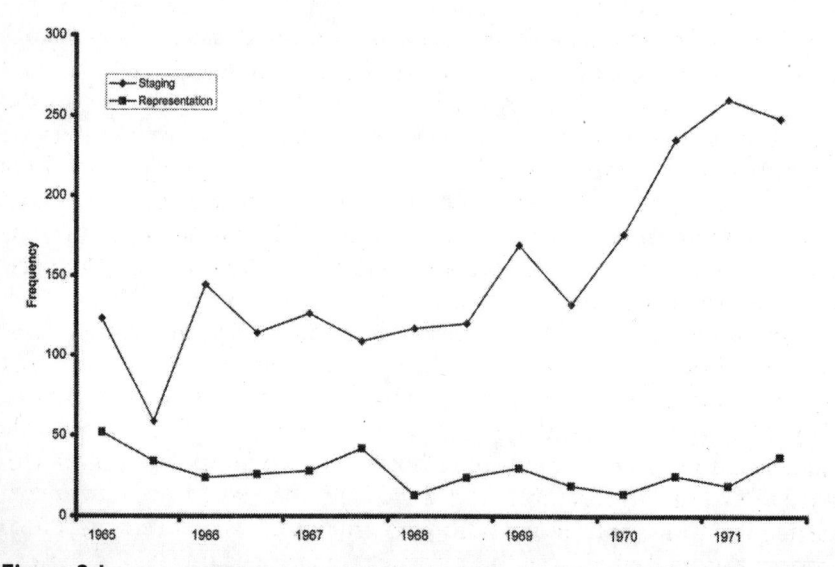

Figure 2.1
Staging and representation, January 1965–December 1971

As a result, I will be circumspect about making any claims concerning the relative importance of Sydney as a centre of protest, the relative prominence of the urban middle class as a political actor, or the precise dynamics between police and demonstrators that result in violent or disruptive behaviour. Such issues apart, these data provide an invaluable record of the changing forms of collective performance in Australia. They demonstrate, moreover, the clear rise to dominance of staging as a repertoire of political performance.

As Figure 2.1 shows, the collective performance of staging became an increasingly important political tool over the late 1960s and early 1970s. Between the first half of 1965 and the last half of 1971, the prevalence of staging more than doubled. Over this same period, the repertoire of representation, the chief competitor for staging, underwent an uneven but definite decline. In short, staging increased in both absolute and relative terms.[10] But if the rise of staging was complete by 1971, its passage was less smooth than we might expect. Reflecting the translation associated with the Freedom Ride in early 1965, the repertoire of staging rises, unevenly, into 1966, and then falls over 1967 and 1968. It is only in 1969 that staging achieves the levels of early 1966. It is only over the next two and a half years, and in particular over 1970 and 1971, that the collective performance of staging becomes a widespread, mass phenomenon.

The curve of collective action shown in Figure 2.1 contrasts with equivalent periods in other countries, and with the models that most scholars have accepted as typical. Sidney Tarrow's *Democracy and Disorder* traced a similar period of collective mobilisation in Italy from 1965 to 1975. His study of contention suggested a 'cycle of protest', in which collective action emerged as a primarily institutional phenomenon, was radicalised by a range of vibrant protest actions, reached a peak in the early 1970s, and then declined as both violence (on the radical wing) and institutionalisation (on the moderate wing) undercut the intensity of popular mobilisation. Over the ten-year period, Italy moved, in a 'cycle of protest', from demobilisation to mobilisation, and again to demobilisation; this was reflected in Tarrow's 'curve of contention'. The rise and decline of collective action in Italy was far smoother than the uneven history we will explore in Australia.

On closer analysis, the divergence from the Italian model increases. Central to Tarrow's account is the role of 'early risers'. He argues that the early phases of the cycle of protest involve the rise of new actors, who use 'expressive and confrontational forms of action' on a wide scale, and thereby demonstrate 'to others less daring than themselves that the system is vulnerable to disruption'. The early risers adopt radical tactics that open up the space for other actors to follow. His data support this analysis. The rate of 'tactical innovation', that is, the number of actions performed per protest event, increases rapidly in the early part of his cycle and reaches a peak as early as 1968. Protest events involving multiple and experimental actions are more likely in the *early part* of the overall period of collective mobilisation.[11]

In contrast, as Figure 2.2 clearly shows, the rate of tactical innovation is not robust in the early stages of Australian contention. It remains at a very low level from 1965 until at least the first half of 1968. Then, suddenly, it increases markedly — a level that is largely maintained until late 1971. In that sense, the Italian experience is both departed from and partly confirmed. Tactical innovation is not evident on a widespread scale in the early phases of collective mobilisation, though it does predate the peak of collective action. There are few 'early risers' in 1965–66. There are, however, the 'not-quite-early risers of 1968', who adopt a wider variety of actions than their precursors and who open up opportunities for the rapid rise in staging over 1969–71.

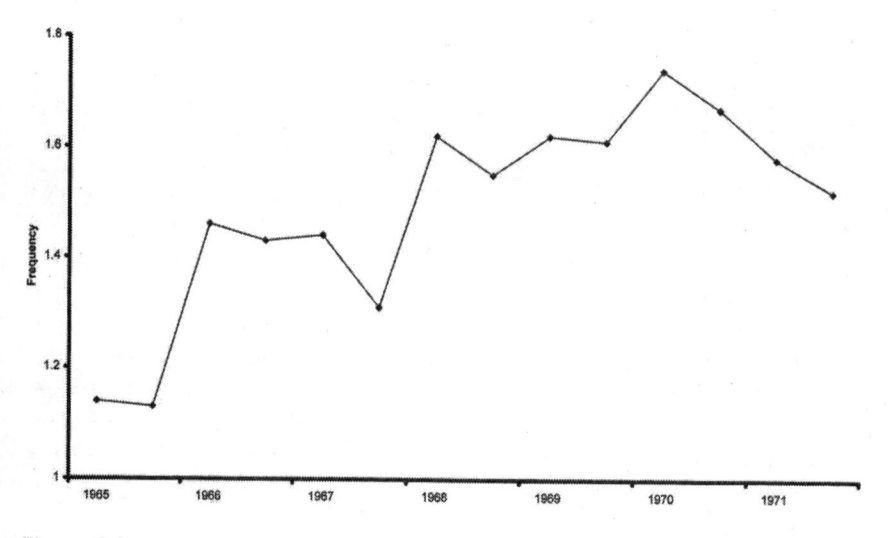

Figure 2.2
Tactical innovation — mean actions per protest event, January 1965–December 1971

What causes this uneven rise in Australian collective action? Why does it rise and fall before widespread mobilisation takes off? An explanation lies in the relations between political actors and the media on the one side, and political actors and the state on the other. That is, the relations at the heart of the political gimmick help to explain the changing overall patterns of collective action. In the rest of this chapter, I pursue these changing relations by drawing on the metaphor of performance and by examining the interplay between actors and audience.

DILEMMAS, PERFORMANCES, AUDIENCE AND ACTIONS

If individuals and teams 'perform' collective action, then who are they performing for? It is now widely accepted that since at least the 1960s, political actors have not performed for those directly present. On the contrary, they have mainly performed for an audience of television watchers, radio listeners and newspaper readers. That is, we have moved from a theatrical mode of publicness, where performers and public meet, to a primarily cinematographic mode of publicness in which performers and public are dissociated and separated.[12]

This has important implications for the organisation of collective action. Three widely recognised principles are particularly pertinent:

1   Only those actions that attain media coverage become widely public.

2   Media coverage tends to increase with the novelty, disruption and violence of collective acts.

3   Media coverage is unlikely to reconstruct the precise interactions between political actors, especially if they involve disruption or violence between demonstrators and agents of the state.[13]

Together, these three principles constitute what could be called the *dilemmas of the activist*. Moderate, routine forms of claim-making are unlikely to attain wide media coverage, and are therefore unlikely to win support or successfully achieve demands. On the other hand, novel, disruptive and violent actions often involve sustained interaction and conflict with police. As a result, the strong media coverage that they attain is likely to be negative and counterproductive. Either way, the broad public support that protesters seek is unlikely to materialise.

The history of staging in Australia between 1965 and 1971 reflects an attempt to grapple with these dilemmas. In effect, it is a history of four moments:

1   A range of newly translated, theatrical political performances are successfully deployed. They attain widespread, sometimes sympathetic media coverage (1965–66).

2   As these political performances become more routinised, and conflict with police emerges, they increasingly fail as political interventions. The performances break down. There is a clear retreat from the more theatrical forms of collective action (1967).

3   Out of the turmoil provoked by this retreat, a group of actors improvise new forms of political performance. Tactical innovation increases and new roles are created (1968).

4   The new forms of political performance are taken up on a wide scale. Two forms of performance become especially important: the staging of public contest and the performance of disruption. Both accept the costs of negative media coverage in preference to political silence (1969–71).

The rise of staging as a dominant political performance emerges as a complex, interactive process. It reflects the changing relations between protesters and police, the changing presentation of protest events by the media, and the changing relations among political performers. That is precisely why the growth of staging is so jagged and interrupted. Political actors were sometimes uncertain, groping and doubtful. Their actions were experimental, sensitive and flexible, and always responsive to the actions and reactions of others. In this way, new performances were gradually developed and reviewed, and a more theatrical repertoire of collective action unevenly rose to dominance.

The importance of interaction among political actors, the state and the media also helps to explain the complex legacies of the period, and its contradictory effects on Australian democracy. The late 1960s and early 1970s increased the tools of political performance available to a range of Australians. Through the spread of staging, conflict, claim-making and disagreement broke out across a range of social spaces, and Australian public life was considerably invigorated. Both public space and the public sphere widened.

At the same time, these performances tended to rely on contest and disruption in order to attain publicity. As a result, the new public 'stages' that were summoned up sometimes lacked the strength to support detailed or balanced discussion. Along with the increasing width of the public sphere sometimes came an increasing shallowness — an absence of rational public debate on the varied issues that were newly raised. In that sense, the rise of staging was neither a simple victory nor a defeat for democratic life in Australia.

APPLAUSE FOR A NEW PERFORMANCE

The successful 'translation' of the Freedom Ride that we analysed in Chapter 1 stimulated a range of collective action in the first half of 1965. A plethora of sit-ins, demonstrations, marches and violations of segregated public space rapidly occurred over issues such as the Vietnam War, democracy in Greece, conscription, apartheid, the civil rights of women, parking privileges, shopping hours, increased wages and conditions, and civil rights for Aboriginal people. Students greeted the South African Rugby team in 'black face'; Aboriginal people demanded entrance to segregated pools and cinemas; and opponents of conscription sat down in shopping malls and city streets.

If some of these actions had a long history of performance in

Australia, that history had been lost, clouded by the twenty years of Cold War. Dorothy Dalton, a former member of the Communist Party, has remembered the timidity with which actions like the march were freshly taken up in the mid-1960s: 'I think we were both self-conscious of marching. I didn't find it easy to march. Communists were the big bogey in Australia and seen as undermining the political system, but Communists were not law-breakers. Those years of [Cold War] experience did not prepare us for that type of action'.[14] The long absence of these performances made their new practitioners brave and daring, but equally it gave the actions novelty and public resonance. Television cameras lurked, anxious to record long-slumbering forms of political action. This was unquestionably news. One journalist somewhat contemptuously observed the eager, stagey interaction between demonstrators and camera crews in Sydney, 25 October 1965:

> The demonstrators moved up steep steps to a higher level midway between street and the courthouse. They turned and posed for television and press cameramen who followed them up the steps ... Young men with long blond hair and bushy beards talked in subdued tones to black-stockinged girls with long hair. 'Are they Vietniks?' asked a woman ...[15]

While the roles and expectations of both actors and audience were clearly still fluid at this stage, it is equally clear that sit-ins, demonstrations and marches which involved comparatively few performers could hope to attain wide publicity. A new political gimmick had been discovered. The repertoire of staging seemed to promise a new era of publicity, and a genuine reinvigoration of Australian democracy.

Six matronly women, members of the Women's International League for Peace and Freedom, could gain front-page coverage by preparing a banner, travelling to Sydney's Kingsford Smith Airport, and greeting Dr Gough, the Anglican Primate of Australia, with demands that he change his attitude to the Vietnam War. Forty students at Melbourne University who demonstrated against Prime Minister Harold Holt, twenty-five opponents of conscription in Sydney, twelve clergymen who distributed an illegal pamphlet in Melbourne, and sixteen students who sat down in the centre of Canberra — all these could achieve the same prominence. In the first half of 1965, when the surprise of these democratic performances was most acute, even brief, peaceful vigils could attract generous media coverage.[16]

Furthermore, much of this coverage was broadly positive. Indeed, the fledgling nature of such performances meant that they often drew angry, irrational and sometimes violent responses from local opponents. When Student Action For Aborigines picketed the Walgett RSL Club on 15 February 1965, local Walgett residents argued violently, and police were forced to intervene. As students left town that evening, their bus was run off the road. When students picketed Moree pool five days later, ten of them were thrown into the pool. When students gamely decided to continue their picket they were jeered and bombarded with fruit. Two students were attacked and local police again interceded in defence of the students, pushing residents back behind a fence and arresting two local people. In this case police even thought it necessary to escort the students out of town, carefully checking the credentials of the cars that followed.

In such situations, actors pioneering new forms of political performance could expect high praise. Like the civil rights activists of the United States, they had effectively choreographed a drama of noble sacrifice and brutal reaction. They were passive, noble, committed; their opponents were racist, violent, unreflective. SAFA's opponents had refused to accept that most cardinal of liberal pieties: the right to free assembly. The actions of students had gained protection from the police, and thus strong normative endorsement. In short, as the *Sydney Morning Herald* saw it, students had 'performed a service' for Australian society. They had shown 'considerable moral and physical courage' in their quest to 'awaken the public conscience'.[17]

Even when staging failed to draw irrational or illiberal response, its sometimes strong emphasis on rationality helped to encourage broad endorsement within the media. Many of the most novel forms of staging embodied a strong rational dimension. This was the case, for example, with one important 'translation' of the mid-1960s: the 'teach-in'. Famously, the teach-in was first developed in March 1965 by students and academics opposed to the Vietnam War at the University of Michigan. It was effectively a marathon debate, with rival speakers and audience members making arguments, posing questions and presenting evidence over several hours. By 23 July 1965, its translation was under way. The first teach-in within Australia attracted more than 500 participants to the Australian National University in Canberra. Subsequent teach-ins at Monash and Sydney Universities were not only reported but were directly broadcast on television for extended periods.[18]

Participants in the teach-in effectively performed their earnest engagement with the issues, their respect for rational argumentation, and their sincere, active commitment to citizenship. In this way they heightened the appeal of the anti-war movement to liberal intellectuals, and they attracted favourable comment within the press. While such a sober method of staging was anything but flamboyant, its newly minted quality and liberal form jointly granted it the bountiful and open media coverage that political actors sought. It soon became a staple of other campaigns, such as the battle for increased educational funding, and its smooth reception powerfully reflects the democratic advances of the mid-1960s.

Over 1965–66, a range of Australians quickly learnt the power of staging. Demonstrations, marches, teach-ins, pickets and protests all increased in number. Not only that, but as the new forms of political performance became routine, claimants began to increase the pace and complexity of collective action. Improvisation was evident, as actors enriched their protests with additional actions: colourful draft card burnings, mass sit-ins and more daring occupations of space began to occur. The quest for fresh forms of political claim-making helped to push actors towards unaccustomed combinations of collective behaviour. The appetite of the media for novel political performances was increasingly sated with fresh and innovative collective acts.

This is reflected in Figure 2.1, notably the clear if uneven rise in staging between 1965 and 1966. A closer analysis of six episodes of staging, spread over the fourteen months between October 1965 and November 1966, powerfully illustrates this interactive, collective process. Indeed, over this period, political actors jointly opposed to the Vietnam War and to conscription showed an increasing dexterity, confidence, and verve in staging their views for a wider public.

The first evidence of this willingness to improvise was evident on 22 October 1965, when students, wharf labourers and peace activists gathered outside the Commonwealth Bank in Martin Place, Sydney. Their demonstration against the Vietnam War and conscription initially appeared to follow the blueprint established in earlier actions, previously held in May and September of 1965. But after around half an hour the protest took an unexpected turn, as a number of participants determinedly advanced into the path of traffic on Sydney's main Pitt Street. Bob Gould of the Vietnam Action Committee has fondly recalled the shock that this transgression caused to local police:

> There was no mall then, and we walked along with the traffic at 5:30 pm on a Friday night. It took the coppers completely by surprise, and we were halfway from King Street to Market Street before they could get in front of us.
>
> About 50 of us got pinched ...
>
> ... It was not a violent demonstration. It was completely passive, except the coppers threw us around a bit, but it was effective in terms of publicity across the nation.[19]

Others similarly began to adopt more confronting political roles. On 14 March 1966, forty students deliberately advanced into the path of the Moomba Day Parade in Melbourne. Two weeks later, demonstrators opposing the Vietnam War and conscription directly contested the appearance of Prime Minister Harold Holt at Kew Town Hall. Marbles were thrown as Holt spoke, and attempts were made to rush the stage. When Holt attempted to speed away in the prime ministerial motor car it was encircled, rocked and pounded. A new performance of commitment and explicit challenge was emerging.

The new mood was evident around the country. On 16 April 1966, peace activists in Sydney again showed their willingness to diverge from past practice, and thereby to construct a more noticeable and terrific public stage. This time an initial Martin Place demonstration was elaborated with a long march through Kings Cross to the Garden Island Naval Dockyard. On arrival a blonde youth threw himself at the dockyard gates. The crowd surged forward. Women in suffragette uniforms attempted to chain themselves to the gates. Bob Gould was present again, and he not only chained himself to the gates, he later climbed onto the office roof, triumphantly flouting the disciplined order of military space. Not surprisingly, his then more nimble form was pictured on the *Herald*'s front page the next day.

Activists in Adelaide also began to extend the range of their political performances at this time. A demonstration and draft card burning outside the US Consulate on 9 September 1966 was supplemented with an attempt to burn the Australian flag. Bystanders were aghast and intervened angrily. The first successful burning of the flag needed to wait for another month. Finally, on 5 October 1966, thirty students outside the Prime Minister's official residence, The Lodge, drew widespread attention (and opprobrium) for the first successful, condemnatory burning of the Australian flag in recent memory.[20]

This intensification of protest reached its temporary peak in late October 1966, with the visit of US President Lyndon Johnson to Australia. The more adventurous approach to the performance of dissent that had emerged over the last year was now taken to a higher level. Demonstrators greeted Johnson with angry, surging crowds at the Rex Hotel in Canberra. When Johnson travelled to Melbourne on 21 October, brothers David and John Langley audaciously splattered his car with the red and green paint of the Vietnamese National Liberation Front (NLF). When the presidential motorcade later sped hurriedly along St Kilda Road, 3000 enraged opponents of the Vietnam War burst onto the street and fell into an extended brawl with police and supporters.

While eight hunger strikers protested outside Parliament House in Adelaide, the 'Vietniks' of Sydney also began to prepare for the arrival of the US President. Demonstrators in Sydney countered Johnson's presence not only with protests but with active civil disobedience. At the corner of Oxford and College Streets, several young women and men lay across the road, blocking the path of the presidential motorcade. At Hyde Park, a placard-wielding activist broke through the barricades and attacked Johnson's car, a young woman threw herself across a police car's bonnet, and police horses were apparently pelted with streamers and stones. This was the protest event immortalised in the Frank Moorhouse short story 'The Revolutionary Kidney Punch', when radical young people first began to clash with police as daring, self-consciously 'revolutionary' actors. Around the city — in Kensington, Paddington, the NSW Art Gallery and Circular Quay — raucous and popular protests deliriously broke out. As the cameras of the American press whirred, the Australian Left seemed briefly, definitively, to be 'on the international map'.[21] Could the new power of staging be bringing it to ascendance?

Functionaries of the Australian state were shocked. Famously, NSW Premier Bob Askin ordered the official motorcar's driver to 'run over the bastards' who lay across the road. Victorian protesters were to complain about incompetence, provocation and assault by local police. New restrictions on popular assembly were quickly signalled.

But while the state decried these new performances, even the conservative press was more ambivalent, slow to condemn. The international press lavished attention on Australian dissidents. The *Sydney Morning Herald* defended the right of protesters to block traffic, 'provided they accept the right of the police to arrest them and charge them'. The cameras continued to attend creative and novel demonstrations, even if they involved genuine conflict with police. A television audience increasingly literate in the 'theatre of protest' began to rank and sort the plentiful images supplied by competing networks. TV critic Harry Robinson, for example, typically displayed this sophistication with his 'review' of the arrest of conscientious objector William White:

> 'Don't push me you b———'. These inelegant but lively words by a bystander came through the ATN 7 News last night [22 November 1966] in the cover[age] of William White's arrest ...
>
> ... ATN 7 News, third on air by a few moments, had a 'down-in-amongst it,' 'blow by blow' film which carried the most vivid sound of all. It was shot on a portable sound camera which makes it possible for one cameraman to get in close with lens and microphone open.
>
> The dividend is realism.
>
> Seven's cameraman was Richard McNicoll, now called the 'riot expert' ... He shot the scoop sound on film of the anti-LBJ demonstrations. Yesterday he was in the thick of the melee at White's house.[22]

As 1966 came to a close, opponents of the Australian Government had good reason to be hopeful. More theatrical forms of political role-playing had been grasped and applied across a range of issues. The mass public of television watchers and newspaper readers, it seemed, could now be reached with political gimmicks and rational pleas. Democracy was enlivened. Not only that, but both political actors and audiences were beginning to show a greater sophistication in the performance and reception of collective action. Surely a dazzling vista of advancing political improvisation and expanding public recognition beckoned into the new year.

A SHAMBLES ONSTAGE

The advances of 1965 and 1966 initially appeared to presage a kind of epochal shift in the resources of citizens. Australian claimants could adopt political gimmicks to reach wide, untapped publics. A new era awaited.

These advances, however, were based on quite peculiar historical circumstances. The apparent novelty of staging at this time helped to produce an accommodating state and a responsive media. The relatively small number of claimants allowed for 'team performances' that could proceed with what would later appear as a remarkable unity and smoothness.

By 1967, these conditions had begun to evaporate. As novelty was replaced by familiarity, and new activists joined the fray, so the performance of collective action began to appear less 'sincere', more stagey and manipulative.[23] Not only that, but police also began to adopt 'more robust' measures at this time. The three largest campaigns of late 1966 and early 1967 — the demonstrations confronting Lyndon Johnson, targeting South Vietnamese leader Marshall Ky, and opposing the hanging of Ronald Ryan — all resulted in complaints from protesters about police violence, mistreatment and provocation. In Queensland, students and unionists were denied the right to march, and a long campaign for civil rights began. In Adelaide, students worried over police interference in the organising activity of their institutions, such as the meetings and rallies of Students for Democratic Action. By 1968, it was a commonplace on the Left that the government had decided to 'get tough' with demonstrators.[24]

As the relationship between political activists and the police soured, so political leaders and the press began to express their distrust of the theatrical techniques with greater vehemence. NSW Premier Bob Askin thought anti-Vietnam demonstrators an 'unwashed' mob. New ALP leader Gough Whitlam expressed doubts over the effectiveness of anti-conscription demonstrations. Central to such doubts was the notion that the intensity of the theatrical performances made them irrational or illiberal. When students disrupted political meetings with confronting demonstrations, they were thought uninterested in debate. When they threw paper darts at the Prime Minister, they were presented as boors, betrayers of the ideals of the university. When the ordered gathering, addressed by 'eminent men and women', was superseded by the more disruptive forms of political stunts, the *Sydney Morning Herald* mourned the tendency of political dissidents to 'go beyond legitimate criticism'.[25]

The very factors that gave the repertoire of staging its force — the theatre, the departure from ordered routine, the active participation of citizens — were now depicted as disquieting symptoms of disorder. Liberal critics lamented the tendency of demonstrations to involve multiple issues and to express opposition and critique rather than alternatives and precise plans. The press adopted an increasingly critical approach to demonstrations. Complaints of distortion were more frequently made by protesters. In fact some students opined that every action was now magnified into a terrible threat to the status quo.[26]

In these circumstances, incipient tactical disputes began to break into open conflict. From within the peace and student movements, doubts were now expressed about the utility of the theatrical techniques. The unstructured nature of these political performances, and their tendency to become vehicles for a variety of claims, began to worry some students. Others thought that the organisation, commitment and disruption associated with the repertoire of staging was too complete to justify the particular issues at stake. Other critics still became doubtful of the frequency of demonstrations, asserting that their overuse had eroded their effectiveness, producing only a collection of 'professional protesters', anxious simply to attack society.

As such criticisms rose in volume, the wider elite dissatisfaction with the repertoire of staging reached a crescendo. As a result, a number of student activists ventured that the disruptive and complex performances that had so recently gained favour were causing more harm than good. As Peter Middleton put it in the University of NSW student newspaper *Tharunka*: 'In the present climate of political opinion formation, student demonstrations do antagonise the public against those involved, and by association, against the views advocated ... The public now has an almost conditioned response against such publicity'.[27]

However, while these critiques expressed a discomfort with the increasing pace and complexity of political performance, the utility of the more unadorned and simple forms of staging was also being undermined. These actions now struggled to attain newsworthiness. They were dull, comparatively routine. Organisers of vigils and rallies came to accept that their actions would not now produce a 'spectacular outcome'. Peaceful marches and demonstrations were often acknowledged as public failures, unable to make an impact 'upon the populace'. As one student concisely put it, in the new conditions the 'publicity' equation had become: 'no violence — no publicity'. It was Humphrey McQueen, the young New Leftist and budding historian, who most strongly asserted the redundancy of moderate forms of staging at this time: 'What could be more grotesque than 5,000 people marching through Melbourne's streets on a Sunday afternoon?'[28]

The team performances of 1965 and 1966 were now breaking down. While actors divided over legitimate tactics, individual team members pursued divergent roles. The process of public staging sometimes dissolved into shambles, as 'moderate' groups insisted on simple and peaceful performances, and younger radicals agitated for more complex and confronting actions. This was the case, for example, in Melbourne on 4 July 1967. Older activists associated with the Congress for International Co-operation and Disarmament clashed with younger members of the Monash University Labor Club. A student plan for a flag-burning and sit-in was stymied, while the older activists worried over public reactions. Neither group was satisfied. The anti-Vietnam campaign was stalling. As Erving Goffman has noted, in these situations of open team conflict, any performance is unlikely to sway its audience. Its reality will not be accepted.[29]

Political actors had been outflanked by events. The tools of newsmaking were suddenly proving ineffectual. In place of a productive new political gimmick, claimants now faced an unfortunate new dilemma. What could they do? Bill Bottomley expressed the dilemma best in 1969:

> Even if there is a decent turnout, the news media manage to obscure the real issues by reporting only the violence — or by not reporting anything if there is no violence to make it 'newsworthy'. If a demo doesn't get coverage, then you're right back to square one; if it does get coverage, it is usually in the form of a 'bad press', and you're back to square one again.[30]

Inevitably, these tensions impinged on the actions of political claimants. The level of staging declined over 1967 and did not surmount the peak of 1966 until early 1969. Existing accounts of the peace and anti-Vietnam movement have explained this decline in terms of the defeat of the Australian Labor Party (ALP) in the 1966 elections.[31] Clearly, this was important — sapping the confidence of activists and causing many to review their previous strategies. However, the decline of staging extended both outside the peace campaign and over a longer period than has previously been acknowledged. There was a general crisis in the repertoire of staging, and it was only when activists improvised new combinations of collective action that its pace and level of performance began to pick up.

In this sense, the dramatic, controversial and varied actions of university students over 1968 would become crucial to both the viability of staging and the wider history of collective action in Australia.

IMPROVISING FOR PUBLICITY: THE RADICALISATION OF 1968

By 1968, a core of radical students had come to believe that moderate forms of staging would achieve 'bugger all'. Conflict with police and 'threats of violence' by the state had caused many of them to develop a more combative stance. The ALP was now seen as a pillar of the 'establishment'. It was time to move beyond 'traditional' forms of political action. The young radicals drew comfort from the positive publicity achieved by the demonstrations against Lyndon Johnson and the struggle for civil rights in Queensland. In these cases, mass, 'militant' action had proved successful. Why could it not be extended and enlarged? As radical student Michael Hamel-Green saw it, past experience showed that civil disobedience and direct action were

> powerful forces in a modern society where the mass media quickly communicate to millions what is happening, and feelings of solidarity may be rapidly generated ... They can provide models of resistance and alternative action for those exploited or excluded groups who come, as a daily occurrence, into conflict with ruling bureaucratic hierarchies of society.[32]

At the same time as Australian students lunged for more adventurous forms of contention, an explosion of radical, sometimes apparently revolutionary, actions broke out across Western Europe, the United States, within the Soviet Bloc, and in the Third World. The marvellous events in Paris in May 1968 encouraged many to believe that revolution was possible in an advanced capitalist society. The growing recourse of European students to 'extralegal' means was understood to be 'increasingly effective'. Others praised the ability of American activists to accept 'hardship and injury', as a way of demonstrating their 'commitment' and thereby awakening the 'consciences' of their fellow citizens. The continuing struggle of the Vietnamese people inspired and radicalised students like Brian Aarons, and the cry of 'Ho, Ho, Ho Chi Minh!' began to be heard across campuses. Some radical students, like Michael Hamel-Green, began to restudy the campaigns of Gandhi, Martin Luther King and the CND, hoping to learn more of direct action techniques. At the same time, other Australian visitors to Britain learnt of and generously praised the action of those British students who had donated aid to the National Liberation Front. Such actions seemed 'very important'. Perhaps Australians, too, needed to take up these campaigns.[33]

Over late 1967 and throughout 1968, a new, more defiant spirit was evident. Although the level of staging remained comparatively low, Figure 2.2 shows that the rate of tactical innovation increased markedly. When activists did hold protest events, they were now marked by a greater variety of actions. There was a willingness to take chances and court arrest, to 'perform commitment' in the cause of public attention. Over a series of notable events, new forms of staging developed. We can trace the nuances of these developments through the brief retelling of a small number of specific events.

On 2 October 1967, eight Monash University students, members of the Aid to National Liberation Front Committee, declared their intention to send $100 to the Liberation Red Cross. As they put it, 'we believe that we have a conscientious duty to aid the National Liberation Front in its struggle for Vietnamese independence'. Albert Langer, one of the students involved, later recalled that this was an act of calculated civil disobedience, a deliberate attempt to violate the law, to undermine the authority of the university's Vice-Chancellor, and to thereby draw public attention: 'It certainly was a premeditated decision to set up this fund. It was done consciously in the knowledge that the Vice-Chancellor had prohibited it. It was done because we thought that the Vice-Chancellor's direction was invalid and we knew that the press would be there'.[34]

This was a new kind of public performance in contemporary Australian political life. The new stage was constructed of shock and disruption. It abandoned the tools of respectability and the hammer of reason for the megaphone of illegality. By performing their open contempt for the policies of the Australian Government, the Monash students were suddenly, powerfully, vaulted to public prominence. They achieved 'tremendous publicity', and the broader radical movement was enamoured of this remarkable and successful improvisation. Doug White of the journal *Arena* thought it 'the first challenge to the Australian rules for many years'.[35] *Arena*'s editors revisited the action early in 1968, elevating it to pre-eminence in the pantheon of recent collective action, confident that it stood out over the 'many campaigns' for civil rights, against conscription, and for university freedom over the last few years. According to them, it signalled to 'many students' a new way of acting politically: '[a] first clear insight into the fact that, when they touch on authority in the State, student politics may be translated into issues with a national impact'.[36]

The intention to 'touch on authority in the state' became the key to the evolving political performances of 1968. On 7 February, the Draft Resistance Movement burst upon the scene. Four members of the new group chained themselves across the gates of the Swan Street Army Reception Centre. When police removed them, a larger group conducted a sit-down demonstration and openly distributed pamphlets on how to resist conscription. The pamphlet extolled the new disruptive stance directly:

> The Draft Resistance Movement has not been formed to oppose conscription, it has been formed to wreck it ... We will hold demonstrations of various kinds with the aim of making conscription as ineffective as possible; we will supply information on how to fail medical exams and other methods of dodging the draft and we will encourage people not to register.[37]

When the new Prime Minister John Gorton addressed the Caulfield Town Hall on 13 February 1968, the atmosphere of defiance was again evident. Thirty members of the Draft Resistance Movement conducted a sit-down demonstration half an hour before the speech began. 'Support the NLF', their placards provocatively announced. Police arrested twelve protesters, but this did not dull the remaining claimants. Gorton's speech was disrupted with boos, chants, and Hitler salutes. When the Prime Minister departed, twenty demonstrators blocked traffic along Glen Eira Road.[38] Such improvisations not only used the techniques of a wide range of discrete political performances, but they were underpinned by a deliberate collective challenge to the state. The role of the disruptive demonstrator, the disobedient citizen, was becoming increasingly popular.

On 19 May 1968, the organisation of civil disobedience came to Australia's capital. Three hundred and fifty anti-conscription actors, representing thirty-seven separate organisations, conducted a march from Parliament House to the official residence of the Prime Minister. This was the first national anti-conscription demonstration that had been called since 1966.

But further improvisations were to come. On arrival at The Lodge, the march was succeeded by a mass sit-in. When the sit-in was not countered by police reaction or arrests, it was deliberately escalated. It was moved to block the main traffic artery to Woden Valley, and sixty-nine protesters calmly submitted to police arrest. The media were interested and impressed by this performance of commitment. Even the *Sydney Morning Herald* praised these 'thoughtful, purposive, and deliberate acts of civil disobedience'.[39] Disruptive staging was about to take off.

On 20 April 1968, students from Melbourne University would conduct a kind of 'Freedom Ride' to the Holsworthy Army Camp in New South Wales — directly challenging the existence of conscription and courting mass arrest. On the anniversary of American independence, Melbourne would be convulsed by a 'mass student riot', with smokebombs, smashed windows, firecrackers, and rocks thrown at the City Watchhouse and police headquarters. When the First Secretary of the South Vietnamese Embassy, Phung Nhat Minh, visited the University of Queensland on 19 July, students held a noose dramatically above his head.[40]

By early August, students at the University of Sydney were confronting the presence of police with confidence and mockery. When the familiar figure of Sergeant Longbottom of the Special Branch was discovered on campus on 2 August, students exacted cheerful revenge. His car was surrounded. A barricade of benches was quickly constructed. One student let down the car's front tyres and demanded to be arrested. Others plastered its bonnet and sides with stickers. Police agreed to erase a tape-recording of the earlier student meeting, and signed a statement agreeing not to attend campus meetings in future.

The humiliation was complete. 'Police carried the car away from Parramatta Road on a trailer. The car had a flat tyre, sugar in the petrol tank, chrome parts and number-plates dangling and was covered in stickers, some in the form of a swastika.'[41]

By the end of the year, the interactions between students and police combined the passion of an arm-wrestle with the calculation of a chess match. The strong process of mutual learning, action and interaction, radicalisation and frustration that Donatella della Porta has identified in Italy and elsewhere was also starkly relevant in Australia.[42] On 25 October, students in Brisbane and Melbourne held militant protests in support of the National Liberation Front. In the northern capital, squads of police and demonstrators fought a 'hide-and-seek battle of wits' over 'many city blocks' for more than an hour. In Melbourne, police prepared with 150 members of the force waiting behind steel barricades at the US Consulate, with their own cameras to record the actions of 'troublemakers', and with a further 150 uniformed officers positioned to shadow student marchers around the city. Students stopped a truck and called for a five-minute 'instantaneous teach-in'. Police responded by entering the truck and pushing it from the road. Students attempted to burn a dummy to show the effects of napalm, and firemen quickly intervened to disrupt their plans. On this occasion at least, the Victorian force could claim a tactical victory: 'Police claimed that the demonstrators tried to turn the incident into one of police brutality, "but we refused to respond" a senior officer said'.[43]

The varied defeats and tactical victories for both police and protesters would multiply over the succeeding months. As these increasingly elaborate contests were held, however, a broader process was at work. The repertoire of political performance was changing. If the shock and apparent novelty of the performances of 1965 and 1966 could not be recaptured, this not only led to indecision and retreat; for some political actors, the conflict enhanced the radical urge to perform.

Especially for some university students, the pace of staging was increased. These actors revelled in their new-found public prominence and were untroubled by the 'dilemmas of the activist'. By adopting more confrontational and disruptive actions, they could claim not only direct victory over local police but also a genuine challenge to the state. In the heady atmosphere of 1968, this connected local actors with their comrades in Berkeley and Turin, Paris and Havana. It made them 'revolutionary' actors, capable of a 'revolutionary thrust', comrades-in-arms with their inspiring Vietnamese heroes.

Certainly, radical Australian students still felt assailed and manipulated by the mass media over 1968. But this became a cause for agitation and propaganda, not moderation and inactivity. Those adopting the most radical poses attained a kind of 'dramatic dominance', to use

Erving Goffman's term. That is, their parts became the centre of attention. They dominated the public reportage of protest, and their political performances therefore became newly central. In these conditions, the more aggressive student performances of 1968 became exemplars for other actors.[44]

Over the next three years, the pace of collective action would increase massively. The pioneering actions of university students would be replicated and extended by a range of political actors. Two new clusters of political performance would be particularly crucial, as the overall level of staging took off. These were the performances that I have labelled the 'staging of contest' and the 'performance of disruption'.

THE STAGING OF CONTEST

Contestation is a classic, scripted performance. Contests range from the Olympics to the federal elections, from the sparring of boxers to the battles of pinball wizards in local parlours. Their domain is sport and politics. Their archetypal form is competitive and masculinist. In that sense, it would appear intuitive, if also 'masculine' for claimants to perform contest, that is, to make their demands in the direct presence of their personal or institutional objects.[45] Why shouldn't citizens opposed to the Prime Minister demonstrate their direct opposition to his presence? Protest outside courts when their judgments are disputed? Target the head office of a business that poses some threat to local wildlife and vegetation?

While this repertoire of performance is more confronting than those 'autonomous gatherings' that occur in *separate spaces* to their objects, it nonetheless appears as a respectable, viable form of collective action. By targeting the personal or institutional locus of their claims, those who 'perform contest' are able powerfully to express the depth and the intensity of their concerns. The political anthropologist David Kertzer has emphasised that officially sponsored rites and spaces have long offered an important setting for counter-rites of opposition and contest.[46]

However, if the performance of contestation has a widely acknowledged utility, it can also offer a widely recognised subversion of the dominant norms of liberal democratic societies. Because it poses a direct challenge to opponents in physical space, it can sometimes be seen as intimidatory; the ability of 'contest' to press claims by direct physical action is sometimes interpreted not merely as the expression of a given viewpoint but as the intention to suppress the viewpoints of others. When it impinges on the actions of other citizens, contestation is depicted as a violation of liberal values, a denial of pluralism. In this way it can be seen as an alien presence, contaminating the (apparently) free marketplace of ideas with the mace of force.[47]

The performance of contestation violates the norms of liberal democracy in other ways. Most obviously, it disrespects the boundaries of 'privacy'. Contests sometimes pop up in places usually regarded as outside the public realm: the residential homes of politicians, the offices of private capitalist firms, the operations of clubs that are reserved for the select use of their members. Because it refuses to be restricted to the domain of accepted political life, contestation therefore looms as a potentially menacing, transgressive force. This, indeed, is sometimes what makes it appealing to those with a cause to advance.[48]

By the early 1970s, many protesters had begun to embrace the new role of contestation. They had become dissatisfied with the structures and assumptions of liberal democratic society. Like radical students of the 'United Front' at Monash University, they felt that they started from a 'powerless position', where debate between equals was impossible. In such a situation, the rational dialogue idealised by liberal democracy was impractical: 'Recent events have shown the impossibility of accepting only mere rational debate (so-called) with no corresponding compromise by those with ultimate power'.[49] According to such a view, Australian society was not democratic. Not only did those in possession of institutional power refuse to give ground, but they could not be swayed by the force of rational argument. As Ian Morrison saw it, the opinions of the mass public and the government had become impermeable, no longer 'amenable to the analysis of facts and their contending interpretations'.[50]

But if rational debate was viewed as ineffectual by many protesters, 'traditional protest' was equally depicted as a weak, flimsy tool. Australian radicals drew from popular theorists like Herbert Marcuse to argue that contemporary society was characterised by an atmosphere of 'repressive tolerance', in which the force of traditional political actions was smoothly integrated and co-opted. As we have already seen, they also drew from local and overseas experience to argue that only the most militant and confronting forms of political behaviour could hope to make an impact. In this way, radical students like Warren Osmond could confidently claim that Australian political life was basically totalitarian, and that the student New Left of 1968 embodied 'the only force in Australian society attempting to crack this authoritarian structure of our society'.[51]

The developing performance of contestation was the joint result of this confluence of enthusiasms, disappointments, theories, and lessons of struggle. As Figure 2.3 shows, the performance of *contestational actions* increased markedly between 1965 and 1971. Contestational actions also rose more rapidly than those 'autonomous actions' that occur in separate spaces to their targets.

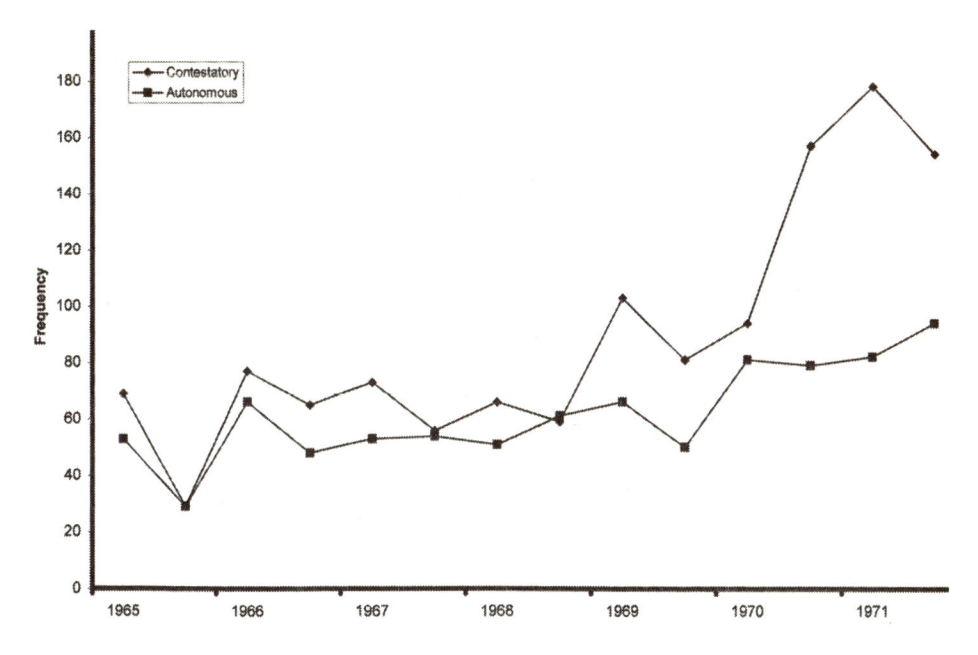

Figure 2.3
Contestatory versus autonomous staging, January 1965–December 1971

The performance of contestation broke out across a variety of social spaces over the early 1970s. In some senses, this was but a confirmation of long-standing democratic practices. Charles Tilly has powerfully emphasised the 'parliamentarisation' of contention in Great Britain over the eighteenth and nineteenth centuries.[52] This carried over to the Australia of the twentieth century, with the Federal Parliament in Canberra and the various State Parliament Houses remaining as crucial sites of protest over issues as diverse as the working conditions of nurses, the level of funding for education, Aboriginal land rights, and local sewerage problems. Given that the state was a frequent object of claims, it should not be surprising that its parliamentary institutions were also frequently the site of popular political contest.

In a broader sense, the state was also directly challenged through actions at other symbols of government power: state and federal office blocks in Sydney and Brisbane; post offices in Melbourne and Port Kembla; and specific departmental offices, such as the Department of Labour and National Service and the Attorney-General's office in Sydney. This same spatial principle of direct contest was also at work when claimants made direct demands on the embassies and consulates of other nation-states, among them those of the United States, South Africa, France, Spain, the Soviet Union, and Yugoslavia. Through the contestation of these official institutions, a platform for issues such as the Vietnam War, apartheid, nuclear testing and the rights of national minorities could all be constructed in Australian space.[53]

Over the late 1960s and early 1970s, however, the performance of contest was also staged at more unexpected locations. The legal system was taken on, with demonstrations both inside and outside courts and gaols. The actions of police were brought under public scrutiny, with demonstrations outside police stations and headquarters. Typically, unionists and students marched on the Russell Street Headquarters of Victorian State Police in Melbourne on 1 April 1971. On this occasion they carried a ceremonial coffin to mourn the recent death of Neil Collingburn, a young militant who had perished soon after being questioned by police.[54]

Perhaps more adventurously, the staging of contest was also used to make claims on many citizens and institutions usually understood as private or apolitical. Civil libertarians and film buffs protested outside cinemas that showed heavily censored versions of films like *Easy Rider* and *Medium Cool*. Opponents of anti-Semitism contested the persecution of Jews in the Soviet Union with demonstrations at the site of the visiting Moscow Circus, or the much-anticipated Russian Ballet at the Regent Theatre, Sydney.[55]

Equally, a great variety of sports stadiums around the country also became the site of contestation. The issue of apartheid promoted a large range of collective action at locations of Australian–South African sporting contact. These included the basketball courts of Moore Park; the tennis courts at Kooyong and White City; the football grounds of Manuka Oval, the Sydney Cricket Ground, Norwood Oval, and Olympic Park, among others; and the beaches of Coogee and Scarborough. Similarly, critics of the Soviet Government's treatment of the Ukraine and its Jewish citizens also protested at the occasion of a soccer match between the Moscow Dynamos and a New South Wales team at the Sydney Sports Ground, 28 February 1971. Through the actions of committed protesters at these and other sites, such sporting contests were transformed into forms of political contest. They became stages on which claims were made concerning the nature of the South African regime, the comparative claims of human rights and sporting competition, and the nature and form of anti-racism in Australia. They became, in short, the location of overt political conflict.[56]

If the staging of contest violated that most sacred of Australian dichotomies, between sport and politics, it also eroded that more typically Western distinction between the 'public' and 'private' realms. From 1969 onwards a cluster of contestational gatherings annexed the previously private spaces of 'the home' and 'the firm'.

On 16 August 1970, forty opponents of conscription appeared at the capacious Bellevue Hill residence of Federal Attorney-General Tom

Hughes. They carried with them a list of 182 people who had refused to comply with the National Service Act. Untrammelled by convention, they 'invaded' the property and placed Moratorium stickers on its door. Hughes threatened them with a cricket bat, and the protesters beat a hasty, tactical retreat. On the following night another thirty protesters returned for a further two-hour picket. When six men were gaoled for the first protest, on 23 August 1970, sixty additional demonstrators appeared at the house. This time they brought their own cricket bat, and played a parodic, impromptu match in the street outside.[57]

To Attorney-General Hughes, this 'invasion' was understandably outrageous and intimidating. It crossed the boundary between his 'public', governmental role and his private, civic life. By violating this boundary, the performance of contest highlighted the radical commitment of his opponents — their determination that the conventional 'rules of the political game' would not be adhered to. It also expanded the scope of 'the political', annexing (in Hughes' house) a new space of conflict and debate for the anti-conscription movement. Finally, the action equally symbolised the advance of 'the political' in these heady times. It expressed the sense of the draft resisters that they had no 'private' life, and it embodied the desire of peace activists to rob the war's supporters of the snug, homely comforts that the inhabitants of Vietnam had for so long forgone. In that sense, it was a compelling, innovative and significant political act.

But if the invasion of Tom Hughes' home was particularly dramatic, a number of more prosaic contests also occurred in a series of other hitherto private homes. On 26 January 1969, for example, twenty-five students marched on the home of Premier Bob Askin, demanding an increase in the number of student teacher scholarships available. In response, Askin defended the sanctity of his castle with blustery if unnecessary passion: 'What they propose is a distinct invasion of my private rights as a citizen. The fact that my wife and I have already made plans to be away on Sunday does not lessen the offence'.[58]

Others were at home when protesters gathered to perform. As Justus Jorgensen entertained the Prime Minister, William McMahon, at his Montsalvat mansion on 1 April 1971, this private, treasured occasion was also challenged with unaccustomed political performances. Sixty opponents of the Vietnam War, including Jorgensen's son Sebastian, descended on his house. Sebastian attempted to admit them to dinner. Police prevented this disruption and quickly ushered him out, but the point had been well made. The homes of the wealthy were no longer safe from politics. In fact they were quite literally under threat. On 1 September 1971, 'The People's Liberation Army' somewhat grandiosely claimed responsibility for the damage done to the boat and dinghy of the South African Consul, which had been moored in apparent safety at his Darling Point home.[59]

Clearly (and thankfully), these actions appear laughable when compared with the violence and menace of the European or American extreme Left. But if mild property destruction substituted for kidnapping and murder, the same direct performance of contest was undeniably at play. In performing contestation on private space, the protesters of the early 1970s offered an important and enduring challenge to Australian political life.

That challenge was strongest, however, when contesting the actions of private firms rather than the sanctity of private homes. In the early 1970s, conservationists protested at the site of environmentally destructive businesses like Australian Portland Cement and the Boral company. Workers anxious to gain industrial victories complemented their strikes with direct contestation at the head office of firms such as Mobil or at the headquarters of employer groups such as the Master Builders Association in Newtown. Proponents of Aboriginal land rights even began to demonstrate and invade the city offices of large rural landowners like Vestey's and Angliss & Company. At times, passionate activists contested the presence of Vestey's goods in suburban supermarkets — blocking cash registers, shouting at customers, abandoning trolleys and distributing leaflets. At the height of anti-Vietnam activity in mid-1970, the makers of 'fragmentation bombs', Honeywell, were even rocked by a shotgun blast at their Melbourne offices on St Kilda Road. Two nights later, another notable producer of military hardware, General Electric, was also assailed. Opponents of the Vietnam War threw Molotov cocktails into the Melbourne offices of this 'private' firm, so closely intertwined with the state's war in Vietnam.[60]

Many of these actions were scandalous and illegal and occasionally they were anonymous. They emerged in the context of strong anti-imperialist and anti-capitalist sentiment. Claimants staged a direct contest with the power of business. Sometimes quite literally, they 'played' at revolution. The apotheosis of these performances was the invasion and liberation of that symbol of capitalist power, the Stock Exchange. On 1 July 1970, around thirty demonstrators invaded the public gallery of the Melbourne Stock Exchange. They set off smoke bombs, threw fake money onto the floor, and shouted insults. There was pandemonium. The next day, twenty Sydney counterparts re-enacted and extended this new popular improvisation. For six minutes around lunchtime, the floor of the Sydney Stock Exchange was invaded. Protesters painted anti-capitalist slogans on the tally boards, painted the carpets, and burned the American flag. Jokingly, they distributed free copies of the Communist Party newspaper *Tribune*, and their cries rang out above the usual melee of trading: 'This is Blood Money', 'Stop the War in Vietnam' and 'Smash Capitalism'.

The direct utility of these actions was questionable. Certainly, they were not serious attempts to organise socialist revolt. Neither were they moderate public protests, calculated to solicit the production of persuasive and sympathetic media images. As participant Denis Freney has recalled, this was not a completely successful example of 'media politics':

> We met at the Criterion [Hotel] for a victory drink and then returned to the Tribune office to listen to the first reports of the raid on the radio news. To our annoyance they were highly coloured, to put it mildly. A spokesperson for the Exchange claimed that we had knocked down some of the staff and even thrown acid. We'd made no attempt to disguise ourselves, and most of us were well known to Special Branch and would have been easily recognised by the workers there. But the Stock Exchange evidently decided that discretion was the better part of valour, believing that any action against us would only lead to more raids and demonstrations. However, the media gave our foray maximum coverage and it even made the BBC News in London.[61]

By this time, the performance of staging had become a well-developed routine. Its use exceeded any particular, local justification. It had become a tool to directly confront those in power, whether or not that confrontation was likely to produce 'good copy'. It expressed challenge, conflict, a refusal to be bound by the norms of liberal democracy. Amid the tumult of 1970, it became the dominant form of staging.

The challenging nature of the performance of 'contest' can perhaps best be understood in terms of the conceptual vocabulary of French social theorist Michel de Certeau. In *The Practice of Everyday Life*, de Certeau posits a famous distinction between what he labels 'strategy' and 'tactics'. For de Certeau, actors that pursue 'strategy' attempt to construct their own place. They isolate this 'proper' place from the outside environment, and they then generate relations between this place and an exterior made up of targets and threats. 'As in management, every "strategic" rationalization seeks first of all to distinguish its "own" place, that is, the place of its own power and will from an "environment".'[62] The pursuance of strategy is associated with the action of businesses, armies, cities and scientific institutions, but it could be extended to include forms of staging that rely on *autonomous gatherings*. When actors perform staging away from the direct object of their claims, they attempt to create their own place of politics. They rally and protest according to their own rules in their own places, and they attempt to generate relations with those outside this place. This is the case, for example, when a group of unionists come together in the Trades Hall to make claims on the government. In these and other similar cases, actors effectively practise the politics of 'strategy'.

In contrast, the 'tactic' does not involve an attempt to construct a proper place. Instead, it 'insinuates itself into the other's place, fragmentarily'. It has 'no base where it can capitalise on its advantages, prepare for its expansions, and secure independence with respect to circumstances'. It must 'constantly manipulate events in order to turn them into "opportunities"'. In de Certeau's work, tactics are witnessed on the terrain of everyday life. They are mobile, fragmentary, eruptive. His key example is the situation of a worker who completes his or her own labour on company time.[63]

Again, however, a political form of 'the tactic' also suggests itself. It is possible to think of the 'staging of *contest*' as the pursuance of tactics. The similarities are striking. In this cluster of performances, political actors subvert the existence of proper places: homes, firms, stock exchanges, sporting ovals, government offices, embassies. They do not attempt to build a base for future actions, but remain mobile, responsive and flexible. They do not attempt to create their own places, but to annex those of others. Finally, they manipulate events in order to grasp political opportunities: exploiting sporting contests so as to raise the issue of apartheid, disrupting a shareholder's meeting in order to emphasise the importance of the environment, and so on. In short, they represent the application of tactics to the political realm.

Apprehending the 'staging of contest' in these terms helps us to understand the distinctiveness and radicalism of these actions. They broke with both the norms of liberal democracy and the long-standing practices of institution-building. They posed a threat to the sanctity of official spaces, and they brought politics to new and unaccustomed realms. Because the performance of contest embodied a form of 'tactics', it did not involve the stockpiling of resources, the permanent change to topographies of power, or the creation of new organisations. But this should not blind us to its very real successes. As the performance spread to new actors, so the spaces of political conflict and debate also widened. Ironically, although the performance of contest expressed a dissatisfaction with liberal democracy and a refusal to accept its limits, the growth of contestation resulted in the reactivation of long silent public spaces, and the reinvigoration of democratic life in Australia.

It shared this complex, contradictory impact with the other dominant performance of 1968–71: the performance of disruption.

THE PERFORMANCE OF DISRUPTION

After the improvisations of 1968, the performance of 'contest' was not the only new role to emerge on a wide scale. A variety of actors also began to 'perform disruption' in a range of innovative and surprising ways. Students openly defied the National Service Act. Academics and politicians openly supported them. Sit-ins became long-running occupations. Properties were damaged, smoke bombs thrown; rarely, shots were fired. Sin-ins and 'festivals of pornography' were staged as deliberate challenges to the censorship of Australian art and literature. The goal posts of the Sydney Cricket Ground were sawn in half; the tennis courts of Kooyong were gouged and smeared with oil and paint. Draft resisters barricaded themselves into Melbourne University and taunted the police to attempt arrest. Student revolutionaries mixed up tear gas and drilled in rifle clubs.

Together, these actions shocked authorities and scandalised public opinion. They drew massive media attention and frequent public attack. They had a disruptive, dislocatory impact on the Australian political environment.

But beyond this commonsense notion, what precisely makes a performance disruptive? In many ways, this is the subject of dispute and disagreement. Disruption is a *normative* category. It relies for meaning on a contrast with 'sanctioned', 'legitimate' or 'conventional' behaviour, and it would therefore appear to be subjective and slippery. For some adherents of liberal democracy, any recourse to non-institutional political activity may be seen as unconventional or disruptive. This notion is even shared by some students of social movements. As Ronald Aminzade has recognised, most definitions of the social movement focus on the willingness of such movements to adopt 'unconventional and disruptive' actions. Scholars such as Frances Fox Piven and Richard Cloward celebrate the political capacities of disruptive social movements and contrast them with those of traditional political organisation.[64] Even Sidney Tarrow, in his magisterial summation of Italian social movements, makes the point that the ability to disrupt is a key aim of all those who participate in protest: 'The aim of protest is disruption, and people achieve disruption by creating uncertainty about how far they are willing to go'.[65] But if disruption is a key aim and a resource, the ability of particular actions to disrupt is by no means obvious. The disruptiveness of any given political behaviour shifts over time. As we have already noted, in 1965 a peace vigil was disruptive and newsworthy to the Australian press. By 1967 this was no longer the case.

Moreover, if 'disruption' is a normative and therefore contested category, it is also necessarily *contextual*. Cultural geographers such as Tim Cresswell have made the point that notions of appropriate behaviour are often linked to notions of place. We are silent in libraries because we believe that this is appropriate; we shout at football matches because we think that this is the way that fans are meant to behave. If we shout 'Go the Eels!' in a public library, we are a disruptive, confronting presence — we are clearly 'out of place'. Equally, anthropologists like Roberto Da Matta have persuasively argued that it is when social objects and actors pass outside their conventional places and enter unaccustomed domains that dislocations and disruptions in the social fabric are likely to occur. Indeed, it is on these occasions that new symbols emerge, that popular rituals can develop, and that previously sacrosanct, reified elements of the social world are opened up to questioning. It is when actions occur 'out of place' that new questions about the organisation of the social order are most frequently raised. In short, the geographical setting of actions plays a crucial role in defining our judgement of whether actions are good or bad, sanctioned or disruptive, and in the likely social impact of those actions.

The spatial dimensions of disruption are particularly relevant to the analysis of collective action. When 2000 Czechoslovakian protesters took to the streets of Sydney on 24 August 1968, they marched proudly along the road, blocking traffic as they went. Police supervised and coordinated the activity — an officially sanctioned protest at recent Soviet action in the Czech homeland. However, to take an extreme example, when around 200 students at La Trobe University attempted a similar march along Waterdale Road, Heidelberg, on 16 September 1970, they were treated as provocative, and violently set on by police. The same action clearly had two very different meanings in two different spaces and times. This divergence is by no means atypical. Historians of collective behaviour have emphasised that even obviously unsanctioned behaviour such as violence can have a different official reception, depending on the precise spatial and political context.

Clearly then, no actions are 'purely disruptive' or 'purely sanctioned'. The identical action in different locations will be more or less disruptive. As students of collective action, we need precise information about the context of political performances in order to judge their disruptiveness: the reactions of police, press and government; the existing rules governing the relevant space, and so on. Collecting this information is likely to be time-consuming, difficult, and sometimes impossible. The results are likely to be uneven and incomplete across a very large sample of events.[66]

In this chapter I adopt a pragmatic approach to such difficulties. Rather than attempting to gauge the subtleties of the *degree* of disruptiveness, I simply code each act of staging as 'disruptive' or 'sanctioned'. More specifically, I code an action as 'disruptive' if it adheres to any one of the following spatial or contextual conditions:

1 It involves deliberate illegality of some kind. In Australian political life, deliberate illegality has been comparatively rare. It clearly transgresses the norms of liberal democracy, irrespective of location, and can therefore be interpreted as disruptive.

2 It draws a direct, reported, negative reaction from police. As the guardians of the state, the actions of the police can be interpreted as a normative signal. When they make arrests, become embroiled

in physical exchanges, or remove actors from a specific space, the action can therefore be considered as disruptive.

3   It prevents the routine use of a particular space by other actors. When politics advances outside its notional 'proper place' and interferes with the actions of others, it violates the norms of liberal democracy. For this reason, actions that block traffic without permission, that prevent university authorities from holding meetings, or that violate 'private' space, can all be understood as 'disruptive' in some way.

Understood in these terms, we can gain a broad gauge of the changing levels of disruptive political behaviour. As Figure 2.4 shows, disruptive staging increased in absolute terms over the period 1965–71. Like the overall level of all staging, specifically *disruptive* actions fell from an early peak in 1966, reached their nadir in late 1967, and began to ascend to higher levels in 1969. The specific increase in *disruptive staging* is, however, somewhat more dramatic. It rises later and more rapidly than the performances and measures that we have already analysed elsewhere in this chapter. Tactical innovation began to take off in 1968, staging in 1969, contestation in 1969. In contrast, the first really large jump in disruptive behaviour that takes it to unheralded levels occurs in 1970.

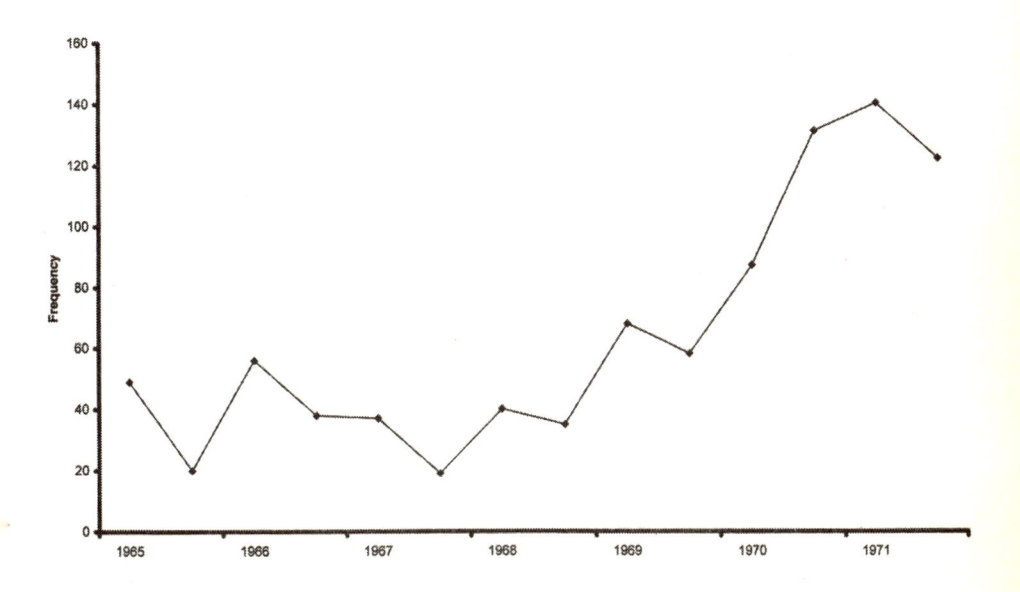

Figure 2.4
Disruptive staging, January 1965–December 1971

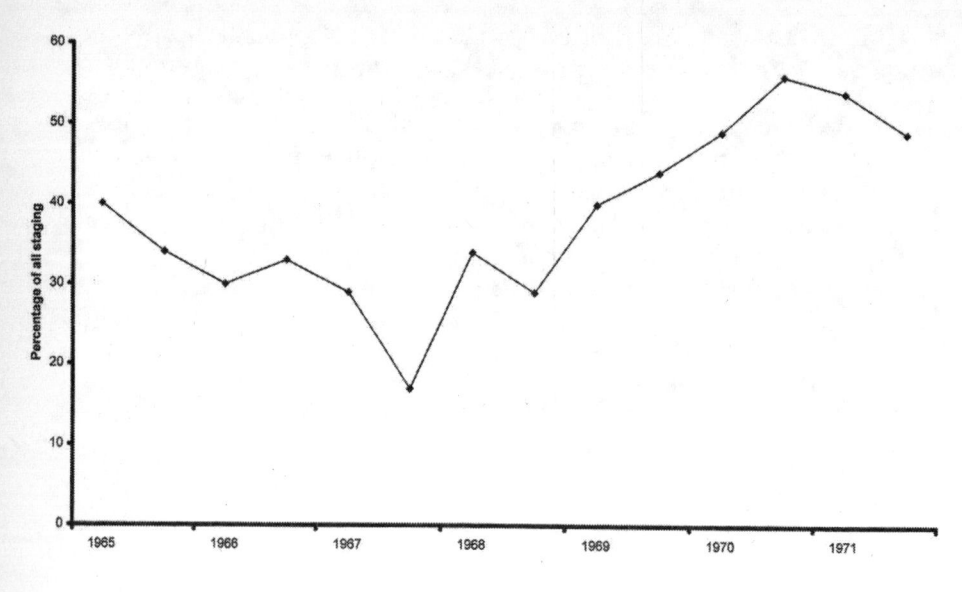

Figure 2.5
Disruptive actions as a proportion of all staging, January 1965–December 1971

Furthermore, as Figure 2.5 shows, over 1970 and 1971 disruptive staging increased in relative as well as absolute terms. Claimants were not only more likely to adopt disruptive staging, they were also more likely to perform disruptive staging *over its sanctioned alternative*.[67]

Why did this happen? In a very direct sense, the performance of disruption grew out of the improvisations of 1968. The history of past interactions tended to fuel ongoing disruptive performances over the late 1960s and early 1970s. The perceived violence of police was used to justify disruption and retaliation among students. Some students felt that they needed to prove that they would not be scared off by police brutality. Others gained impetus from television footage that showed police indulging in violent and unnecessary behaviour. For some activists, there was a special satisfaction to be gleaned from 'outwitting' police. Others fantasised about vengeful showdowns: 'If the cops get nervous and start to use that $500,000 worth of riot equipment we will be ready for them. They won't be expecting the type of retaliation we have in store'.[68]

By the early 1970s, a romantic cult of revolutionary action had clearly emerged. Activists were encouraged to connect imaginatively with guerrilla movements elsewhere. They saw the intervention of the police as confirmation of their revolutionary credentials — their status as antipodean insurgents. Frank Moorhouse catches the most extreme edge of this mood in his discontinuous narrative *The Americans, Baby*.

Here the character of Turvey is convinced that 'people are becoming molten'; he keeps a Bren machine-gun in his garage and fervently believes that Chinese guerrillas are beginning to land on the Australian mainland.[69] While not every activist with a poster of Che Guevera on the wall also had a bomb under his bed, direct action was clearly 'in', and the outrage of officials was proudly courted rather than shamefully acknowledged. As Silas Grass put it in *Tharunka*, 'What's the use of a protest that offends no one?!'[70]

The continuing appetite of political actors for wide media coverage also encouraged the sustained performance of disruption. The radical figure of the outlaw draft resister energised otherwise tame protests and provided the frisson to lure camera crews and interested journalists. Draft resisters emerged mockingly at a variety of sites over the early 1970s: at the Moratorium march of June 1971; at the Melbourne University Draft Resistance siege; on the television program *This Day Tonight*; and even at Sydney and Melbourne University orientation weeks. As Michael Hamel-Green recalls, these disruptive interventions functioned as beacons for the mass media: 'Immediately resisters started going underground, there was an amazing increase in the awareness of issues and the amounts of publicity'.[71] In other campaigns, too, deliberately disruptive behaviour resulted in mass publicity. The strong relationship between violence and publicity, in particular, continued to work for activists.

But if the expanding performance of disruption involved a continuity with the improvisations of 1968, it also involved a genuine development. After five years of struggle, the anti-Vietnam and anti-conscription campaigns had failed to achieve any significant victories. There was a growing recognition that the old methods were not working. As draft resister Geoff Mullen put it, 'conventional marches might provide their participants with an emotional pleasure, but to think that is enough is insane'.[72]

Anti-war actors were frustrated, alienated. The Australian state lost respect with every dead soldier shipped home, every revelation of injustice and infamy in the waging of the war. The My Lai massacre, in particular, became both a powerful symbol of the conflict in Vietnam and a spur to more trenchant opposition. As a result, the escalation of legal protest to illegal resistance seemed the most logical and appealing prospect. Indeed, the growing recourse to disruption increasingly became the staple form of contention in radical political circles between 1969 and 1971.

Radical students invaded the office of Minister for Immigration Billy Snedden on 1 August 1969. They used the phone and messed up the papers that lay across his desk. They refused to leave and even locked the Minister inside his own office. A month later, on 8 September, a gang of young men raided the National Service office in

Adelaide, throwing animal blood and cutting through telephone cords and cables. By the end of September 1969, the 'People's Liberation Army' had hurled paint and bricks at the Commonwealth Offices and Magistrate's Court of Adelaide city. A spokesperson told a local radio station of the growing radicalism of the war's opponents: 'It is true we have gone beyond the bounds of mere demonstrations and we are going to carry out terrorist activities until capitalism is overthrown'.

The performance of disruption continued into 1970. On 11 June 1970, anti-war demonstrators stormed into the National Parliament, holding up proceedings for thirty-seven minutes. By 1971, the very administration of the court system was facing persistent disruption. After being found guilty under the National Service Act, draft resister Phil Golding set fire to the summons dock in Adelaide on 9 March; on 27 August draft resister Gary Cook occupied the magistrate's chair in Perth. The frustration of political powerlessness was being transformed into the satisfaction of deliberate disruption.

Students in particular revelled in their ability to demystify the powerful, expose the petty human motives that lurked beneath the most official, sacred surfaces. One Sydney protester, for example, fondly recalled the invasion of the office of Federal Minister (and soon to be Prime Minister) William McMahon:

> Nobody could fail to enjoy his file of girlie magazines, or to take note of the copies of Oscar Wilde's Fairy Tales and Stendhal's work on Love which were on his shelves. It's a way of getting close to great men, and of finding out something about their inner selves.

Not surprisingly, in this disruptive context the Federal Government soon worriedly contemplated new penalties for the violation of official Commonwealth offices, institutions and properties.[73]

But just as the anti-conscription and anti-war campaigns had faced defeat and setback, so the long campaign for democratisation of the universities had also produced increasing frustration for student activists. As 1970 came to an end, Monash University students had also come to believe that only the most disruptive acts, such as the 'occupation' of university buildings, could hope to make an impact. They also presaged and defended this action with a definite emphasis on the failure of past, sanctioned actions:

> It WILL disrupt and this disruption has become necessary because the university authorities have treated our 'reasoned arguments', our resolutions, our petitions, our delegations and even our lecture boycott with contempt. We have been forced to answer the university authorities with the only language they understand ... direct action.[74]

Disruptive behaviour gave disappointed activists a sense of tangible achievement after years of apparently fruitless struggle. If they could not end the Vietnam war, they could 'liberate' the South Vietnamese Embassy in Canberra. If they could not make the revolution, they could invade the Stock Exchange. If they could not win Aboriginal land rights, they could install and defend the Aboriginal Embassy on the front lawn of Parliament House. If they could not end apartheid, they could delay a football match between South Africa and Australia.

In short, the performance of disruption sometimes worked. By directly challenging the enforceability of some laws, it eroded their public legitimacy. By 1971, over 300 draft resisters around Australia openly defied the government, thus posing a direct threat to the system of National Service. Similarly, the disruptive performances that dogged the Springboks around Australia in 1971 undeniably had a direct political impact. The planned spectacle of Australian–South African sporting contact actually became a spectacle of political contest and civil dissent. Matches were played behind barbed-wire fences, violence broke out among enraged sporting crowds, games were marred by interruptions. By performing disruption rather than merely signalling their disagreement, protesters could be sure of at least partial success. While still amid the Springbok tour, John Wentworth accurately forecast the more hopeful potential impacts of the performance of disruption:

> In point of fact, whichever way it goes South Africa and the Rugby Union lose. If the tour is called off they lose. But if the tour goes on, the anti-apartheid movement will surge with renewed vigour, and if demonstrations do not actually wreck the tour, they will damage it beyond repair at the least.

The Springbok Rugby tour ended in chaos. It was not surprising that the upcoming tour of the South African cricket team was cancelled in September 1971.[75]

Of course the performance of disruption tended to accept direct victories 'in the field' for eventual defeats in the public sphere. As contention became more innovative, affective, and unaccustomed, so its risk-taking agents became increasingly inward-looking, morally autonomous, and unruffled by the norms of 'straight' society. Anthropologist David Kertzer has suggested that most successful popular movements are generally accompanied by the development of 'rituals' — forms of repetitive, standardised, symbolic behaviour. According to this view, rituals (like demonstrations, for example) involve public identification with a political group, release large reservoirs of *communitas* or affection for fellow participants, and therefore increase the attachment of individuals to the wider collective. They provide for the development of a sense of *esprit de corps* among social movement members. Not only that, but as collective action increasingly annexes new social spaces, and thereby overflows the boundaries of conventional politics, so the disruption of the 'normative order', the intensity of symbolic display, and the sense of joint marginality from existing society are all likely to increase.[76] Under these conditions, the immediate group rather than the wider public becomes the moral yardstick. The comrade-in-arms becomes the citizen to impress rather than the suburban television watcher.

Clearly, such a process was at work within the insurgent movements that galvanised Australian political life in the early 1970s. Demonstrators took up 'fancy dress' and revelled in their ability to shock the 'middle-class shits'. Participants in large events, like the Vietnam Moratorium march of 8 May 1970, were surprised by the genuine warmth that seemed spontaneously to rise up for fellow protesters. With increasing frequency, these actors began to see their own actions as involving the creation of a kind of 'liminal space' existing in the cracks between the structures of conventional society.[77] Massive crowds like those on Moratorium Day simply disregarded the wishes and conventional controls of the police and, in their view, transcended them. The crowd determined its own form. People's lives changed forever, making their break with conventional society and family. 'Business as usual' was at a (temporary) end. The question 'what is 'normal life' anyway?' began to be thrown up in the aftermath of disruptive, inspiring collective acts.[78]

Contention was increasingly seen as a release from the frustrations of everyday life. Instead of enduring a crushed bus ride, you walked down the middle of the street; instead of watching ads on television, you chanted 'DOWN WITH THE ARMY, DOWN WITH THE STATE!' The collective event was a place where new forms of behaviour, not acceptable within the 'official community', were possible: the joining of hands, the display of affection and love for others, the use of 'four-letter words', the ability to 'generally be human'. This sort of action increased your level of 'political commitment'. Such behaviour was freely acknowledged not to 'communicate very much to the bourgeoisie in their Valiants'. Frank Starrs articulated this mood at its most extreme in the Adelaide University student publication *On Dit*:

> demonstrations do not exist for the appeasement of those watching them, but for the emotional stabilisation of those taking part in them.
>
> they are pubic ritualistic rejections of the bureaucratic paper-ridden impersonal vote-seeking politics of the status quo in favour of a politics of personal interaction and confrontation.
>
> the ideal demonstration is a love-in.[79]

In short, the moral judgements of the press and the establishment became gradually less relevant to the self-image of the most radical activists. In their own terms, they had taken the moral high ground and this was a victory of a kind.

However, it remains true that if radical political actors were increasingly untroubled by the 'dilemmas of the activist', this did not make those dilemmas any less real. If they willingly chose disruptive, sometimes infamous prominence over sanctioned, respectable marginality, this did not make the public critique any less trenchant. Disruptive protesters were described as 'authoritarian', 'anti-intellectual' and threatening. While they successfully demonstrated their particular commitment to causes and policies, they were not always able to generate wider debate on these issues. The medium of political action became the message. The methods of activists became the issue.[80] Even committed political activists, such as Dennis Altman, conceded that the new repertoire of disruption raised distinct issues. It embodied a direct challenge to the activity of others, and the imposition of a kind of 'injustice' on other Australian citizens. Altman analysed the anti-Springbok campaign in 1971:

> The crucial argument, however, was over the right not to demonstrate but to disrupt, and the calculus that each individual had to make was whether one perceived injustice (playing a racially-selected team), justified another (hindering the Rugby Union from playing whom they wished). Ordinary arguments in favour of civil disobedience hardly helped, for there the protest is directed against a law or system of laws that impose on those who protest. Such arguments would, of course, justify disruption, and indeed revolt by non-white South Africans, but they were not relevant to the Australian protest.
>
> In the end I supported the strategy of disruption — if not all its methods — for two inter-related reasons: the horror of racism and the Australian government's unwillingness to translate their platitudes about racism into reality.[81]

In this sense, the long popular journey from 1965 had a strange, recursive feel. Novel actions, departures from routine, remained an important political weapon. They attained newsworthiness and attracted camera crews. They gained public attention and sometimes even endorsement. At the same time, by 1967 a persistent tension had asserted itself. In order to depart from routine, claimants found it necessary to depart from the key assumptions of liberal democracy: to bring political activity to new spaces; to offer direct contest to the objects of their claims; to impede the routines of others; to court arrest with deliberate illegality. As the complexity and range of staging increased, so the state and the media moved to explicit opposition. Each new improvisation brought notoriety and vilification; advance and retreat. It stretched the fabric of Australian political life and offered sometimes difficult choices to Australian citizens. Some actors grasped the new opportunities and performances with glee; others recoiled from their unconventional and disruptive implications. In a jagged, messy way, the level of collective action increased. New performances were routinised. New forms of more disruptive and confronting political action became the norm. New stages of debate and discussion were constructed.

But these victories remained temporary, sometimes unstable. In his classic study of the American New Left, Todd Gitlin has argued that the attention of the mass media undercut the breadth and range of student radicalism in the United States, fostering a politics of display and sometimes violent illusion in place of the grinding activism of practical achievement. By analogy, some Australian students also thought that this could be said of the local, antipodean context. By 1969 one of the architects of the Freedom Ride, Jim Spigelman, had begun to question the developing direction of student insurgency. In his view, confrontation had become a kind of universal strategy, and the tools of education and rational debate were now unjustifiably rejected. The atmosphere that characterised the 'translation' of theatrical protest during the mid-1960s — the coexistence of display and debate, performance and rationality — had now been superseded by a series of dangerous developments: 'It is fairly clear that a vicious circle has developed between student radicals and the Press. This is seen in the constant search for gimmicks to ensure continued newsworthiness'.[82]

In this context, the performance of collective action was by no means a simple expression of democratic will. The manner in which the new forms of performance fitted together was still uncertain, their repercussions doubtful. If staging had become a dominant repertoire of political action, its precise impact on Australian democracy was itself still very much open to question, contest and debate.

STAGING AND DEMOCRACY: AN UNEXPECTED LEGACY

How did the rise of staging change Australian democracy? For the liberal critics of this cluster of new performances, staging was a threat. When its practitioners had recourse to contestational or disruptive behaviour, they were thought illiberal and undemocratic — an 'authoritarian minority', as the *Sydney Morning Herald* put it.[83] By refusing to rely simply on representative democracy, they seemed to reject democracy in *toto*. By performing commitment and contest over polite citizenship, they threatened the rule of law and order. By insisting on the popular activity of frequently small groups, they sometimes contradicted the apparent will of 'the silent majority'. Of course these arguments gained strength from the open declarations of a range of movement participants. Many were critical of the merits of pluralism, enamoured of Mao Zedong rather than John Stuart Mill, fans of 'direct action' rather than 'direct democracy'. Revolutionaries first, democrats second.

Nonetheless, despite the attacks of some critics and the motives of some political protesters, it remains possible to see staging as a stimulant rather than a depressant of democratic life. The development of this cluster of political performances enlivened Australian democracy and reconstituted popular participation. It made the *practice* of democracy newly possible. We see this impact most clearly when we examine the question in historical, comparative and spatial terms.

Before the rise of staging, a great number of nominally 'public spaces' in Australia were effectively zones of non-politics. Under the pressure of Cold War, Australian citizens had been shepherded out of the public sphere and into the embrace of private commitments. Political institutions such as the Communist Party were frequently denied the right to hold street meetings. Repeatedly, town halls and civic spaces were denied to opponents of the Vietnam War. The distribution of leaflets in cities like Melbourne was effectively outlawed. In the State of Queensland, marching and placarding were tightly policed. Even where these practices were extended greater official tolerance, they remained rigidly demarcated. If citizens in other states were allowed to march, the necessity for activists to keep to the footpath was at times violently enforced. The depoliticisation of public spaces in this period was so complete that elite figures like NSW Governor Sir Roden Cutler even asserted that 'physical demonstrations' were not 'part of a university's liberty'.[84]

Following the radical art critic Rosalyn Deutsche, we might conceptualise these apparently 'public' spaces as effectively 'private'. Deutsche has recently argued that public spaces are sites of political debate, discussion and struggle, 'a realm not of unity but of divisions, conflicts, and differences resistant to regulatory power'. In these terms, particular places can move from 'publicity' to 'privacy' over time. If conflict and debate flourishes, the space is public; if it is repressed, the space is private. Within any specific site 'lies the potential to be transformed into a public or, for that matter, a private space'.[85] When smoothness and unity are imposed, publicity is lost. When conflict and contest break out, publicity is attained.

From this perspective, the democratic virtues of staging can be clearly grasped. When protesters took to the streets, they reactivated them as public spaces. When they brought political contest to previously private spaces, they claimed them as public. By performing staging, Australian actors learnt to perform democracy. The vigils and demonstrations, the marches and sit-ins, the paint lobbed and the goal post sawn, all involved the construction of a conflictual public space — a zone of democratic practice.

As the pace of contention increased, the boundaries of acceptable public behaviour shifted outwards. The meaning of democratic practice was expanded for all actors. Opponents of the Vietnam War challenged and overturned the local ordinance forbidding the distribution of political leaflets in Melbourne. Unionists and students reclaimed the right to march in Brisbane. In Victoria, the right to march on the street was even claimed. As Save Our Sons activist Jean McLean remembers:

> When we had the first demo in town, the police said we couldn't walk down the street, but had to walk along the footpath in single file so as not to block cars. No one had gone off the footpath before, but we just said, 'Why not? Who said cars have supremacy over people?' No one had ever thought of that before.
>
> ... Now everyone who gets angry, whether it's shooters, cattlemen, or the Right to Life, marches on the streets.[86]

The rise of staging therefore had varied and surprising consequences. If it grew out of radical student practices and expressed a radical critique of both liberal democracy and capitalism, it resulted in the enrichment of liberal, capitalist democracy in Australia. If it seemed threatening and violent to the elites of 1970, it ultimately performed and extended democracy more usefully than their fulminations or worries, restrictions or regulations. This militant performance not only created publicity for a range of important issues, it brought publicity to a range of previously private spaces. Its legacy of actions, issues promoted and spaces liberated therefore expanded the scope of democratic Australian life. In short, the radical critics of Australian democracy in the 1960s may have been its greatest friends.

CONCLUSION

Over the seven years from the beginning of 1965, the terrain of popular political action in Australia was almost completely transformed. An enormous experiment in collective action was organised. Long-slumbering forms of popular claim-making were reawakened, new techniques were translated, newly translated tools were renovated, changed, remade. In the course of halting, ongoing collective campaigns — often groping, ineffectual, failure-ridden — a largely successful change was orchestrated. Indeed, as battles were held and tactics reviewed, the techniques of collective action were undergoing fundamental alteration. A tremendous change was in process.

The petition and the delegation were increasingly supplanted by the march and the demonstration; the march and the demonstration were rapidly complemented by the 'invasion' and the 'occupation'. The available forms of contention multiplied. In a moment of sustained interaction, tension and improvisation, new clusters of political performance became available. By the early 1970s, staging had become the dominant repertoire of collective action. A great variety of Australians had learnt to 'stage contest' and to 'perform disruption'. Tools of direct democracy were now in wide circulation.

We are accustomed to thinking of these tools in relation to the somewhat heroic campaigns of the period: the Moratorium against the Vietnam War, the battle against conscription, and so on. But it was crucial to the development of these tools that they were used and adapted by a range of actors, across a wide array of movements. Sometimes they were unsuccessful. Their utility was often open to question. Frequently they involved small rather than large numbers, contested rather than transparent issues.

In this way, their use has extended into our most recent history. The theatrical performances first improvised in the late 1960s continue to divide citizens, to inspire conflict rather than agreement. As in the past, many doubt their applicability, question whether the particular issues justify the disruption, defend the existing order on the grounds of privacy and consensus. This seems intrinsic to their use and to their success — a continuation rather than a departure from the history of collective action. As we will show in the next chapter, it is precisely the capacity to shock, to disrupt and to confront which makes the 'performance of staging' such a powerful resource. It is this capacity, indeed, which allowed new performances to feed widespread political mobilisation, and thereby to nurture the movements for women's liberation, Aboriginal rights, gay liberation, and protection of the environment.

3
DIFFUSION

> diffuse: [to] disperse or be dispersed from a centre; spread or be spread widely.
> — *Concise Oxford Dictionary*

> One police wit said last Wednesday that the police force were considering holding a sit-in in the Great Hall of Sydney University for higher wages, and asked if the students would support them ...
> *Tribune*, 26 August 1970

In April 1972, students at the University of Melbourne announce the emergence of the Exam Resisters' Movement. The methods developed to challenge conscription will now be applied within the university itself, put to work in a battle to end the servitude of the student. A Manifesto is released to spearhead the novel campaign:

> Let it be understood by all members of the University that we seek the complete abolition of the present exam system as an initial step towards the revitalisation of University teaching and learning, and beyond that to secure a democratic, open and humane University. We urge all students to help bring this about through debate, through departmental reform and if necessary through the threat of boycotts. We must and shall resist examinations, abolish examinations now.[1]

A Melbourne tram-driver, Clarrie O'Shea, follows the example of conscientious objectors within the student movement. When his union is financially penalised for strike action by the Arbitration Commission, he refuses, as an office-bearer, to pay the fine. He is imprisoned in May 1969. Massive strikes and demonstrations occur in the major cities, and students join with trade unionists in militant protests. It seems to some observers that a 'fusion' of student and industrial working-class 'styles of activity' is under way.[2]

In 1974, students at the Gordon Institute of Technology in Geelong become concerned with the construction of a staff car park. The new seven-car facility poses a threat to a 100-year-old tree that adorns the campus. Over 300 students and staff hold a demonstration and begin to replace a number of trees already removed. They further threaten a kind of 'guerrilla warfare' to prevent any further trees being chopped down. The cause of 'Tree Liberation' rings out confidently.[3]

Fresh from the success of the Vietnam Moratorium Movement, the methods of the Moratorium are applied to the movement for indigenous rights. A new campaign to stop work and march on National Aborigines Day, Friday 14 July 1972, begins. This is a 'Black Moratorium' to succeed the 'Vietnam Moratorium'. It targets a war that predates the horrific Vietnam conflict but that European Australians have been slower to admit or oppose:

> The Government is unable to face the truth about this country's past. The people must be willing to concede that there has been a 200 year war going on, and that it is still going on, with Blacks dying while Whites don't even realize that there is a war going on right in their back yards ...
>
> Call an end to this racist war which is going on here in Australia.
>
> End the Australian war NOW.[4]

On May Day 1973, the traditional Sydney march is disrupted. Women's Liberationists who have begun to march in recent years have decided to stage a boycott. Members of Sydney Gay Liberation quickly move to support them. The young revolutionaries of Gay Lib distribute a leaflet that explains their motives and position:

> 'Sexual revolution' is itself part of a total movement to change society at its roots. May Day is part of this movement for that new society. So to be consistent with its stated objectives, the Sydney May Day Committee must:
>
> 1 stop insulting homosexual women by holding 'Miss May Day' contests
>
> 2 stop insulting non-homosexual women by holding 'Miss May Day' contests
>
> 3 shed itself of the mentality that places the Women's Liberation contingent second last and the Gay Liberation last, as they did last year.

> If it doesn't, then we should get rid of it.
>
> Workers, end sex roles! End male dominance! Fight for the acceptance of homosexuality as a valid form of sexual expression.[5]

All of these events represent the process of diffusion. The tools, images and rhetoric of one movement are spread to others. Resistance moves from 'the draft' to 'the exam'. The Vietnam Moratorium becomes the Black Moratorium; the imprisoned student becomes the imprisoned worker. The battle for liberation spreads across race, gender, sexuality, nature. The official occasion that marks the battle to end workers' oppression becomes the site of new challenges to the oppression of women, lesbians and gays. One after another, new movements appear, raising new demands: Black Liberation, Women's Liberation, Gay Liberation, Male Liberation, Children's Liberation, Tree Liberation. In short, a diffusion of protest to new campaigns and locations is under way.

The students who were most closely associated with the improvisation of new forms of political behaviour were highly conscious of this process. They even hazarded early interpretations as to the causes of diffusion. As early as 1969, a young student, Patrick Morgan, observed this action somewhat cynically for the readers of *National U*:

> Agitators can fall back on old dependables (like conscription) but new issues are needed all the time to keep up the interest and excitement. The changeover rate is incredibly fast. Many of this year's freshers wouldn't know what an Ibo or a Gurindji was, and doubtless next year's lot will live the rest of their lives in total ignorance of By-Law 418. Issues used to foment dissent are becoming more domestic and petty, such as prolonged protests over parking conditions.[6]

Conservative opponents of political protest were equally quick to decry the process of diffusion. When the anti-apartheid movement took off in 1971, the *Sydney Morning Herald* vehemently denounced this development. According to the *Herald*, the campaign against the Springboks had only arisen because the anti-Vietnam movement was 'running out of steam'. It was little more than a convenient new target for dedicated, professional activists. Young protesters were searching for an issue around which they could perform their newly improvised actions; they were not sincere opponents of the South African regime: 'Apartheid has got very little to do with the issue. The louts who carry weapons and dangerous explosives ... are out to stir up trouble against authority and one pretext is as good as another'.[7] Similarly, when Patricia Giffney of the *Sydney Sun* heard of the new campaign for a course in Women's Studies at the University of Sydney in June 1973, she was dismayed. 'What on earth is this all about?' she asked. 'I must have my Women's Liberation philosophy all wrong.' Giffney wondered how a movement dedicated to equality could justify a 'special course on women's thoughts'. It seemed 'illogical'. Perhaps more fearfully, she noted that the energies and methods of the Vietnam movement were now being transferred to other causes: 'I've been wondering, incidentally, now that the anti-Vietnam War cause has been won (or lost) what stirrer would think up another one to disrupt student life'.[8]

Even some students were uncomfortable with this process. There was something disorienting, outflanking, destabilising, about the rapid multiplication of movements and causes. Those who felt themselves to be at the centre of radical campaigns strongly resisted their slide from centrality. For these actors, student power and 'stop the war' needed to remain the key demands. Any attempt to raise other claims was diversionary and self-defeating, a move away from 'fundamental student needs' to 'peripheral' and marginal issues. From the perspective of some male 'revolutionaries', the rise of women's liberation was enough to provoke apoplexy — images of dirt and disorder, infantile references to faeces, even the adoption of revealing, fearful pseudonyms. 'Glorfindal Eunuchwarbler', a contributor to *Honi Soit*, angrily bemoaned the passage of political energy and performance from the campaign for 'university democratisation' to the campaign for 'women's liberation' over the course of the Women's Studies dispute: 'oh no, the heavy handed Women's Lib. fuckwits jumped on the band wagon and "sexism" was splattered round the campus until it ran diarrhoea like, from everyone's assholes, which seemed to be the part most people were using as a mouth'.[9]

Clearly, the rise of new political movements was a disturbing, often threatening process. For conservative critics, it signalled that the pace of political contention would not decline, and that selective compromise would not be enough. A thousand political flowers were beginning to bloom. Where would it all end? For the adherents of the student and peace movements, the diffusion of political performance was sometimes equally troubling. Surely 'the movement' was fragmenting? The new campaigns would undermine the old. The 'new' issues were less pressing and central than their precursors. This was irrational, unsolidaristic. How and why could it happen?

EXPLAINING THE DIFFUSION OF PROTEST

Students, of course, had their own explanation for the rise of new campaigns and the rapid diffusion of political protest. Patrick Morgan noted that there was a constant need for 'new issues' to 'keep up the interest and excitement' of the student political world. Silas Grass of the University of New South Wales noted that as radical campaigns were 'commandeered' by more moderate groups, so the 'good ship Revolution' — the spirit of disruptive political challenge — was forced to move on to new waters. In this conception, the new political performances were constantly under threat of capture. An exhilarating chase occurred across social space, as radical actors joyously opened up new issues, and moderate, institutionalised actors followed relentlessly in their wake. Diffusion was the product of a continual battle between the new forms of political performance and the older methods of institutionalised struggle. The radicals were perpetually escaping to new terrain, and the new campaigns therefore proliferated.[10]

Recent scholarship has provided additional explanations. The 'political process' school of social movement study suggests that the level of political opportunities decisively shapes the likelihood of open political contention. The greater the access to power, the availability of influential allies, the extent of divisions among elites, and the instability of political alignments, the greater the likelihood that citizens will become involved in collective action. On this basis, Sidney Tarrow has suggested that the action of innovative and militant political actors is likely to *increase* the likelihood that other actors will follow suit. 'Early risers' are likely to create the conditions for those less rapidly out of their 'apolitical' beds — to make elites more vulnerable, to foment divisions, to open up previously closed political systems. The first movements for change create the spaces through which their successors will emerge.[11]

Clearly, both explanations are cogent and highly persuasive. In this chapter, however, I want to provide an additional explanation for the rapid diffusion of political protest and the emergence of new movements that challenged racial, gender and sexual oppression. I want to argue that the diffusion of protest to a range of 'new movements' would not have been possible without the *specific* contribution of the political gimmick. The newly improvised forms of 'theatrical political performance' provided actors with powerful, recently forged tools of claim-making. Their ability to construct new stages of political demand, to contest the powerful in previously 'private' spaces, and to disrupt the routine operation of ordered, 'proper places' would prove decisive. The staging of contest and the performance of disruption seemed particularly well attuned to the new demands that were beginning to ring out.

More specifically, the repertoire of staging provided three key resources for the mobilisation of new movements:

1 New spaces for the public emergence of previously apolitical actors and identities.

2 Tools to demand cultural and institutional recognition of previously overlooked oppression.

3 The means to bring previously private matters into the public realm.

Thought of in these terms, the repertoire of staging was an important contributor to the emergence of social movements that opposed gender, racial and sexual oppression. Certainly, the need to maintain the pace of political action was an important contextual factor. But without the tools to maintain that pace and to perform new sorts of demands, the momentum of political activity would have rapidly and inevitably abated. Similarly, the ability of the student and peace movements to 'break through' and open up opportunities for other movements should not be forgotten. However, if the opportunities were undeniably present, this did not mean that 'new' movements challenging newly recognised forms of oppression would inevitably grasp them. It was in this context that the political gimmick became central.

Indeed, thought of in this sense, the political gimmick not only shaped the rhythms of collective action in the 1960s but allowed new movements to emerge that would challenge and shape the rhythms of political and social life for the next three decades and beyond.

SPACES OF POLITICAL EMERGENCE

Participants in the demonstrations and protests of the 1960s presented themselves proudly, openly in public space. As Chapter 1 showed, sometimes this was a continuation of previous forms of public activity: the student Commemoration Day stunt became the creative student sit-in and demonstration. In the same way, industrial workers and other members of the labour movement had a long tradition of public assembly, meeting, and routine participation in party politics. But for women and for Aboriginal people in particular, this routine political participation had often been denied. Although a cluster of political institutions had fought heroically to assert their demands, open political activity 'on the streets' was a comparative rarity.

As a result, when the new repertoire of staging became dominant, the public, political presence of these groups also, slowly, increased. In February 1965, it took great bravery for fifty Aboriginal residents of the Toomelah Reserve to cheer and farewell the Freedom Ride of Sydney University students. When Aboriginal riders were denied the service of alcohol at the Brunette Downs rodeo in June 1965, and they staged a boycott, white observers refused to concede that this could be a political action. When eighty Aboriginal workers went on strike for award wages at Newcastle Waters Station in late April 1966, the *Herald*'s reporter portrayed them as listless, still apolitical actors:

> Last week the entire camp was almost out of food for several days. The men lie about all day doing nothing. They are an unhappy, bewildered group, some of whom at least would like to return to work if they could.
>
> But that is not possible before they get the word from [trade union organiser] Dexter Daniels.[12]

However, if this patronising reception of Aboriginal action remained, the growing incidence of political activity by sympathetic whites gave Aborigines the space to launch their own campaigns. Drawing strength from the earlier visit of Student Action For Aborigines, Aboriginal residents of Moree and their white supporters launched their own deliberate violation of racial segregation at the local pool. Together, Aboriginal protesters and supportive, mostly non-Aboriginal students demanded equal pay for Aboriginal workers in a demonstration outside the Commonwealth Arbitration Court on 7 July 1965. When SAFA returned to country New South Wales in August and September 1965, local Aboriginal people in Walgett and Coonamble eagerly crossed the dividing lines of racial segregation in hotels and cinemas. By November 1965, the Freedom Ride had been diffused into a purely self-directed form of political action by indigenous groups. On 31 November, the Federal Council for the Advancement of Aborigines and Torres Strait Islanders (FCAATSI) launched a bus trip to the Federal Parliament in Canberra. All in all, thirty-six Black protesters turned out to powerfully demand the trilogy of equal rights, Commonwealth control of Aboriginal affairs, and increased funding to address Aboriginal disadvantage. One of the Black leaders, Faith Bandler, eloquently expressed the growing, public confidence of indigenous people: 'We're coming here with dignity. Remember, we have a right to speak. Our taxes pay for Parliament. We will attend quietly outside on the lawn. We will show what we feel'.[13]

As Aboriginals and Torres Strait Islanders increasingly became politically visible in public space, so women, too, began to emerge from the 'private home' over the course of the 1960s. Women participated in the very early phases of anti-Vietnam activity. Members of the Women's International League for Peace and Freedom demonstrated openly in early May, 1965. As the USS *Vancouver* sped into town, a hundred members demonstrated their pacifism, shaking their fists in opposition on the shores of Sydney Harbour. In November 1965 they asserted themselves again, this time greeting the Anglican Primate of Sydney, Dr Gough, with a demonstration that clearly repudiated his hawkish views on the escalating war.[14]

However, it was within the anti-conscription movement that the presence of women was most ubiquitous and effective. Indeed, the Save Our Sons organisation was a powerful spearhead of the campaign from 1965 onwards. As the moniker attested, members of SOS were generally older women who self-consciously identified themselves with the role of motherhood. They wore sashes and gloves. Their language was calm and measured, and they represented a sort of 'genteel' occupation of public space. They acted as a kind of moderating force on younger activists, and the initial actions of members were typically constrained and respectful. The repertoire of 'representation' was evident, with petitions and delegations. However, demonstrations and contestational gatherings were also increasingly evident as the campaign gathered strength in 1966, 1967 and 1968. By the early 1970s, five members of Save Our Sons— 'The Fairlea Five' — had been imprisoned for trespass, and a number of committed women had participated in other apparently disruptive and illegal political performances.[15]

This was an unaccustomed sort of public performance for many women. Of course, important if now distant historical precedents *did* exist. When women chained themselves to the public bar in the Regatta Hotel, to the Garden Island Dockyard gates, to the exterior of the Commonwealth Building in Melbourne, and to the railings of the public gallery in Parliament House, Canberra, they all clearly followed in the manacled footsteps of the British suffragettes. Some even wore suffragette uniforms. Nonetheless, there was something new in the assertiveness and apparent aggression of many young, politicised women. They threw themselves on car bonnets. They sometimes abused police. They disrupted Australian–South African surf carnivals with brave sallies. They demanded the right to wear the clothes of their own choice while attending tertiary education. The change from only half a decade ago was obvious and important. In the course of participation in innovative and sometimes disruptive protests, a new form of public female identity was emerging. By 1967, lurid tabloids like *Pix* magazine were running articles promising to uncover 'the girl behind the demonstrations'. The *Sydney Morning Herald* was driven to admit that many 'modern young women' were 'prepared to demonstrate publicly on issues about which they feel strongly'. A 'new woman' was ascendant, not for the first time, and was now increasingly visible in the rising tide of collective political action.[16]

Nonetheless, a contradiction lurked. While women performed in public demonstrations, they typically remained minor members of the chorus rather than lead actors on the main stage. Men, by and large, 'set the priorities'. The main issues, theories, even cultural icons were masculinist in nature: conscription, war, imperialism; Marxism, Socialism, Libertarianism; Che Guevara, Danny Cohn-Bendit, Lenin. Women performed most of the unpaid labour that occurred 'backstage' — stuffing the envelopes, making the tea, typing, organising. They endured male, sometimes sexist leadership, and they were typically dominated both within the organisations and actions of the Old Left and the New.[17]

Some male leaders bragged of their ability to 'liberate' women, and the fact that there were no complaints from 'all of the girls concerned' (!). They propounded theories that ranked the oppression of class as more fundamental than that of gender. Some if not all of them intervened in political campaigns to insist that feminist demands were 'diversionary', 'trendy' and damaging. Others produced publications that failed to focus on the 'Women of the Left'. At their most extreme, some male leftists mocked feminists as sexless dowagers — as when the *National U* caricatured Germaine Greer as a kind of desperate witch, asking plaintively: 'Won't Anyone Screw Me?'[18]

Similarly, the student New Left often failed to accept the independence of racial or sexual oppression. For many, it remained crucial to insist on the economic and class determinants of racial oppression. Capitalism was the enemy, and the 'working class' the inclusive, exclusive agent of history. Wayward Aborigines were to be corrected. Many gays and lesbians were 'too frightened' to declare their sexuality openly, and remained 'closet queens' among their 'politico friends'. They complained of overt and continuing oppression within student organisations, such as the Australian Union of Students, and socialist organisations, such as the Socialist Youth Alliance. As late as 1974, some Communists, like Leonard Amos, declared their homophobia in Marxist-ese: 'What I am saying is that homosexuality, originally engendered by non-communist social environments, is inherently retrogressive, as it is socially subversive in relation to species procreation'.[19] Of course, not every male protester was a homophobic sexist who thought that racism was a capitalist construct. But while many (straight, white) men did show a willingness to discuss and to support emergent campaigns, the primary political energies and issues remained under their hegemony.

Paradoxically, while the new political performances allowed for a novel, more assertive form of public visibility, they did not necessarily deliver political independence to all of their performers. When (gay and straight, male and female, black and white) marchers proceeded to authorised rallies, they typically listened to speeches from white, straight and male leaders, standing on upraised stages, wearing suits and ties, and shouting directions to those below. This was a clear relationship of power within the movement. To one marcher in the Vietnam Moratorium in Sydney, the leaders seemed to want only to 'set themselves up with microphones to harangue the poor plebs who had assembled at their feet'.[20]

Participants felt pressured to 'unite in activity' and to 'conform to the demands of those on the platform', as Wendy Bacon put it. They stared upwards at speakers who did not resemble them. In 1971, for example, thirty-two of the thirty-three speakers at an anti-war conference in Sydney were men. And in public meetings and movement forums, the act of leading was similarly male (white and masculinist) by assumption. Indeed, even during sustained political performances that aimed to address women, male student leaders attempted to wrest control. Their attempts to dominate the 'Women's Studies' action at Sydney University and to transform it from an issue about 'Sexism in the University' to one about 'Student Control in the University', were often remarked on. Similarly, when an occupation of the Melbourne University Council Chambers occurred over the issue of childcare on 6 May 1974, the assumption of male leadership was equally evident. One woman activist noted that:

> As usual the old male student heavies crawled out of the woodwork from everywhere (we haven't seen some of them for years!!) and told us that this was not just an issue of childcare, oh no, this was an issue of student control!! etc. We've heard all this before. It was only thanks to the strength of the women that the men who came along expecting to dominate it, or expecting to see it dominated by men, were frustrated.[21]

What did this mean? If the repertoire of staging allowed for theatrical forms of political performance, they were most often directed by white, straight men. If the process of 'staging' allowed for the construction of a variety of spaces upon which claims could be made, those claims tended to focus on the demands of a narrow section of the population. The political gimmick had had a contradictory impact. It allowed a range of citizens to emerge as public, political actors. But it did not allow all of them to direct and star in performances of their own devising. If new stages of debate had been constructed, they were not equally open to all demands. To pioneer new roles, some actors had, quite literally, to seize the stage. Shamelessly, openly, they needed to challenge directorial power, and to demand the spotlight themselves.

Suddenly, around the year 1970, this began to occur.

TRANSITIONS: SEIZING THE STAGE

As students of Sydney University prepared to march in the first Vietnam Moratorium of 1970, a woman, Kate Jennings, angrily annexed the role of speaker. Amid the hubbub of 'Victory to the NLF' and 'Ho, Ho, Ho Chi Minh', a new voice was heard:

> Watch out! you may meet a real castrating female or you'll say I'm a man-hating bra-burning lesbian member of the castration penisenvy brigade, which I am. I would like to speak.
>
> It's the Moratorium. I would say, oh yes, the war is bad, a pig bosses' war, may the NLF win. I also say VICTORY TO THE VIETNAMESE WOMEN. Now, our brothers on the left in the peace movement will think that what I am about to say is not justified, this is a moratorium ...[22]

Jennings went on to articulate the new cry of Women's Liberation. The 'stage' of the anti-war movement had been seized, and new demands were tumbling forth.

A day later, when a program of marches, demonstrations and rallies had seemingly reinstalled the primacy of the 'stop the war' cause, a further eruption occurred. Around 10 000 people gathered in Hyde Park, Sydney, sheltering their candles in the light wind. This time, a young Aboriginal, Paul Coe, shouldered his way to the microphone and demanded the right to speak. As Denis Freney, one of those in attendance, remembers, this seizing of the stage would have profound implications for many of those present:

> It was a brilliant speech, perhaps one of the best I've ever heard. Paul had no great rhetorical flourishes, his voice had a clipped broad accent, and he dropped his aitches, and his final 'g's. He showed no generosity to his audience. His tone was brutal. You are our oppressors. You worry about Vietnam, about the Black struggle in the USA or South Africa. But what about us, here? You raped our women, you stole our land, you massacred our ancestors, you destroyed our culture, and now — when we refused to die out as you expected — you want to kill us with your hypocrisy ...
>
> ... When he finished, a storm of applause broke about, in most part to assure ourselves that we were not the 'you' he was talking about. We were not like that, the applause said, as though if it was loud enough it would smother the brutality of his speech. But soon it faded away and an uneasy calm settled on the crowd.[23]

Clearly, the actions of both Jennings and Coe displayed a frustration with the selectivity of existing student concern and interest. Both marked a powerful, eloquent cry for the recognition of other campaigns and oppressions. As political actions, however, their historical novelty seemed to lie in another direction. In both cases, the stages of the existing 'Left' were seized. The newly public spaces created by mass political performance were themselves being challenged, criticised and complicated. The challenge to the powerful embodied in demonstrations and mass gatherings was itself being contested — now apparently a source of power and authority in its own right.

This moment represented an historic transformation in the uses of the political gimmick. It had emerged as a tool of political challenge to the state and to powerful if apparently private interests. A range of new performances had been improvised, and the student and wider Left had been energised. Citizens previously unable to assert themselves politically had begun to appear and to act in public space. But now, suddenly, the political gimmick seemed to turn on itself. It began to be applied not only in 'proper' places, in squares, city streets, businesses and homes, but also on the terrain of 'the Left' itself. The spaces of the movement were increasingly contested and disrupted, shaken by sit-ins, boycotts and demonstrations. Through the adroit use of the repertoire of staging, the existence of previously overlooked oppression was highlighted. The hierarchies, theories and practices of the existing Left were now threatened. Movements for political change, and indeed, Australian society itself, would never be the same again.

DEMANDING THE RECOGNITION OF OPPRESSION

Unexpectedly, some of the traditional cultural practices of the student and industrial Left found themselves under attack. In early 1970, the traditional 'Miss Fresher' contest at Adelaide University's 'O' Week was disrupted with a sit-in and demonstration by seventy male and female proponents of Women's Lib. The contest was denounced as little more than a 'yearling sale' and an agent of the 'dehumanization process' that blocked women from realising 'their full potential'. The tradition was opened up for critical scrutiny, and the audience of male students was both astounded and angry:

> When an attempt was made by a speaker to explain the aims of the Women's Liberation Movement and why they were pursuing this particular course of action, the speaker was drowned in abuse, and pelted with paper darts and fruit ... Despite the fact that this was a fairly normal kind of demonstration, the hostile feelings that were aroused between the two groups of students was [*sic*] far greater than any experienced, by this correspondent at least, on the Adelaide campus (which proves something, I suppose, about the point the W.L.M. were trying to make).[24]

Other students were soon to be similarly challenged. In early 1971, Michael Wright, the president of the Students' Association at the Australian National University, looked forward to his judging of the Miss ANU Competition. Wright let other students in on his key criterion of quality, apparently noting that he would 'be voting for the one with the biggest boobs'. However, he was forced to review such a carefully formulated principle when the Labor Club entered its own candidate: a calf. The feminist journal *Mejane* reported the scene ironically:

> The Labor Club candidate, Miss Daisy Bovine of Fyshwick, made up in number what she lacked in size — she has four though, as she is quite a young thing, they are not overly developed as yet ... Daisy made quite an impression on the judges and other entrants, and because she was somewhat nervous, had quite an effect on the T.V. Room carpet.[25]

As already noted, these traditional beauty contests were similarly 'sent up' by Gay and Women's Lib activists at the Sydney May Day march, 1973. Not only was a boycott staged and an explanatory leaflet issued, women's liberationists and gay liberationists even 'stormed the speaker's platform' at the May Day rally. The crowd cheered, and conservative union officials looked on, surprised. How could May Day, the symbol of workers' ongoing struggle, itself become a site of contest?[26]

But more fundamental challenges were soon to be made. The apparent sexism of student publications was contested with ritual burnings of *Honi Soit*. The dominance of the male editor of the *National U* was questioned by young feminists, who exposed the tasks that they were relegated to: 'sticky tapers, pencil sharpeners, bottle washers, feet kissers'. The unthinking homophobic critique of prisons as 'breeding-grounds' for homosexuals was challenged and criticised by articulate young proponents of Gay Liberation. [27]

Indeed, the institutions of the peace movement, the trade unions, the student movement, and the Communist Party all found themselves challenged by the force of the new demands. The marginalisation of women to 'defined' roles within the peace movement was taken on, and the Moratorium was even forced to concede that it would henceforth attempt to 'help break down sexist, chauvinist and discriminatory practices and attitudes to women'. Leading women members of the CPA began to note that the conventional role of women was seldom challenged within the party, and that political campaigning for women was typically 'peripheral to the main stream of radical action'. The creation of special 'Women's Committees' was criticised.

On the broad Left, the challenges to existing theories and practices were manifold. The need for theoretical examination of the family, sex, and gender oppression was postulated. The status of women as central social actors, and the need for an 'autonomous women's movement' was theoretically established. The apparent racism of student organisations like the Australian Union of Students was trenchantly exposed. The previously unacknowledged homophobia of the student Left began to be grasped — the reliance on 'machismo', the refusal to accept those who had 'come out', or even to broach the issue of sexuality.[28]

In a few short years, from 1970 onwards, the existence of unacknowledged oppression *within the Left itself* was forced into recognition. Aborigines, women and gays all used the political gimmick to target the institutions of the Left, and to politicise previously uncontested practices. The changes were disorienting.

In a notable case of translation, Aboriginal leaders now declared their allegiance to Black Power, and the need for Aboriginal leadership of Aboriginal organisations. The colonisation of Aboriginal institutions by sympathetic whites was contested with a variety of demonstrations, marches, and tactical disruptions of institutional space. In November 1971, the office of the Foundation of Aboriginal Affairs in George Street, Sydney, was angrily attacked. The front door was smashed, a fake bomb threat was phoned in, and slogans were proudly daubed. Less than two weeks later, fifty 'Redfern blacks' sat down in front of the building again, chanting 'Down with Uncle Toms' and 'This organisation is white dominated', wearing red headbands and hoisting Black Power banners. They attempted to storm the building, and five protesters were arrested. Before the year was out, the office of the Aborigines Advancement League in Northcote, Melbourne, had also been directly challenged. The slogans painted on the building's side in red, black and cream gained front-page headlines:

'Black Power Aint Here'

'Join the Revolution'

'AAL is a Flop'

'To Be a Honkie is to be a No No'[29]

This offensive extended to other terrains. At the Easter 1970 conference of the Federal Council for the Advancement of Aborigines and Torres Strait Islanders, a number of militant indigenous delegates booed and hissed at previously dominant white delegates, sought constitutional changes to guarantee indigenous leadership, and eventually withdrew to form an alternative organisation — the National Tribal Council. Aboriginal activists such as Len Watson challenged religious conferences that addressed Aboriginal politics, in 1973 disrupting the Eucharistic Congress in Melbourne and the Quaker Conference in Sydney. Together with a range of other Aboriginal actors, including Bob Bellear, Lyn Thompson and Gary Williams, he also contested the powerful Australian Institute of Aboriginal Studies in 1974. Applying the tools of the political gimmick, the operation of the Institute was opened up for criticism and debate, the discipline of anthropology was criticised as exploitative and objectifying, and the absence of any direct political connection with Aboriginal people was lambasted. New questions were posed of 'sympathetic whites'. Old practices were challenged, familiar understandings questioned.[30]

Of course, this application of theatrical performance to the conferences and gatherings of the Left was not limited to Australia's indigenous peoples. Women, too, flexibly applied a range of political gimmicks. Peace congresses were disrupted with demands for babysitting and greater representation of women. Communist-run conferences addressing issues like worker control were marked by the eruption of somewhat startling new issues. The demand went up for childcare arrangements that would allow women to participate fully, for a greater balance of male and female speakers and chairs, and for an acknowledgement of the problem of 'sexism'. By the late 1970s, the disruption of the conference by demonstrations had itself become routinised — parodied in Frank Moorhouse's acute social comedy *Conference-Ville*.

Perhaps the most striking of these contestational, disruptive gatherings was organised in opposition to the Australian trade union movement. In August 1971, the Conference of the Australian Council of Trade Unions, the paramount trade union gathering in Australia, was met by a shocking contingent of eighty Women's Lib. activists. They demonstrated for equal pay and employment opportunities. They jostled new ACTU president Bob Hawke, and they caused a substantial commotion. When one delegate from the Australian Workers Union tried to pinch a protester, he was whacked emphatically with a placard. Another was called a 'bourgeois ——', according to the *Herald* reporter present. The matey clubbiness of much of the trade union world was definitively challenged. The gatherings of the 'Old Left' were politicised by creative, contestational actions. Feminist activists of the time felt the ACTU protest to be 'an encouraging and stimulating indication of how powerful sisterhood can be. If we needed further proof of this, it was certainly given by the wary looks on the faces of the male delegates who waited in the distance for their mates, to avoid walking alone through our reception line'.[31] In this case, at least, the ease of the male within the industrial movement was thrown a strong challenge. The demands of women could, quite literally, not be ignored.

Of course, calculating the success or failure of these inventive acts was a hazardous endeavour. They seemed to defy accustomed logic. They targeted, as their practitioners clearly realised, their apparent friends, allies and sympathisers: the concerned whites who organised conferences to investigate race relations; the unionists who officially endorsed the aim of equal pay; the Communists who believed that socialism would grant equal rights to women. Not the Prime Minister, but the union militant; not the summit of male power, but the president of the students' association. Was it not their friends that these protesters were turning on?

These actions seemed, furthermore, to concern issues that teetered between the wildly utopian and the trivially specific: No Miss ANU Contest and an End to Sexism; No Miss May Day contest and the dismantling of sex roles; changes to specific Aboriginal institutions and the promulgation of Black Power. How would such mundane aims change anything at all? How could the larger aims ever hope to be achieved? How could the local and the general ever hope to be connected?

Doubtless, such hard-headed questions deserve to be asked, but they overlook the direct political impact of many of these actions. Often the very confusion of aims and objects, aspirations and targets helped to give the performances additional drama. By demanding the impossible, they disrupted the routine space of Left politics. By posing apparently unrealistic demands of the existing Left, they forced the Left to re-examine its priorities.

In effect, a new political role was being improvised. This could be called the role of *the self-defining movement dissident*. The new role had three elements. First, it drew on the repertoire of staging, in particular the actions of contestation and disruption. Aborigines, women, lesbians and gays all showed a willingness to demonstrate, march, chain themselves, break the law, and to disrupt in a variety of ways.

Second, it was a performance directed against existing 'progressive institutions'. Its target was the existing Left rather than the state, business, or other obvious opponents. That is, this role not only represented a form of creative staging but also took on previously sacrosanct, 'proper' left-wing places. It not only involved sit-ins, graffiti, invasions and jostling, it also directed this ensemble against the supposed champions of social change.

Third, the new role demanded the recognition of previously overlooked oppression. Racism and 'Sexism' (understood as the oppression of both women and homosexuals) needed to be understood, accepted as realities, and opposed. The existing theories of exploitation and injustice needed to be reformulated to take account of new demands. The priorities of those on the Left needed to be reformed.

By bringing these three elements together, the new role of the 'self-defining movement dissident' allowed for the public, political emergence of new collective actors. One after another, the Aboriginal, women's and gay movements were able to mobilise. The political gimmick was applied on unaccustomed terrain, and newly independent movements for social change diffused. This was, indeed, a role that was available to a range of actors. Just as the movements for Women's and Gay Liberation performed dissidence within the straight, male Left, so other actors would take up this role within the institutions of the new feminism and Gay Liberation. As early as 1972, a range of lesbians began to criticise the sexism of Gay Lib. Indeed, the role of movement dissidence was powerfully performed at the Women's Liberation Theory Conference in Mount Beauty. At this gathering, the Hobart Women's Action Group famously claimed that lesbians were oppressed within 'the movement' — sometimes abused, told they were a 'media problem', discriminated against, and marginalised by practices such as consciousness-raising. The complaints of lesbians were even framed with deliberate reference to the history of Women's Liberation and the male Left: 'Just as women in left-wing movements became dissatisfied with waiting in the wings until the socialist revolution solved everyone's problems, lesbians have become increasingly dissatisfied with the Women's Liberation Movement that demands the same of them'.[32]

These roles would be performed again in later years: by lesbians, by Aboriginal women, by migrant women, and eventually by bisexuals. Microphones would be seized and lecture theatres occupied. Indeed, the world of the simple, worthy, united, committed and popular demonstration had been left far behind. New roles had been improvised to perform new sorts of demands: the right to difference rather than unity, the need to question larger causes in the name of their smaller, irreducible elements.

This was a significant if unexpected evolution in the history of the political gimmick. A political tool developed to gain the media's attention had been developed into a cluster of new political performances, and then into a role performed on the terrain of 'movement space' itself. The quest for political change was itself changed. The demands of the 'periphery' could now be constantly performed, and the necessity to respect difference within mobilising social movements would become a central political principle. The quest for a decentred, 'postmodern' politics would become an important new current on the Left.[33]

How could the three young men, proudly burning the draft cards in Wynyard Park in 1966 have predicted the tremendous transformations that would follow?

BRINGING PRIVATE ISSUES INTO THE PUBLIC REALM

If one set of performances included the new role of 'movement dissidence', then many continued to involve more familiar applications of the repertoire of staging. Indeed, the very novelty of many of the demands of the 1970s made the performances of contestation and disruption particularly apt. As Dennis Altman argued in the typical language of 1972, women, Blacks and homosexuals were fighting 'a personalized and internalized oppression' which contrasted with the more 'impersonal' concepts of capitalism and imperialism.[34] Precisely because these 'personal' experiences were at the heart of the new movements, the performance of contest proved of immeasurable value. It allowed 'private', personal matters to be diffused into the public realm, across a great variety of issues and spaces.

WOMEN'S LIBERATION

We can see this process most starkly with Women's Liberation — that movement most famously dedicated to bringing the previously personal and private into the public, political realm. Three of the most fundamental demands of Women's Lib — the right to safe, legal abortion, the right to adequate sex education, and the wide recognition of the depth of sexual violence in Australia society — all involved the politicisation of previously 'private' issues. In each case, the performance of contestation helped to challenge the personal shame felt by many women concerning these matters; it fostered public awareness and debate and it forced public authorities to respond.

As historians of the women's movement have noted, the campaign around abortion was a dominant presence in the early years of Women's Liberation. Women demonstrated outside courts when surgeons were prosecuted for performing abortions. They marched on Sydney's Parliament House in April and November 1971 and disrupted the operation of the Legislative Assembly. They adopted street theatre, demonstrations, marches and protests over the early and middle 1970s. For many participants, the value of these actions lay not only in their ability to change government policy but in their challenge to the 'internalized oppression' that Altman had earlier identified. As Deb Shnookal argued in March 1974:

> One of our greatest obstacles to overcome in our struggle for abortion on demand is the terrible stigma attached to this operation. To destroy this guilt, it is important to build a loud, determined, and MASSIVE movement around this demand. Women must get up in the streets and publicly proclaim that they have had abortions and that they believe that it is EVERY WOMAN'S RIGHT to decide to terminate her pregnancy. Such a campaign would not only accomplish the repeal of the abortion laws but it would also help women change their attitudes about themselves and their role in society.[35]

Similarly, political performances around sex education and birth control were also able to transform the self while they demanded the transformation of government policy. Hilariously, a birth control booth was established outside St Francis Xavier Cathedral in Adelaide. In Brisbane in September 1971, Women's Lib activists distributed sex education pamphlets to female students. In October 1971, a similar campaign was staged in Sydney high schools. Official silence was contested with movement initiatives; private shame was challenged with bold, public behaviour.

But it was around the issue of rape that the most profound shame existed and the most rigorous public silence enforced. Through their brave adoption of the repertoire of staging, some feminists were able to bring this issue, too, into wider public debate. Some early movement actions were local and halting. For example, in mid-1974, a 'rape vigilante squad' known as the 'Feminist Action Front' was formed. Women who had been raped were instructed to leave messages at Sydney Women's House, with the promise that anonymous action would be taken. Newspaper and television reporters showed considerable interest in the fledgling organisation; at the very least, the culture of private guilt was clearly being challenged by a more assertive, public presence.[36]

But it was in the early 1980s rather than the 1970s, and in the context of non-violence rather than violence, that the most sustained public opposition to rape was evident within the feminist movement. Beginning in Canberra in 1978, feminists contested the excision of the suffering of women from the official commemorations of Anzac Day. For these feminists, rape was seen as a 'weapon of war' which was officially condoned by the silence that surrounded it. The aim of their public performance was therefore to break that silence, to mourn the losses borne by women, and thereby to publicise the ubiquity of sexual violence in Australian society. As one pamphlet issued by the collective put it:

> Women Against Rape mourns women raped in war and brings to public attention rape as a violent act of oppression used against women in both war and peace time. Rape is a part of a whole spectrum of sexual harassment used to oppress women to keep us in our place as the collective property of men. Our male dominated society ignores, hides and finds excuses for the sexual harassment of women. In doing so this society generates an acceptance of such oppression and gives men the right and power to act on women's bodies without our consent.

The actions taken by women were themselves usually respectful and moderate. From 1980 onwards, the major actions in Canberra consisted in nothing more than a dignified, non-violent march and an attempt to lay a wreath at the War Memorial Cenotaph.

However, even such a simple action challenged the established, masculine meaning of Anzac Day. In 1980, when only sixteen women attempted to lay a wreath, fourteen were arrested, and the magistrate accused them of practising 'terrorism'. By 1981, the Federal Government has rammed through the *ACT Traffic (Amendment) Ordinance 1981*, which allowed for the arrest of anyone who acted in a manner 'likely to disturb or disrupt' the Anzac Day Parade, or likely to 'give offence or cause insult' to those taking part in 'such a parade'. That year, sixty-one women participating in the mourning ceremony were arrested. In response to such a vast police mobilisation, the 500 women who gathered to participate in the 1982 ceremony decided to stage their own action of mourning before the official ceremonies were held. Arrests were mostly avoided in this and later years.

By the mid-1980s, the campaign had spread around the country and had even been radicalised in Melbourne, as a number of young women began to campaign explicitly for the abolition of Anzac Day. As Marilyn Lake has argued, the 'masculine custodians of national memory' were outraged by such acts. But amid the public bluster and anger, the issue of rape — in war and outside it — was politicised and publicised. In this sense, the actions had an undeniable utility for the developing movement.[37]

Of course, because sexism was understood to exist on the everyday terrain, the adherents of Women's Liberation applied the tools of the new repertoire to a range of everyday places. Repeatedly, they contested their eviction from hotels with 'drink-ins' and deliberate violations of gender segregation. This action was originally taken in the Regatta Hotel, Brisbane, as early as 1965. It was followed by similar actions in Canberra in 1969 and in Sydney in 1970 and 1971. As late as 1975, women were still being excluded from public hotels and were organising counter-actions to 'liberate' them.[38]

In other everyday places, the repertoire of contestation was also applied. Educational institutions that practised gender segregation were gleefully targeted with 'invasion'. Supermarkets were invaded, and their restrictions and policies deliberately subverted. Sticker raids occurred across shop windows: 'This Exploits Women', 'Women Unite', 'Better Dead than Wed'. Groups of women boarded public transport together, refusing to pay more than 75 per cent of the allotted fare, and thereby highlighting the absence of equal pay. Young Women's Libbers emphasised that 'male chauvinism must be challenged persistently', and even social gatherings and parties became sites of feminist contest and intervention.[39]

GAY LIBERATION

Just as feminists used the new repertoire to challenge their own, personal oppression, so lesbians and gays also posed their own challenges with the performance of contest and disruption. As Dennis Altman put it with remarkable understatement, homosexuality was not valued as a 'valid part of human experience'. Gays and lesbians not only faced legal discrimination, police harassment and economic exploitation within the 'subculture' but they also remained largely invisible to the wider public. The gay world was a taboo subject, and homosexuality the object of ridicule, hatred and medical intervention. Even when lesbians and gays asserted themselves with moderate political activity, it was often simply ignored by the mass media.

For the proponents of gay liberation, this censorious silence not only had implications for the shamed self-image of lesbians and gays but it also had a wider significance for the straight world. Indeed, on this conception, non-gays had been straitjacketed into a heterosexual existence, unable to accept the 'homosexual within' or to embrace the 'polymorphous perversity' inherent in us all. Precisely for this reason, the repertoire of staging was a particularly apt tool.[40]

Certainly, the political gimmick could be used to challenge specific cases of discrimination — like the victimisation of Macquarie student Penny Short, or the dismissal of Peter Bonsall-Boone from a position within the Church. Audacious invasions by 'radicalesbians' could also be used to challenge the high prices charged by gay bars. But the main virtue of the theatrical forms of political performance was their ability to present new, more positive models of gayness in public, to increase the self-confidence of those who had not yet come 'out', and to destabilise the existing sex roles of Australian society.[41]

The first public homosexual demonstration occurred on 8 October 1971. A new organisation, the Campaign Against Moral Persecution or CAMP, organised the action, which targeted the headquarters of the Liberal Party in Angel Place, Sydney. The ostensible motive for this gathering was the preselection for the federal seat of Brewora, where the sitting member, Attorney-General Tom Hughes, had been accused of being 'soft' on homosexuals, and was facing a challenge from fundamentalist Jim Cameron. But the unheralded gathering of about seventy people and hundreds of multicoloured balloons proved to a have a wider, less limited ambit. The Liberals, including Tom Hughes himself, were apparently 'terribly puzzled by the whole thing'. There was an atmosphere of fun and hedonism which contrasted with the more sober and macho nature of many anti-conscription actions. Gay identity was celebrated in public. Indeed, according to one participant, Colin Gray, 'the whole value of the demonstration lay in its high-spirited assertion of campery — people were vivaciously and imaginatively asserting their right to be gay, validating their experience as gays, and, for a moment, both tasting and portraying the possibilities of a sexually pluralist society'.[42]

As Graham Willett's impressive history of gay and lesbian activism shows, by June seventy-two Gay Liberationists were marching in the streets of Sydney, holding pink helium-filled balloons, passing out boiled lollies and 'gay apples' for passers-by. In December 1972, same-sex demonstrators noisily tested the beds in Myers department store in Melbourne, and in April 1973 Dr Harry Bailey, the prominent psychosurgeon who used brain surgery to 'cure' homosexuality, was shocked by a disruptive demonstration that burst into his offices, denounced his 'psychobutchery', and dramatically emptied a bucket of sheep brains on his waiting room floor.[43] Such assertions of Gay Pride were to become a staple of the new political movement. In September 1973, Gay Pride week was marked by demonstrations in Adelaide, Melbourne and Sydney, and a host of other minor but significant events. As Terry Bell remembered, 'we did not simply defend a sexual preference, we were angry and we were proud and above all we were gay in the best traditions of racial minorities'.[44]

Of course, the overall movement for gay liberation was not without its vicissitudes. It declined in the mid-1970s, and was only revived in 1978, when a march on International Homosexual Day, 24 June, was violently set upon by police. This harassment provoked further demonstrations — on 26 June, when the fifty-three who had been arrested faced the Central Court of Petty Sessions, and again in September 1978.

In 1979 the march was defiantly held again, and in 1980 it ended with a dance at Paddington Town Hall. By 1981, the growing action had been moved to summer, and the Sydney Gay and Lesbian Mardi Gras began to develop its distinctive and spectacular flavour. That year, as the now 5000 participants passed the cinemas on Sydney's main George Street, the disruption to routine city life was gloriously evident: 'There was a feeling of confrontation with the onlookers but not hostility. Here were the feminists, the socialists and drag queens, [the] leathermen and the clones declaring that these streets were theirs too'.[45]

The Gay and Lesbian Mardi Gras has developed into a massive celebration of marginal sexual identities, a site of religious counter-mobilisation, an international tourist drawcard, and a marker of Sydney's promotion as a so-called 'global city'. Not all participants are happy with the changing form of the Mardi Gras, but its public assertion of pride and its overt challenge to homophobia cannot be doubted. Indeed, the ability of the repertoire of staging to shift homosexuality from a kind of private shame to a fount of public, sometimes joyful identification, is surely beyond doubt. In the process, the range of public political activity, the scope of public sexual identity and the very geography of Sydney as a city have all been challenged.

ABORIGINAL PEOPLE

Just as Gay Liberation developed a new form of political performance with the Mardi Gras, and women pioneered a new role with their interventions into Anzac Day, so Aboriginal people developed improvisations of their own. As historian Heather Goodall has rigorously documented, the right to traditional lands has remained the central political aspiration of Australia's indigenous people throughout the history of European settlement, but this has been neither acknowledged nor respected by the majority of the white Australian public. Even sympathetic whites, such as many of the members of Student Action For Aborigines, tended to emphasise civil rights issues inspired by struggles and barriers in the United States rather than local, land-focused issues.[46]

The repertoire of staging allowed this to change. First, because it involved the eruption of politics into previously apolitical spaces, and even the invasion of private 'proper places', the repertoire of staging explicitly raised the issue of land. When protesters used the sit-in, they claimed the right to occupy particular places. When the Federal Government contemplated legislation that threatened new penalties for the sit-in and for invasion of property, angry students offered a quick retort: 'Is not the taking of land from Aborigines by large companies a breach of this law, as the Aborigine [is] the lawful occupier of the land?'[47]

Not only that, but the flexibility and confidence offered by the repertoire of staging allowed Aboriginal people to advance the cause of land rights themselves. While the strike, walk-off and struggle of the Gurindji at Wave Hill were largely unconnected to the developments in urban Australia, they were enthusiastically supported by a wide range of other actions. There were repeated vigils outside Federal Government offices demanding land rights; marches; petitions; even rolling, forty-day fasts. The president of FCAATSI, Faith Bandler, was impressed with the utility of such actions, suggesting to members that 'there is tremendous work involved in acts of public protest, and they should make some effort to unite and organise together, making the impact greater'.

Increasingly, over the late 1960s and early 1970s, the dispossession of Aboriginal people by whites was itself 'performed' by supporters of land rights. Marcia Langton claimed 100 square feet of land opposite the Commonwealth Offices in Brisbane. Charles Poynton took out a mining claim to the land around the Perth Shrine. The offices of the Vesteys company in Sydney were invaded and occupied, and other demonstrations targeted the Australian headquarters of Angliss & Company.[48] Aboriginal demonstrators and their white supporters marched proudly along George Street, Sydney. Protest leaders Paul Coe and Dexter Daniels provided a 'running commentary' through a portable loudspeaker, and shoppers looked on, startled, as the unfamiliar words and images tumbled forth: 'You white Australians who go home to your comfortable homes, your families, your TV sets ... do you think about the thousands of Aboriginal children who sicken and die in poverty?'[49] By 1972, the growing tendency of *all* actions to disrupt existing spaces began to combine with the developing ability of Aboriginal people to perform politically their desire for land rights. An exciting new political performance was the result: the Aboriginal tent embassy.

When Prime Minister William McMahon disappointed the expectations of Aboriginal people for land rights in his Australia Day address, 1972, a number of activists took immediate action. Quickly, tents and outdoor furniture were gathered, cars borrowed, and a small group thundered towards the national parliament.

The establishment of an Embassy for Aboriginal people on the front lawns of Parliament House cogently portrayed the failure of white governments to respond to Aboriginal demands. At its most basic, as one participant put it, the Embassy dramatised the truth that 'foreigners had more representation than us'. Statements were issued and a 'ministry' named. In diverse regions around the country, the battle for indigenous rights was enlivened, and the international mass media gravitated to Parliament House.[50]

The Embassy quickly became more than a conventional demonstration. The lawns of Parliament House were virtually taken over by Aboriginal protesters. For more than six months, the Embassy persisted. Government ministers were seriously embarrassed; when they announced their intention to remove it, supporters pointed out that the tent site was clean, orderly, and infinitely superior to the squalid conditions on many government-run reserves. When politicians complained of its 'unsightly' presence, supporters emphasised the 'miserable conditions of life of the majority of black people in this country'.[51]

More broadly, the new Embassy directly performed the strong desire of Aboriginal people for land rights. The first public statement of protesters expressed this directly: 'The land was taken from us by force ... we shouldn't have to lease it ... our spiritual beliefs are connected to the land'. Not only that, but when the Minister for the Interior called the protesters 'campers', and argued that the Embassy transcended the right to protest, the issue of land was brought into the mainstream of political debate. Aboriginal people emphasised that they would not leave until their demands for compensation and land rights were met. Whites were puzzled by this stubborn insistence, and began to appreciate that an alternative understanding of land ownership was being enacted. As Gordon Bryant, the shadow Minister for Aboriginal Affairs, tentatively put it:

> the Embassy represents an effective and unique demonstration of the Aboriginal people's concept of land and ... until some arrangement in Canberra expresses a different 'proprietorship' from the usual leasehold-freehold tenure of land, its presence is valid and necessary.
>
> I recognise that this is a difficult concept for non-Aborigines to grasp and admit that my own expression of it is imperfect.[52]

When the police moved in and destroyed the Embassy on 20 July 1972, the violence of Aboriginal dispossession was played out for television cameras. When the Embassy was re-established, and again removed on 23 July, this wide publicity was regained. On 30 July 1972, the Embassy was again reconstituted, and the symbolism of Aboriginal resistance and survival was made clear to all.

Ultimately, the Embassy became a 'modular' political tool, available to all manner of protesters. When Aboriginal people felt the need to assert themselves politically in 1974, 1979 and 1992, an Embassy was re-established on the front lawns of the Old Parliament House. An Aboriginal Consulate was established outside the Western Australian Parliament to demand improved housing in 1972. When environmentalists aimed to press for an end to logging in the mid-1990s, they established a 'Forest Embassy' in Canberra. When the cause of Gay Rights was asserted in New South Wales, they established their own Embassy outside the Premier's residence. When new industrial relations legislation threatened the freedom of Western Australia trade unions, they decided to establish the 'Workers Embassy' in Perth.[53]

In a sense, the world of Australian protest had now been inverted. In the mid-1960s, white students had been enamoured of American civil rights protests and had carefully translated them into the Australian environment. Although SAFA was led by Aboriginal student Charles Perkins, for the most part indigenous people were the cause of collective action rather than the active subjects themselves. Slowly, however, the political confidence of Aboriginal people increased, and the range of political performances expanded. The cause of land rights was championed by Aboriginal people themselves in a range of surprising and exciting ways. By the early 1970s, they had developed their own, specific forms of political performance to dramatise their particular demands. Political issues that whites had been unable to grasp were being played out in front of the national parliament with subtlety and flair. A new political role, increasingly available to other Australian actors, was now in circulation. The politics of social change had literally turned upside down.

CONCLUSION

As the 'new' social movements enter their third decade of existence, and contemporary historical work emphasises the longevity of campaigns for women's, Aboriginal and gay rights, the profound changes of the early 1970s are in danger of being forgotten. In half a decade, the landscape of the Left was utterly changed. New demands were stridently championed, new theories enunciated, and new identities publicly expressed. The concepts, hierarchies and practices of the existing Left were all questioned. The politics of difference and diversity quickly became pre-eminent, and the older quests for unity and order were henceforth under challenge.

Such a profound transformation is likely to be overdetermined — the product of a variety of economic, political and social changes. The histories of individual movements are likely to be complicated and varied, and their trajectories riddled with temporary setbacks and minor triumphs. Their joint history is likely to be even more labyrinthine and entangled. Clearly, this chapter has not offered such a history. Its aim has been more limited and conceptually focused — a history of how political protest was diffused to a range of newly mobilising actors.

While the political gimmick was not the only generator of change on the Left, there is no doubt that it contributed to the ferment of the early 1970s. The theatrical forms of political performance were important in at least three ways. They created spaces for the public emergence of previously invisible actors, they granted those actors the tools to demand the institutional recognition of previously overlooked oppression, and they provided the means to bring previously private, apolitical matters into the public realm.

The dizzying changes that followed not only allowed a range of new movements to develop but also enriched the tradition of Australian political protest. As the 1970s stretched into the 1980s, it seemed to be in the women's movement, the gay and lesbian movements, and the Aboriginal movement that the most exciting and innovative forms of political performance were being staged. The mourning on Anzac Day, the Mardi Gras and the Embassy were (along with the Green Bans of the BLF)[54] perhaps the most outstanding improvisations of contemporary Australian political history.

How did this impact on the key ideas of the Left? What did the diffusion of the political gimmick mean for the dominant theories of social life? What were its implications? What were the consequences of such performances for the debates over social change and social structure that continued to punctuate the intellectual life of the Left? What, in short, did it all mean?

We turn to these questions in the next chapter.

Above Staging for the cameras at a Palm Sunday rally. Courtesy of the *Tribune* Collection, State Library of New South Wales, PXA: 593, vol. 31.
Below The peaceful spectacle of mass rational commitment in the Sydney Domain. Courtesy of the *Tribune* Collection, State Library of New South Wales, PXA: 593, vol. 31.

Above The theatricalisation of protest. Courtesy of the *Tribune* Collection, State Library of New South Wales, PXA: 593, vol. 31.
Below Contesting corporate-led globalisation — the WEF protest on 11 September 2000. Courtesy of the *Age*.

104 •

Above The mass gathering as public mourning — Sydney women on Anzac Day 1985 mourn the losses of all women from all countries raped in wartime. Courtesy of the *Tribune* Collection, State Library of New South Wales, PXA: 593, vol 31.
Below The peaceful spectacle takes to the streets on Palm Sunday. Courtesy of B Hennessy and the Australian Society Archives.

Above Claiming Land Rights with confidence, Sydney 1982. Courtesy of Margaret Olah/Rapport and the Australian Society Archives.
Below Claiming the streets — anti-Vietnam War marchers leave Treasury Gardens in Melbourne. Courtesy of the John Ellis Collection, Melbourne University Archives, UMA/I/30.

Above The theatre of conflict — police and protesters clash as camera crews eagerly follow, Canberra 1991. Courtesy of the John Ellis Collection, Melbourne University Archives, UMA/I/936.

Below Staging debate — Jim Cairns addresses the crowd in Melbourne City Square, 1975. Courtesy of the John Ellis Collection, Melbourne University Archives, UMA/I/142.

Above The Women's Liberation Movement mobilises on May Day 1976. Courtesy of the John Ellis Collection, Melbourne University Archives, UMA/I/170.
Below Gay Liberation makes new demands, May Day 1978. Courtesy of the John Ellis Collection, Melbourne University Archives, UMA/I/414

Left Claiming Land Rights through contestation — Captain Cook's cottage is claimed on 26 January 1976. Courtesy of the John Ellis Collection, Melbourne University Archives, UMA/I/162.

Below Contesting Hansonism — an anti-racism rally and march in Melbourne, 8 December 1996. Courtesy of the John Ellis Collection, Melbourne University Archives, UMA/I/926.

4
THEORY

> theory: a supposition or system of ideas explaining something; a speculative (esp. fanciful) view.
> — *Concise Oxford Dictionary*

> To squeeze meaning out of (at best) ambiguous results was a large part of what a movement leader did.
> — Todd Gitlin

In 1969, a dispute broke out on the pages of the Australian student newspaper *National U*. Kelvin Rowley, Terry Counihan and Douglas Kirsner, three students at Melbourne University, decided it was necessary to intervene in what they understood to be disturbing trends within the student movement. As they saw it, the rise of the political gimmick had not been entirely beneficial. As the theatrical techniques of political performance developed, so a kind of obsession with publicity had emerged, and genuine theoretical analysis of Australian society had therefore lagged. Demonstrations were becoming an end in themselves, a 'fetish'. It was Kirsner who attacked the strategy of the leading student organisation Students for a Democratic Society with the greatest insight and penetration:

> An acute sense of publicity cretinism is obvious. The success of a demonstration is not only by the number of arrests (a tactic which has become a strategy for SDS) but by the extent of newspaper or TV coverage. The fact that responsibility for the effect an action will have has been handed over to a scarcely politically neutral press seems to elude SDS. A non-ideological SDS deals with matters as they come up.[1]

If students were to pose a more powerful challenge to the injustices of Australian society, they would need to start again. In place of the demonstration there would need to be the journal; in place of the draft card burning, the study circle. Their heads buzzing with the newly accessible work of Louis Althusser and Antonio Gramsci, Rowley and Counihan suggested that the most important political act would be to pursue 'radical reeducation within and through the University itself'. According to this view, the circulation of radical research, theory and analysis was of 'vital importance'. The act of theorisation was at the summit of political potency. As they put it most concisely, 'essential for the "New Student Left" is the creation of a theory of itself, and of the role of the university in society'.[2]

But what would this 'theory' be? And how would it relate to the political gimmick? Clearly, the young Melbourne theorists thought of their own work as operating on a distinct, deeper level. It would penetrate to the fundamental forces that animated Australian society; it would analyse capitalism as a distinct social formation, illuminate immanent social trends with the 'labour of the mind'. Those more prosaic questions to do with the mobilisation of numbers or the likely interactions between students and police would be bypassed. The 'unthinking adulation of heroes and "gurus"' and the apparently rampant 'abuse of terminology' among the Student Left would all be sidestepped.[3]

On the other hand, without the energy and momentum provided by the political gimmick it would be hard to imagine that the conditions for this intervention would exist at all. It was when campus politics began to adopt the repertoire of staging that the infrastructure of political debate also began to develop. It was only then that the roneoed leaflet was passed to the eager hand, only then that the student rally attained a broad, critical mass of interested listeners. If 'publicity cretinism' loomed as a serious deficiency, then the fruits of the political gimmick still provided bountiful sustenance for the 'student as theorist'. If the demonstration was becoming a 'fetish' then even the critics of the demonstration (such as Kirsner, Rowley and Counihan themselves) still organised their theoretical sallies against and in relation to its political prominence. The 'theory' that they produced would be informed by the political gimmick, shaped by its ubiquitous presence and apparent power. It would be a 'new' theory that reflected a new political moment of opportunities and actors — demands staged and energies diffused.

But how, precisely, did the theory produced at this time differ from its precursors? How did the actions of the political gimmick disrupt the ruling social and political propositions of the Australian Left? Answering these questions helps us to trace the varied impacts of the political gimmick as it filtered through from the public square and the evening news into more discrete and alternative 'public spheres'. It also touches on wider issues concerning the process of 'theory production' and the important, seldom scrutinised connections between social theory and political events. It brings the study of the political gimmick from the outer reaches of political science into the mainstream of the sociology of knowledge.

Unquestionably, the widespread political mobilisation of the mid-1960s and early 1970s was also a moment of distinctly theoretical change. Alongside the development of theatrical forms of performance and the diffusion of protest energies to 'new movements', the ruling propositions of left-wing thought also faced consistent challenge. Among the many theoretical principles that would emerge from the 1960s would be the new importance of intellectuals as social actors; the rolling back of classical Marxism for post-Marxism; the elevation of culture as a central category of sociological analysis; the increasing emphasis on the political action of non-class actors; and the need for an increasing, international circulation of texts and concepts.[4]

For the Australian Left, this represented a quite fundamental change. But how and why did these new propositions so successfully challenge the old verities? How, exactly, was apparent political change converted into intellectual development? Existing accounts have failed to take these questions seriously. Rather than seeking to explain *how* theoretical change has occurred, they have focused instead on arguing about whether or not this was a good thing. Rather than analysing, they have advocated. Rather than chronicling the detailed, shifting connections between changing theories and changing events, they have resorted to polemical disputes over the political and intellectual efficacy of the rival positions. Explanations written from within 'old' Marxism have insisted on explaining the transformation of social theory as part of broad developments within capitalism and self-interested strategies by ascendant intellectuals. Explanations written from within 'new' post-Marxism have told a different story — as society, culture and politics developed, so new forms of theory became more appropriate, and the boundaries of Marxism became too restrictive. Thought advanced 'beyond Marxism' towards more delightful pastures.[5]

If we are to learn more about how theoretical change occurs and how the political gimmick shaped it, then we need to avoid these argumentative stand-offs. Tracing the impact on social and political theory of the political gimmick and the emergence of widespread contention can only become something more than an impossibly broad, inevitably impressionistic exercise if it focuses in on specific examples of theorisation in rigorous detail. As with the study of 'translation' in Chapter 1, the analysis of 'theory' and its connection to the political gimmick can most usefully be organised as a discrete, carefully documented case study. But as with Chapter 2, we can only understand the precise dynamics of this change and avoid polemical exchanges if we have recourse to social science tools such as statistical analysis.

ARENA AS A CASE STUDY OF THE PROCESS OF THEORISATION

Established in 1963, the journal *Arena* offers a useful window on the prominence and impact of the political gimmick on social theory in Australia during the 1960s and early 1970s. The Melbourne-based journal was an important point of connection between different elements of the New Left and the Old Left. It contained contributions both of highly abstract and more empirical interest. It was consistently engaged with the political activities of radical movements in Australia and overseas, and with the elucidation of their theoretical significance. It began life as a journal dedicated to 'rethinking Marxism', yet it had moved a decade later to a position far distant from the classical Marxist tradition. It was, in fact, the source of a distinctive and innovative social theory — the '*Arena* thesis' — that the 'intellectually trained' were possessed of certain cultural characteristics (autonomy, rationality, ethical concern) that made them pivotal social actors in the emerging society.

While *Arena*'s specific history is by no means representative of the reaction of all social theorists to the political gimmick in Australia, it does provide a fertile case study of how 'events' became the fodder for theoretical innovation during the 1960s and early 1970s. While not all theorists interpreted the rise of the political gimmick and the new movements in the same way, analysing the theoretical vision and insight within *Arena* can teach us more general lessons about how events are handled in theory, and how they can legitimate theoretical change. In short, if *Arena*'s conclusions were singular, its responsiveness to the eruption of collective action was not. If its theory of political change was distinctive, its use of political change to develop social theory could not have been more typical of the time.

THEORETICAL INVESTMENT IN POLITICAL EVENTS: A SOCIAL-SCIENTIFIC APPROACH

How is it possible to reconstruct the connections between political events and theoretical propositions? How can we find out whether particular demonstrations lead theorists to change their mind about the role of classes or the need for particular strategies? How can we discover if particular theoretical interests predispose intellectuals to emphasise the importance of a specific cluster of collective events?

The methods used in Chapter 2 offer us scant assistance. The simple counting of concepts or events is not supple enough to give analytical purchase on either the process of cognition or the dynamics of culture. If we need to understand how theory and events connect, then we need a coding method that locates and records such connections. We need to focus not only on the frequency of concepts but also on the interrelationships among them, and the frequency of both concepts and interrelationships. Such a coding method has recently been developed by American linguist Kathleen Carley. It is called 'map analysis'. Whereas traditional content analysis counts specific *concepts*, map analysis counts *statements*: 'A pair of concepts form a statement if they are part of a semantic unit such as "robots are nice", "comedies can be satires", "boy walks". Within a statement there is a "link" between the two concepts'.[6] The links between two concepts to make a statement can be *directed* (e.g. from first concept to second), *signed* (e.g. a link such as *a* is *b* or *a* is not *b*) or possess a certain *strength* (e.g. a degree of emphasis). For Carley, the primary benefit of map analysis is its ability to analyse meaning, and in particular to remain attentive to changes in the meaning of concepts over time. But these techniques are also of immense benefit for those interested in exploring the connections between collective action 'events' and theoretical frameworks.

Drawing on map analysis, this chapter's analysis rests on a coding of two sorts of concepts and two kinds of statements on every occasion that they appeared in the journal *Arena* between 1963 and 1973 inclusive. Two concepts have been coded:

1   *Endorsements* of political or discursive events, for example:[7]
    'The Moratorium March was a success'
    'Marx's insights in *Capital* remain invaluable'

2   *Critiques* of political or discursive events, for example:
    'The violence of the Moratorium March made it counterproductive'
    'Humphrey McQueen misunderstands Australian history'

In addition, two forms of statement have been coded:

1   *Positive justifications*
    These are statements that forge a positive, directed link between one political or discursive event and another. To put it more simply, a 'positive justification' involves the authority of one event being used to justify another.

    'The success of students in Paris shows us the need for theoretically informed student action in Australia.'

    'Lenin's writings showed the importance of the Party for revolution. Without a Marxist Party, we cannot hope to make revolution.'

Positive justifications are made up of two concepts. I call the first concept in the statement a *referent*. In the first example cited, the referent would be 'students in Paris', in the second, 'Lenin's writings'. The referent of a positive justification is an expression of the authority and legitimacy of a political or intellectual event. I call the second concept in the statement an *object recommended*. In the first example, the object recommended would be 'theoretically informed student action', in the second, 'a Marxist Party'. The object recommended of a positive justification is an expression of the interests and engagement of a journal and its contributors.

2   *Negative justifications*
    These are statements that forge a negative, directed link between one political or discursive event and another. To put it more simply, a 'negative justification' involves the lack of authority of one event being used to justify another, subsequent event.

    'The failure of the Moratorium emphasises the need for a new project of sustained theoretical rethinking.'

    'The failure of the Communist Party's recent statement to grasp the growing middle class shows that we need to recast class analysis.'

Negative justifications are made up of two concepts. I call the first concept in the statement a *referent*. The referent of a negative justification is an expression of the lack of authority, the problems and imperfections of a political or intellectual event. In the first example, the referent would be 'Moratorium'; in the second, 'the Communist Party's recent statement'. I call the second concept in the statement an *object recommended*. In the first example, the object recommended would be 'sustained theoretical rethinking', in the second, 'recast class analysis'. The object recommended of a negative justification is an expression of the interest and engagement of the journal and its contributors.

Applying this coding framework to *Arena* over the period from 1963 to 1973 has produced over a thousand discrete records. Each record is a specific instance where an event is either endorsed, critiqued, used as part of a positive justification or as part of a negative justification. While the long explanation of this method may have appeared burdensome (and the process of coding certainly was), the records accumulated provide invaluable data on the connections between theory and events. They provide information not only on which particular texts or political occurrences were praised and criticised, but on how these events were used to justify future forms of intellectual and political work. That is, they provide original data on the relationships between theories and events during a period of political and theoretical invention. By drawing on these data, we can hope to reconstruct how the political gimmick was used to stimulate and legitimate theoretical change.

This chapter draws extensively on these data in order to explain the development of *Arena*'s distinctive social theory over the 1960s and early 1970s. But before we move to this detailed analysis, we first need a broad understanding of *Arena*'s intellectual and political transformation.

THE BROAD HISTORY OF ARENA: THE DECLINE OF MARXISM

From its beginnings, Marxism was a key element in the discourse of the journal. The texts of Marx, Engels and Lenin were either specifically *endorsed* or used as the *referent* for a *positive justification* on 115 occasions between 1963 and 1973. However, positive references are far stronger in the period between 1963 and 1971, where Marxism was referred to on 110 occasions, than in the period after 1971, where Marxism was referred to on only five occasions.

Figure 4.1
Endorsements and positive justifications using Marxism as a referent

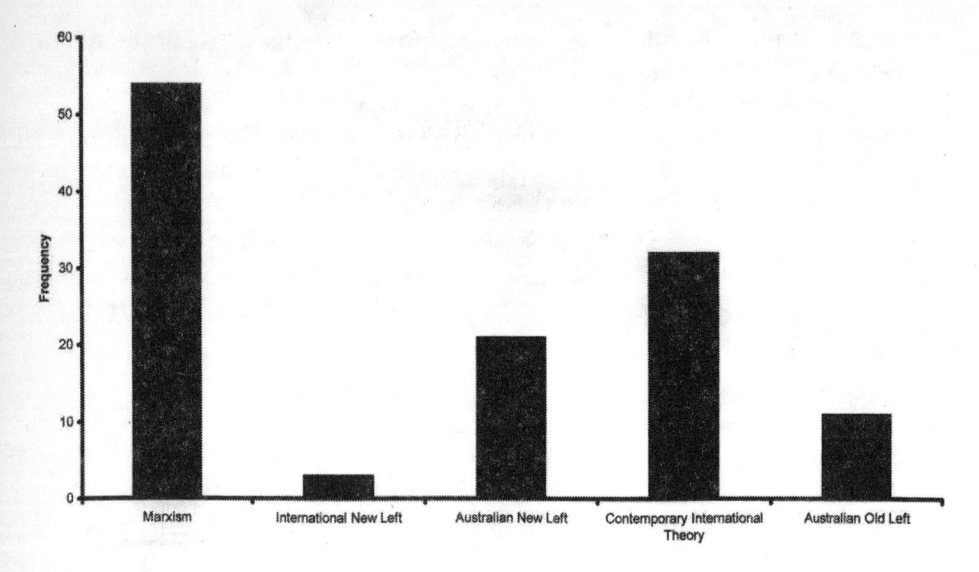

Figure 4.2
Endorsements and positive justifications in *Arena* 1963–67

The extent of this decline is even starker when viewed in relative terms. The authority of Marxism within the intellectual networks of the Communist Party of Australia in the first two decades after World War II had been such that Marxist references were necessary to ground both political strategy and further intellectual work. Marxism was established as 'essential for an understanding of any political question'. It could be thought of as a kind of 'master discourse', through which party intellectuals were forced to express themselves if their contributions were to be favourably received.[8]

This continued until at least 1967 within the discourse of *Arena*. Between 1963 and 1967, Marxism was either *endorsed* or referred to as a *referent* for a *positive justification* on fifty-four occasions. The authority of Marxism, as measured in *endorsements* and *referents* for *positive justifications*, outweighed all other sources, including collective events associated with the Australian New Left, the Australian Old Left, and the International New Left.

It is 1968 that marks the relative decline of the authority of Marxism within *Arena*'s conceptual economy. In that year, Marxism was *endorsed* or used as a *referent* for a *positive justification* on eleven occasions; events associated with the international New Left were *endorsed* or used as a *referent* for a *positive justification* on thirty-one occasions. Similarly, events associated with the Australian New Left were *endorsed* or used as a *referent* for a *positive justification* on twenty-six occasions. Even other forms of social theory challenged the established Marxist classics of Marx, Engels and Lenin at this time. Contemporary international theory, a capacious category that includes both newly accessible Marxists for Australian audiences, such as Antonio Gramsci, and Marxisant or even non-Marxist intellectuals outside Australia, such as Herbert Marcuse, Mario Savo and Arthur Koestler, quickly supplanted the older purely Marxist authorities associated with the master discourse of the CPA. This contemporary international theory was *endorsed* or used as a *referent* for a *positive justification* on twenty-one occasions during 1968.

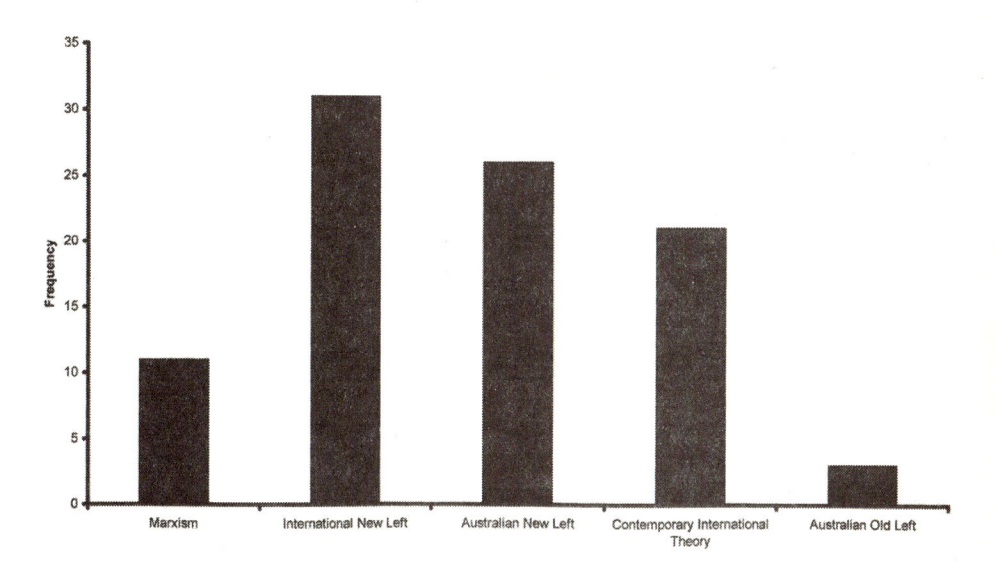

Figure 4.3
Endorsements and positive justifications 1968

Clearly, Marxism declined as an authority over the later 1960s and early 1970s. For the first time, it no longer became necessary to refer to Marxism to ground other propositions concerning intellectual and political events. Perhaps even more strikingly, Marxism itself also became an object of less intellectual interest. This can be demonstrated by a careful reading of the category of *object recommended* for both *positive* and *negative justifications*. Between 1963 and 1973, it was recommended explicitly, on the basis of either a positive or a negative justification, that some form of rethinking or intellectual production occur on 525 occasions. Between 1963 and 1967 the rethinking of Marxism was explicitly recommended as an object on 20.4 per cent of all occasions when intellectual production of some kind was recommended. However, between 1968 and 1973, it was recommended explicitly on only 5.1 per cent of all occasions when intellectual production of some kind was recommended. Plainly, Marxism had declined as both an object of direct interest and engagement, and as an authority for other intellectual and political interventions during a decade of intense political change and improvisation.

HOW DID IT HAPPEN? AN EXPLANATION OF THE TRANSFORMATION OF ARENA

The decline of Marxism and the rise of alternative intellectual and political authorities was directly tied to the changing political events of the 1960s and early 1970s. Indeed, events affected *Arena*'s theoretical development in three crucial ways. First, intense interest in a small cluster of collective action events in 1968 led to the importation of a substantial body of international social theory and the development of an indigenous local theory to explain their upsurge. Second, this new theory relied on the prestige of collective action events in order to gain legitimacy and to supersede previous theories. Third, as the pace and the direction of collective action shifted over time, that theory was extended and modified in important new directions. In short, the sustained use of the political gimmick provided the impetus for the development of a new, non-Marxist social theory on the Left. The prestige and excitement of these events also provided the legitimacy and authority necessary to challenge a previously sacrosanct Marxism. Finally, the continued eruption of collective action, and the process of diffusion discussed in Chapter 3, forced changes to the nature of the developing new social theory. The impact of the political gimmick was felt not only in the formation and legitimation of *Arena*'s new theory but also in its eventual modification.

In order to explain this detailed interplay between theory and event, a more focused, historical analysis will be necessary. This chapter will reconstruct the connections between *Arena*'s changing theories and erupting political events over seven discrete analytical phases.

PHASE ONE: RETHINKING MARXISM 1963–67

Arena began its life as a journal committed to rethinking within a Marxist methodology. Between 1963 and 1967 an extensive range of Marxist texts were drawn upon or discussed, among them *The German Ideology*, *The Economic and Philosophical Manuscripts of 1844*, *Critique of Political Economy*, *Theories of Surplus Value*, *Capital*, *The Eighteenth Brumaire*, *The Communist Manifesto*, Lenin's *Philosophical Notebooks* and Engels' letter to Joseph Bloch.[9]

More broadly, Marxist concepts were used as authorities for other propositions: the concept of alienation; the equation of freedom with the recognition of necessity; the need to reach truth through praxis;

the rejection of mechanist history; the rejection of rigid economic determinism; the conception of 'man' as free, conscious activity; the need for high-level generalisations; and the primacy of 'material relations' in the 'field of production'.[10]

Alongside this flexible use of Marxist authorities was an equal engagement with the substance of Marxism, and an attempt to rethink Marxist propositions in the context of contemporary Australian society. It was acknowledged that the industrial working class was becoming a diminishing force within the Australian social body; that there was a strategic need for a 'higher' consciousness among Australian workers; that a rapid transformation of the 'employed strata' was currently under way; and that there was a need to take account of social changes brought about by technology and the expansion of education.[11]

The failure of Marx to conceptualise the 'intermediate classes' adequately was conceded and the need for critical analysis of those classes within a Marxist framework was suggested. There were diverse attempts to understand the basis, nature and political orientation of these intermediate classes during the early 1960s, with an especially pronounced interest in the 'new stratum' of the intelligentsia. Definitions of the intelligentsia proliferated, from the 'objective', to the 'subjective'; from the cultural to the functional. However, amid such diversity there was a relative consensus that the intelligentsia, whatever its precise boundaries, was politically left-wing or radical, currently testing ideas, implicated in a 'transitional consciousness', or groping in common towards an understanding of the 'technical-scientific revolution'. That is, if the intelligentsia was in some ways analogous to the industrial working class, it was also strongly influenced by the ethic of education towards values such as rationality, universalism and communality, and thereby towards ethically motivated political action. The 'new stratum' was part of a humanistic culture, even if that culture was not respected in the course of the intelligentsia's working life.[12]

Much of this tentative theorising reflected current fears about the future of universities — the rise of the so-called 'multiversity', the growth of a credentialist orientation to education among new students, and the hegemony of human capital theory.[13] In the teeth of these practical threats, the assertion of a common identity and distinctive culture among university graduates and teachers became particularly urgent. Somewhat remarkably, however, although this theorisation of the intelligentsia responded to the hostile educational context during the early 1960s, it *did not* connect with the broader social and political forces then galvanising Australian life. Most surprisingly, this nascent conceptualisation of intellectuals was not tied to the political actions of the Australian New Left — actions which were also beginning to define this unstable period of change.

As Chapter 1 showed, Australian students had begun to take up the tools of theatrical protest pioneered by their British and American counterparts by 1965. Political protests organised by Australian students against racial discrimination in the United States had provoked international media interest, local versions of the Freedom Ride had created widespread engagement with Aboriginal disadvantage, symbolic marches and draft card burnings had opposed conscription for the Vietnam War. None of these political campaigns were invested with authority by *Arena* contributors, save for a single reference to political action against the Vietnam War by Doug White, and a timid assertion that this might reflect the importance of education as the transmitter of a specific cultural ethic. It was as if, for these political theorists at least, the political gimmick was yet to appear in Australia at all.

But this strange blindness to unfolding political events was not to persist. Indeed, the eyes of *Arena* contributors were to be opened wide during 1968, as the political actions of students and workers in Paris blazed brightly, and as fears of a hostile social environment were superseded by the promise of an immanent, complete social transformation. In the aftermath of these events, the political vision and theoretical production pursued by *Arena* contributors would take a decidedly more open and novel turn.

PHASE TWO: INTERNATIONAL EVENTS

Political events in Paris during May 1968 gained immediate, unrivalled prestige and authority. Suddenly they were significant. During the previous five years, only three actions of the New Left in countries other than Australia had been *endorsed* or used as a *referent* for a *positive justification* by *Arena* contributors. However, during 1968 alone, thirty-one separate *endorsements* or *positive* references were made to this category of international events.

This category of events was clearly the most authoritative referent for contributors to *Arena* during 1968 (see Figure 4.3). Perhaps even more importantly, almost half of these references to the international New Left (many of which referred to 'overseas student revolts' in general), referred *specifically* to events in France during May. The only other series of events that received repeated reference were those in Berkeley, which were specifically referred to on three occasions.

If references to the struggles in Paris were plentiful, then their apparent significance for Australian writers was equally expansive. The new struggles in France were interpreted as a signal of 'upheaval' and 'deeper striving' for social change. They were seen as revolutionary, as the harbinger of a new level of social development, as indicating the new importance of intellectuals, and as expressing the close connection between socialism and intellectual culture. For some contributors, they expressed social changes in progress elsewhere, and they therefore symbolised the beginning of a new era of 'new revolts'. For others, they posed new and pressing questions for the socialist movement everywhere, and required deep examination of French political sources. Their general significance was uncontested.[14]

Of course, the persistent theoretical interest in 'May 68' has often been remarked on. But its prevalence and authority as a *referent* mark it out as what historian W. H. Sewell Jr has called a 'transformative political event'. For Sewell, historical events have the power to transform social practice, stimulating a chain of subsequent happenings and ushering in new cultural frameworks. For example, he has recently traced how the historical events surrounding the storming of the Bastille led to the invention of the political concept of 'revolution'. In the same way, the chain of happenings identified as 'May 1968' also transformed social practice and cultural frameworks in Australia, destabilising the 'social vision' of contributors to *Arena* in a number of fundamental ways.[15]

PHASE THREE: INTERNATIONAL THEORY

Between 1968 and 1971 the writings of contemporary international scholars played a newly central role in the work of *Arena* contributors. As Figure 4.4 illustrates, between 1963 and 1966, contemporary international scholars were referred to on only nineteen occasions as the subject of *endorsements* or as *referents* for *positive justifications*. From 1967, this began to climb, but it was only in the context of the prestigious eruption of collective action in 1968 that this international theory was imported in sustained fashion.

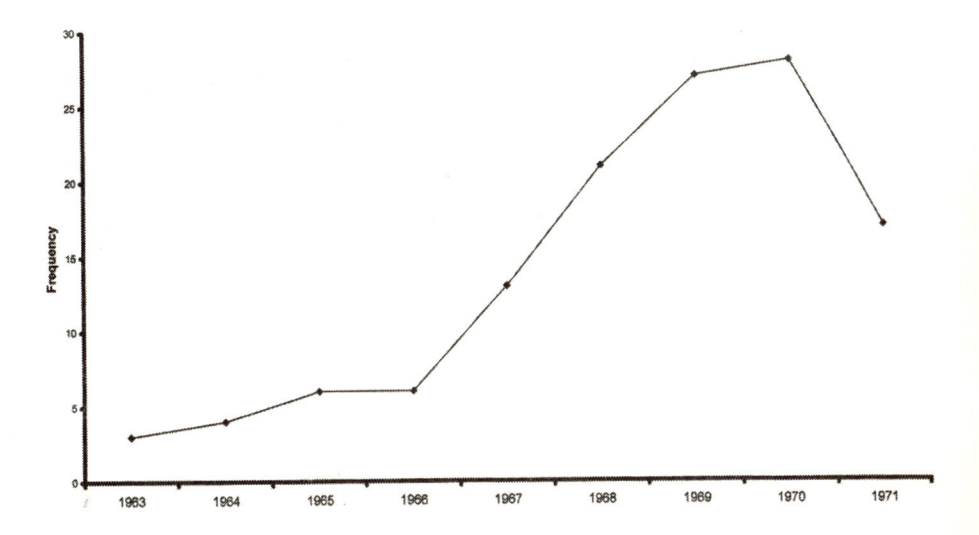

Figure 4.4
Endorsements and positive justifications with contemporary international theory as a referent

The tie between international (particularly French) political action and international (particularly French) theory was foregrounded by *Arena* contributors. First and most obviously, partisans in the 'events in May', among them the Cohn-Bendits and anonymous banner-hangers in the Sorbonne, were positively cited as theorists. Second, and perhaps more starkly, the need for French writing to comprehend these exciting French political events was explicitly recognised. A separate publication, containing translations of French theorists who engaged with that country's political dissent, was both produced and publicised by the *Arena* collective. Under the title 'The Events in France', it was even advertised for those interested: 'Several articles from French journals have been duplicated and are available from *Arena*'.[16]

A number of French theorists connected with political dissent in that country became immediately fashionable and authoritative: Sartre, Althusser, Lefebvre, the Cohn-Bendits, Poulantzas, and anonymous 'leading French Marxists'. Others who wrote about the events in Paris were also used as authorities, among them Mandel, Quattrachi and Nairn, writers in the English journal *New Statesman* and the French newspaper *Le Monde*.[17]

It was Althusser who was most central. His views on the history of Marxism were accepted, his claim that Marx represented a qualitative transformation of philosophy was endorsed, and his reworking of the base-superstructure argument was proclaimed. His ideas were discussed and explored in expository articles and in polemics. Drawing prestige from events in Paris, Althusser became a new source of intellectual legitimacy. No longer were the Marxist classics of Marx, Engels and Lenin the primary arbiters of theoretical rightness. Herbert Marcuse, a figure frequently associated with the American student movement, also became a key authority for *Arena* contributors. His work was repeatedly used to justify other propositions, as was that of Gramsci.[18]

This was an enormous change in the conceptual economy of the Australian Left. Certainly, Althusser, Marcuse and Gramsci all worked within a Marxist tradition. However (as the work of Rowley and Counihan itself showed), they were now sources of independent authority. Drawing on the prestige of international political dissent, they mandated a new sense of intellectual flexibility and iconoclasm. The determining power of the 'base' could be questioned; the role of the party could be rethought; and the political priority of intellectuals could be pondered. Quotations from Lenin and Marx were no longer enough. The British journal most closely associated with the introduction of these new thinkers to Australian audiences, *New Left Review*, was also enthusiastically received. Other contributors, such as Perry Anderson, Gareth Stedman Jones, Fred Halliday and Juliet Mitchell, were also cited as *referents* for *positive justifications* over 1968–71. As

Australian universities made photocopying available to students for the first time, so articles, action plans and theories were reproduced and passed on. The older, singularly powerful connection between classical Marxist authorities and the Australian political environment was now supplanted by a series of competing connections. Not only overseas political events were a powerful source of authority, so were contemporary international theorists. The basis for a more radical challenge to Marxism, and for a new form of social theory, had been laid.[19]

PHASE FOUR: THE IDENTIFICATION OF EQUIVALENT LOCAL EVENTS AND THE RECOGNITION OF THE AUSTRALIAN POLITICAL GIMMICK

The transmission of prestige and authority from international political events to international theory was matched by an equivalent transmission between international and domestic political events. In the five years from 1963 to 1967 inclusive, the actions of Australian students, intellectuals, the peace movement and the new social movements had attracted only limited interest. The political gimmick had not been seen as worthy of theoretical interest. Indeed, these political actions were only *endorsed* or cited as a *referent* for a *positive justification* on twenty-one occasions. However, between 1968 and 1972, an equivalent five-year period, these actions were *endorsed* or cited as a *referent* for a *positive justification* on 101 occasions.

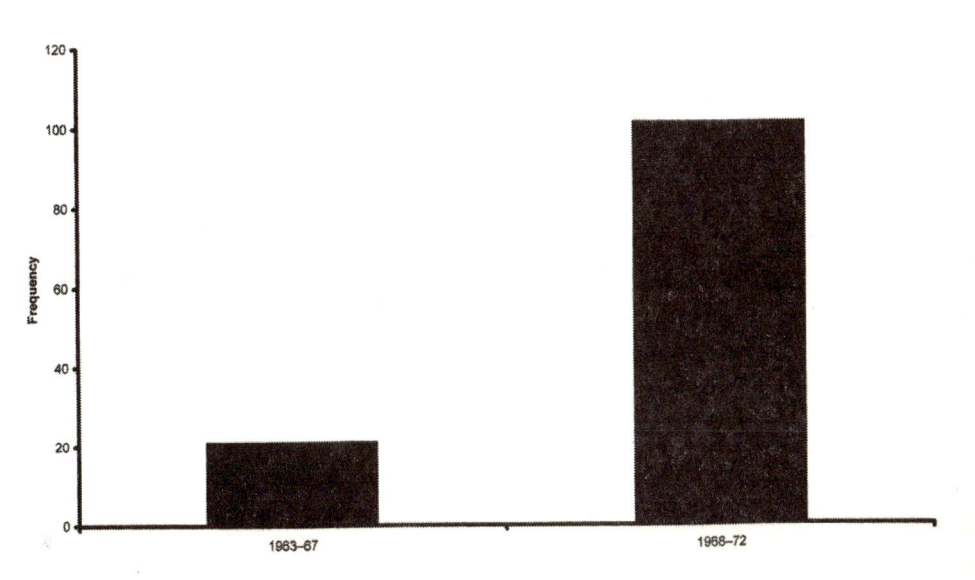

Figure 4.5
Endorsements and positive justifications with the Australian New Left as a referent

These actions quickly became authoritative during and immediately after 1968. Importantly, their new authority was a reflection of the prestige of *international* events. Indeed, it was only when Australian manifestations of the political gimmick were deemed to resemble international political events that they became authoritative. *Arena* contributors attempted to construct a direct tie between a small range of domestic events and those unfolding in France and the United States. The 'growing quality' of Australian campaigns against the Vietnam War was equated with that of the American campaigns. The ability of students and intellectuals to 'set a new course' in Australia as well as in France, the United States and Czechoslovakia was heralded. The similarity of the mass protests against the gaoling of Australian militant Clarrie O'Shea and on the streets of Paris during May 1968 was confidently announced. In both cases, forms of political gimmick forged among student activists were believed to have attained integration with mass working-class mobilisation.

Equally, the campaign of students at Monash University to raise funds for the NLF in Vietnam was compared with the actions of Columbia University students. On other occasions, the tie with an international event was constructed, only to be denied. Warren Osmond raised the apparently common question — 'When will students at Monash organise a campaign that parallels that of Berkeley students?' — only to deny its relevance: 'We will have, and *are having*, a 'Monash' at Monash!'.[20]

These domestic events involving the use of the political gimmick by the student movement were consistently praised. They were seen as 'the first challenge' to Australian rulers for many years, and to stand out over and above other forms of political action. Whereas *Arena* had traditionally avoided the precise description and analysis of political events, during 1968 this privileged attention was focused on Monash University students. The political improvisations that led to the expansion of the 'Australian repertoire of staging' were quickly identified and proclaimed. Mass meetings of students, sit-ins, mock crucifixions, campaigns for aid for the NLF and for university freedom were all detailed and endorsed. Even less theatrical actions, such as attempts by students to distribute literature to migrant workers, to organise in the local community and to participate in local electoral politics were all hailed.[21]

Not only were these manifestations of the political gimmick now praised, but they were also constructed as *theoretically significant*. Humphrey McQueen developed the concept of a 'revolutionary thrust' to describe the actions of Monash students and to emphasise that they represented a direct attempt to assist enemies of the Australian state. But more than that, because student actions like the collection of aid for the NLF could be described as a 'revolutionary thrust', they were also deemed to deserve thorough intellectual examination for their 'theoretical implications' and 'tactical lessons'. This description and analysis would eventually be extended beyond the Monash campaign for NLF aid to embrace specific student-led 'militant' demonstrations in Melbourne and Brisbane during 1968–69. Other *Arena* contributors similarly emphasised that the action of 'militants in universities and schools' was theoretically significant, expressing a new fusion of thought and action and presenting lessons for self-management and for organisational practice on the Left. The editors of *Arena* even made the unprecedented step of soliciting theoretical analyses of events at Monash in 1968: 'It would be of value to the whole of the Left if recording and dissection could take place while the events are still fresh in the minds of participants. *Arena* invites first-hand accounts and social and political interpretation'.[22]

Clearly this was a selective theoretical investment. As already noted, earlier manifestations of the political gimmick on the part of students did not receive the same theoretical attention. But neither did the ongoing actions of the Australian labour movement receive sustained theoretical investment. Workers had led early campaigns against the Vietnam War. Seamen had even organised and maintained a boycott against the supply ship *Boonaroo* in mid-1966 — an action that at the very least rivalled the 'revolutionary thrust' of collecting funds for the NLF. However, as one *Arena* correspondent was to lament, this worker-led action did not receive equivalent approbation of analysis.[23] Because it did not resemble or follow the prestigious student actions of Europe and America, it simply fell outside *Arena*'s theoretical vision. Only student improvisations that extended the repertoire of staging were deemed as exciting, revolutionary, and worthy of the gaze of the 'theorist'.

PHASE FIVE: THEORISING LOCAL/INTERNATIONAL EVENTS

If the authority of both Australian and international manifestations of the political gimmick has now been established, then the obvious question beckons — what was this authority used to justify? Through the application of the techniques of map analysis, and an examination of the category of *object recommended* in particular, it is possible to chart the shifting intellectual concerns of *Arena* contributors and to grasp precisely this question.

Of course, those prestigious political events that relied on the political gimmick were used to justify a range of political plans, tactics and strategies. They were also linked to a plethora of specifically theoretical propositions, concerning such topics as Australian society, culture, revolution, the economy, the university, and the working class. But by far the most important of these propositions concerned the status and significance of intellectuals and students as social and political actors.

As already noted, the sociological analysis of the intelligentsia had long been of interest to *Arena* contributors. As early as the mid-1960s there was a relative consensus that intellectuals were politically radical and sympathetic to such values as rationality, universalism and communality.[24] In the context of the flourishing of the political gimmick in the latter 1960s, however, these tentative propositions were reformulated with a striking degree of certainty and sophistication.

A series of theses concerning the 'features of the intellectually trained' were asserted by editors Geoff Sharp and Doug White in issue 15 of *Arena* in 1968. These theses together insisted that the intellectually trained were the fastest growing and most important grouping in advanced societies; that their work and training was characterised by a specific intellectual technique, social relationship and connection with universal values; that they possessed a heightened individuality; and that their places of work and training (the universities) were likely to become a primary point of future social conflict.[25] The nub of these interconnected theses was summarised by Geoff Sharp a year later: 'the intellectual culture carries within its basic structure the prototype of the socialist society'.[26]

The year 1968 was again the decisive period during which this newly found prominence and certainty first crystallised. As Figure 4.6 shows, during 1968 alone it was *recommended* on forty-three occasions that the position and theoretical status of intellectuals be rethought in some way. This frequency towers over previous years and expresses the apparent emergence of intellectuals as decisive social actors in the new environment.

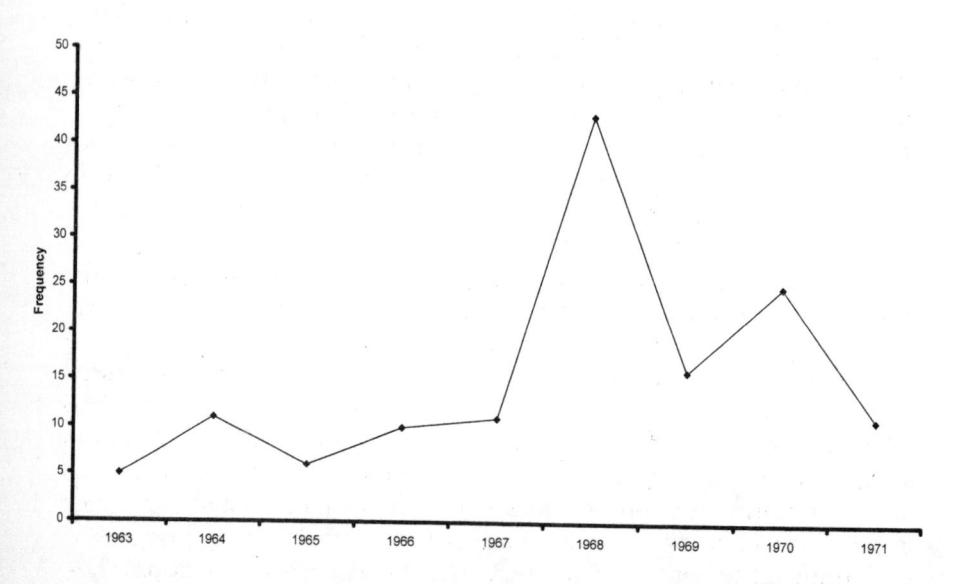

Figure 4.6
Rethinking intellectuals as an object recommended

The challenges to existing social theory on the Left were fundamental. For *Arena* contributors, the practice of intellectuals was now understood to conflict fundamentally with the class relations of capitalist society; the relationship between intellectually based practice and the formation of social consciousness was now presented as in urgent need of 'fuller understanding'; the independence of the 'scientific culture' was now accepted; the ability of 'intellectual culture' to penetrate, disintegrate and absorb the structures of conventional society was now validated; the ability of intellectuals to function as an independent rather than a subordinate base for the socialist movement was now proclaimed. Equally, the ability of intellectuals to 'detonate' or lead the workers onto the political battlefield was now also frequently endorsed.[27]

Clearly, this attempt to rethink the status of the intellectual overturned many of the most treasured verities of Marxism. But it overturned this older intellectual authority by reference to a more recent one — the political events associated with the New Left in Australia, Europe and America. Indeed, it was by constructing a direct link between the actions that deployed the political gimmick and the new theorisation of the intellectual that this radical cluster of ideas became accepted.

Of the forty-three occasions when the rethinking of the intellectual was *recommended* during 1968, it was justified by *referents* associated with the international New Left on eighteen occasions. Most of these references to the international New Left were to events in Paris (twelve occasions) or the USA (four occasions). That is, the prestige of international (particularly French) uses of the political gimmick was directly used to justify the rethinking of the intellectual, and the recognition of this actor's new centrality. As Geoff Sharp put it in a symptomatic intervention, events in Paris managed to 'underline the existence now of two distinct yet interlocked bases for a socialist movement in the advanced capitalist states' — the intellectuals and the workers.[28]

In the same way, the prestige of Australian student improvisations at Monash and elsewhere was also used to justify the rethinking of the intellectual on eleven distinct occasions during 1968 alone. For example, the apparent prominence of intellectuals in the campaign against the Vietnam War in Australia was used to justify an account of the 'intellectual culture' which emphasised rationality and universalism; the rise of campus dissent was used to justify the importance of intellectuals to contemporary capitalism; and the success of the Monash students was used to justify the proposition that campus-based campaigns that focused on university–society relations could mobilise large numbers and trigger the action of both students and workers. With amazing speed, the prestigious political actions of students in Europe, America and Australia had stimulated a radical new social theory. A powerful new set of theoretical propositions now circulated within the Australian Left. Warren Osmond labelled them the '*Arena* thesis' in his contribution to the 1970 anthology *The Australian New Left*, expressing both the intellectual and institutional authority of this very recent production.[29]

PHASE SIX: ASSERTING AND EXTENDING THEORY

Creating a new theory is one thing, asserting its dominance at a moment of political and intellectual change is another. Adherents to the budding *Arena* thesis concerning intellectuals needed consciously to assert the value of their new theoretical framework over other explanations. During the late 1960s and early 1970s this took two primary forms: criticising alternative explanations and treating the *Arena* thesis as an authoritative *referent*.

The chief competitor which the *Arena* thesis faced was that brand of Marxism associated with the Communist Party of Australia. If the centrality of intellectuals was to be accepted, then both older conceptions of the centrality of the proletariat and newer attempts to forge a coalition between students and workers through a political party needed to be resisted. As a result, it is not surprising that the Old Left in Australia — a category that included the Communist Party, the Australian Labor Party, other fringe communist parties, and the trade union movement, came in for increasing criticism over the later 1960s. As Figure 4.7 shows, the Old Left was the subject of regular *critique* or else was used as a *referent* for a *negative justification* by *Arena* contributors from the mid-1960s onwards. But it was in 1968 that this opposition reached a new plateau.

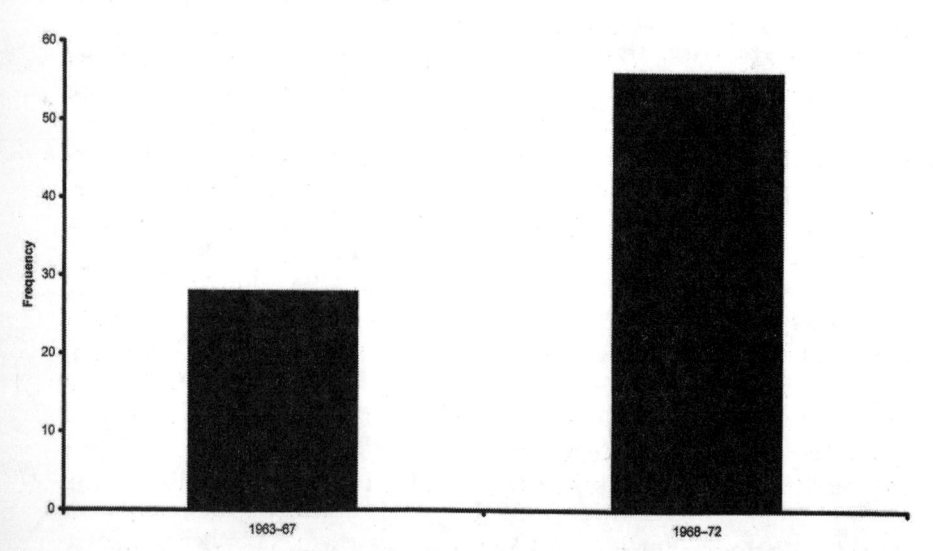

Figure 4.7
Critiques and negative justifications with the Australian Old Left as a referent

The bulk of this disparagement emphasised the backwardness of the Communist Party of Australia. Some of the rising criticism enunciated traditional deficiencies in the communist political project: an inability to accept criticism, poor behaviour by the leadership, or a merely formal commitment to revolution. However, much of it settled on the absence of adequate theoretical discussion and development on the part of Australian Communists. The forms of discussion practised within the party were attacked, and the dominant factions condemned. The failure of the CPA to encourage theoretical renewal was a common theme, and it also led to a common conclusion — the apparent need for 'intensive discussions' outside the party, emphasising theory and positing a distinctive 'New Left' approach to social change.[30]

This criticism was not gratuitous. The theoretical capacities of the CPA needed to be questioned if the new theory developed around *Arena* was to be legitimated. *Arena*'s interpretation of recent political events needed to be unchallenged if the prestige of those events was to be effectively tied to the nascent *Arena* thesis. This is why a number of *Arena* contributors explicitly criticised the CPA's interpretation of French political dissent in 1968. Australian Communists were accused of simply following the line set down by their French comrades, and their tendency to criticise 'ultra-leftists', to overlook student groups and to deny the existence of a revolutionary situation were all rejected. For those intellectuals affiliated with *Arena*, it was necessary that French events express the ability of Left activists outside the party, be dominated by the action of students, and represent a genuine challenge to the social order. If they did not, then the power and the prestige of *Arena*'s new theory would similarly decline.[31]

The *Arena* thesis also needed to be endorsed and legitimated by fellow intellectuals if it was to attain conceptual hegemony. This also began almost immediately after the new thesis was proclaimed. Indeed, over the period 1968–71 inclusive, the centrality and distinctiveness of the intellectually trained that had so recently been codified in the thesis was either *endorsed* or used as a *referent* for a *positive justification* on nineteen distinct occasions.

In the same issue of the journal that Geoff Sharp and Doug White first sketched out their key propositions, these arguments were already being taken up by other scholars. In the next issue, Geoff Sharp himself took up his own earlier arguments as an intellectual authority, and Doug White followed suit in the subsequent issue. Others, such as Jack Blake, would come to accept the force of intellectual consciousness or, like Nonie Sharp, would argue that equivalent processes were at work among other social actors, such as farmers. Others still would also come to use the authority of the *Arena* thesis to justify the introduction of other texts and intellectual quests, among them the usefulness of Leavis and the need for an ongoing examination of technocratic labourism. What had only recently been expressed as a theory rapidly became a legitimate authority. Indeed, as early as 1969, Geoff Sharp had reinterpreted his earlier theses as now demonstrated beyond question — 'the fact' that 'the intellectual culture carries beneath its basic structure the prototype of a socialist society'.[32]

However, this fact/theory would be challenged over the next few years by ongoing collective action. In particular, the diffusion of the repertoire of staging to a range of newly mobilised actors would soon begin to destabilise and threaten the dimensions of the existing *Arena* thesis.

PHASE SEVEN: CAPTURING ONGOING COLLECTIVE ACTION

As Chapter 3 showed, political dissent in Australia did not reach its peak in the late 1960s. During 1971 and 1972 contributors to *Arena* continued to remain responsive to unfolding political activism, as the tools of the political gimmick were diffused to a range of newly mobilised actors. Indeed, actions associated with the New Left and the new social movements were either *endorsed* or used as a *referent* for a *positive justification* on forty-five occasions during these two years alone.

These political events, however, were wider than simply campus-based dissent. The Women's Liberation Movement declared its dissatisfaction with the existing male Left and launched a radical assault on existing cultural concepts and social relationships. The political mobilisation of indigenous people began to receive its own independent attention by the white Left and to provoke critical self-reflection among many. Educational movements promised to cultivate new forms of social relationships. The Gay Liberation Movement began to redefine sexuality. The ecological movement raised the issue of the relations between humans, their environment, and each other. Prisoners and builders' labourers began to agitate for reform and change.[33]

As Chapter 3 showed, these new movements were most frequently hostile and contestational towards other 'left-wing' institutions and campaigns. They were defined and motivated precisely by their distinctiveness and singularity. Not surprisingly, then, none of these key political actors closely resembled the intellectually trained that *Arena* had so stridently championed. In most cases they were not defined by their intellectual training, but sometimes by its absence. They did not so much express the values of universality, humanism and rationality as they did their limitations and inappropriateness. Clearly, therefore, this wave of political dissent posed a troubling dilemma for adherents to the *Arena* thesis. If it was the 'intellectual culture' that produced political dissent, then how could these other movements of the early 1970s pose such radical and independent challenges? If the new theory developed by *Arena* was to be justified by recent, prestigious political events, then how could its theorists ignore the still erupting political field in the years after 1968?

Contributors to *Arena* managed these difficulties in four ways. First, they embraced the new actions as significant. Second, the varied movements associated with these actions were apprehended as of the same general family. Rather than emphasising the cultural specificity of each of these movements, the differences in their aspirations, methods and priorities, those contributors most associated with the *Arena* thesis attempted to depict them as movements of the same general type. They were described as 'students, women and other groupings'; 'state subordinated persons' who had stood up 'behind the black caste barrier, in the prisons, within the family, the schools and the universities'; movements 'like women's liberation, gay liberation and black power'; or else as part of an elaborate checklist that included students, the occupations that students frequently moved into, Women's Liberation, movements 'among blacks', and movements among 'untypical proletarians' ('typical' proletarians amounting to just about the only social group left out).[34]

Third, if these movements could be described in common terms, then their aims could equally be depicted as nothing more than the common disruption of culture. Because these movements were typically evoked in checklist form, their aspirations could also be portrayed in broad, common terms. In nearly all cases, the movements that mobilised in the early 1970s were portrayed as common movements that posed a common challenge to existing culture. Any interest in or engagement with structural questions by these movements was elided. Any sense of cultural conflict between these 'cultural movements' was de-emphasised. For Geoff Sharp, these 'new revolutionary groupings' were seen to express a 'cultural rather than a specifically class form', and to throw up issues concerning 'the cultural suppression of the person'. They struggled for a 'fuller recognition of their oppression' and took up issues of 'self-development in a context of mutual fulfilment'. They disrupted the traditional cultural framework within which the Left had practised politics, and they expressed the need for a thorough renovation of the language of culture and politics. That is, 'they' could be treated within the same cultural vocabulary rather than by a series of different vocabularies. Only Dennis Altman raised the thorny issue of the difficult and contradictory relationships between the 'new' movements that redefined race, gender and sexuality, and even this admission was within a broad contrast between such 'personalised' movements and those that challenged 'impersonal' forces such as 'capitalism'.[35]

Fourth, this common challenge to culture on the part of these common movements was linked to the *Arena* thesis. It was argued that the opening up of the question of culture was a function of the rise of the intelligentsia. To put it precisely, the 'new class' was seen as a force that reordered the ties between 'culture and class domination', and therefore as the 'bearer of a new culture' in a period of 'revolutionary ferment'. That is, the 'intellectual culture' that *Arena* contributors had so vigorously championed in 1968 and 1969 was now seen as a 'preliminary model' for a 'cultural revolution' that could be expressed in the interventions of a range of actors. The emergence of so many new actors did not reflect the fact that the *Arena* thesis was misplaced but that the 'intellectual culture' was beginning to 'break up' and to partially incorporate the 'old proletarian culture', thereby becoming the 'universal human culture'. According to this view, the cultural radicalism of the intellectually trained was the stimulus for the cultural radicalism of other groups. The emergence of vigorous campaigns off campus expressed the strength and centrality of the intellectuals rather than their transcendence. As Geoff Sharp would put it baldly, 'newer movements find their roots in the emergent personal and cultural forms of the intellectuals and the intellectually-trained'.

Consolidating this flexible extension of the *Arena* thesis, the past concerns of the journal were now creatively reinterpreted. That is, rather than presenting itself as a journal for rethinking Marxism, or even as a journal concerned to examine the status and nature of intellectuals, editor Geoff Sharp now argued that *Arena* had always been concerned to examine culture anyway. For Sharp, *Arena* had a 'distinctive standpoint', which consisted of an attempt to develop a 'politics of culture'. Certainly, he conceded, this standpoint had been 'somewhat muted' in the past. But it was evident nonetheless and it mandated an ongoing engagement with the movements exploding around him — movements that expressed in common a 'practice of cultural politics which no one had anticipated'.[36]

FROM A DOMINANT NEW THEORY TO A DOMINANT NEW PRACTICE

Even in 1972, the *Arena* thesis had by no means reached its maximum point of extension. As the mobilisation of the new social movements turned to demobilisation, the journal's attempt to forge a politics of culture would take new directions, and the common project for theoretical renewal would fan outwards. With the election of the Whitlam Government and the decline in political activism, the question of the nature of 'intellectual culture' would be reassessed, and the tendency for that culture to separate the abstract from the practical would be mourned. This concern with the ethical and the general, it was argued, had actually constrained the ability of activists to pioneer new forms of action and new ways of achieving political change. New questions, such as the examination of subjectivity, now became a priority.[37] However, if the specific arguments of the journal would continue to expand, the model of intellectual practice pioneered between 1963 and 1973 would remain.

This was a form of intellectual practice that valued the production of 'theory'. It sought to explain developments in collective action in Australia and overseas by the development of highly abstract concepts rather than close, strategic political analysis. Shifts in political action were to be explained by fundamental transformations in the subject, in the forms of social organisation and in culture, not by more limited changes in political opportunities, resources and tactics.

Equally, it evinced a close engagement with international theoretical discussion, and it adopted a cosmopolitan model of 'the intellectual'. Events in Australia could be placed alongside those in Paris and San Francisco. Apparent advances in conceptual understanding could illuminate all of them. In the mid-1970s this would be extended as *Arena* published translations of important European thinkers such as Jurgen Habermas, complete with expansive introductions; in the 1980s this would help to ground *Arena*'s emergence as an internationally prominent journal of cultural studies.[38]

Third, this was a model of intellectual work which emphasised a collective, institutional process of sustained innovation. It was now established that there was an *Arena* thesis, and that the dimensions of that thesis would be reworked in response to ongoing political events. Contributors to the journal would refer to that thesis, and would work in common towards its extension.

This was a co-operative intellectual enterprise. Indeed, if the intellectually trained have often been treated as members of the new petit bourgeoisie, then *Arena*, ironically, seemed closer to the model of the old petit bourgeoisie. Through their very attempts to argue for the novelty of intellectuals, the *Arena* writers came to develop a small-scale enterprise. This enterprise would contest the market for intellectual work, would attempt to expand its customer base outside Australia, and would use its capacity for innovation as a point of consumer appeal. At stake were not simply the sales of the journal, but its academic reputation — its symbolic capital, and therefore the position of its key contributors. In 1975 this existence as a small enterprise would become economic as well as intellectual. *Arena* would purchase its own printing machinery and make a direct appeal for the capital of readers and supporters.

It was this model of intellectual practice that became most influential among Australian knowledge producers. In a process that resembles Ron Eyerman's account of 'the intellectual' as an historically reproduced role, the innovatory rethinking of the *Arena* collective would be taken up by a new generation working in Australian universities as a new form of intellectual practice. The movement from rethinking Marxism to transcending and even critiquing Marxism would be replayed a decade later in the journal *Intervention*. The attempt to forge a connection between prestigious intellectual events and new forms of theory would be used by other new writers and publications. The strategy of linking Australian theory with prestigious European theory in the same Australian publication would be taken to new levels by the 'Working Papers' Group, and by the journal *Thesis Eleven*. The importance of familiarity with European events, theory and even language would come to be widely accepted among radical Australian intellectuals. At the same time, the attempt to develop a common Australian intellectual project and to market this project to international audiences would also become hegemonic, eventually being expressed in the international prominence of a specifically 'Australian Cultural Studies' and 'Australian Feminism'. In all of this, a new form of Australian intellectual — a cosmopolitan, theoretically adept and ritually iconoclastic figure would emerge.[39]

CONCLUSION

This chapter represents a kind of cyclical journey from the earlier concerns of this book. Continuing to focus on the history of the political gimmick, it has pondered its impact on theories and political ideas in the 1960s and early 1970s. It has examined the multiple connections between collective action events and theoretical development. Drawing equally on the sociology of knowledge and on advances in textual analysis, it has applied the new techniques of map analysis to the history of *Arena* journal in the period 1963–73. Cumulatively, this analysis has suggested the decisive influence of the 1968 'events in May' in France.

The political dissent in France changed the whole direction of intellectual work in *Arena*. International political events became legitimate referents for theoretical deduction. Constructing a tie with these events helped to legitimate international theory and domestic political events as similarly authoritative referents. It was on the basis of these new forms of authority that contributors to *Arena* began to challenge the central tenets of Marxism, and to develop a radical new form of social theory. It was by maintaining an intimate connection with these events that this new social theory was buttressed and extended, and the *Arena* thesis became a dominant new form of social theory in Australia. In this complex historical process, a new and successful model of intellectual work was established, and this came to be emulated by an emergent generation of Australian intellectuals. As a result, *Arena* came to produce not only a new social theory but a new historical form of the intellectual in Australia.

More generally, this suggests that theoretical innovation may rely on the prestige of political events, even when those theories are presented as meta-theories of societal transformation or are pitched at a high level of abstraction. That is, major processes of theoretical innovation may be responses to short-term strategic imperatives and interpretations. It is by capturing a new political event, such as a successful protest or campaign, and establishing a hegemonic interpretation of its significance, that new forms of theory can become legitimate. It is in the context of these strategic skirmishes that fundamental changes can occur.

This analysis also suggests that social movements and political events may come to matter less because of their transformative success or local relevance and more often because of their theoretical construction as important and powerful exemplars of underlying social trends. Indeed, it was the ability of *Arena* contributors to focus on a selective range of political events, and to emphasise their connection with 'intellectual culture' that justified the new *Arena* thesis. Other actors, such as the working class, also mobilised successfully, and other interpretations of Paris 1968 existed, such as those associated with the Communist Party of Australia. However, they were successfully marginalised within the journal, and the new theory was therefore successfully asserted. In this sense, it could be argued that the institutions and conditions of a diverse range of public spheres need to be regarded as central to the analysis of social movements and to the examination of how they come to matter. The ability to construct an event as significant and representative may ultimately come to be as important as the ability to stage the event at all. The power of the political gimmick may ultimately lie in the eye of the beholder and the mouth of the onlooker.[40]

This is cause for humility, celebration, and renewed intellectual purpose. First, humility. As new attempts to theorise contemporary politics multiply, and confident predictions as to the future of the Internet, 'the intellectual', and the 'post-human subject' fly forth, it is worth recalling the inevitable blindness of even the most apparently omniscient of these dazzling thinkers. Social theories are typically built on a particular range of events seen as both exemplary and prophetic. While *Arena*'s willingness to engage with changing forms of collective action was laudable, its focus on a specific class of political events was to have tremendous implications. Its praise for Australian and international New Left actions was unbalanced and for the most part unjustified. Its presentation of a grand new theory of political change was soon undermined by ongoing events, and required a quite inspiring form of political dexterity in order to be saved. In this sense, more humble forms of analysis, which work outward from a variety of political events and seek their causes in more immediate and varied factors, may ultimately serve as a better guide to the future of political change and activism. In this sense, too, we can pose the question whether those 'new theories' that so confidently announce a post-Marxist age should really be so confident as to the existence and the characteristics of the apparent 'new era'.

Nonetheless, there is also cause for a kind of celebration. Without question, the actions associated with the political gimmick had quite profound theoretical implications. While no successful revolution ensued, no Bastilles were seized and no governments overthrown, this does not mean that the development of new political campaigns had no long-term intellectual repercussions. On the contrary, the improvisations pioneered by students and diffused to others caused the existing hierarchies of the Australian Left to be overturned. It became far more difficult to insist on the primacy of the working class or even the validity of once sacrosanct political ideas. It became newly possible to ponder different kinds of political questions and to postulate the general relevance of a diverse range of social movement activities. Certainly this was not without its dangers. For many, 'class' became simply anachronistic, investigation of material inequality deeply unfashionable.[41] But the possibility still shimmered that the new theories would have more enabling implications, and the quest for a political coalition that refused to impose hierarchies and that allowed for the full play of different aims began to appear on the Left's agenda. Whether you liked it or not, things would never be the same again.

Finally, the ultimate synergy of the theory–event axis is also cause for renewed intellectual purpose. It suggests that those fumbling, often self-important, publicity-seeking forms of political gimmick may be quite significant after all. It suggests that their continued eruption and analysis in the contemporary period may have quite profound impacts. And it suggests that the analysis of how such collective events are received and used in the development of theory across a range of fields may prove to be an exciting and rewarding intellectual endeavour.

I take up some of these questions in the final chapter, analysing the history of collective action in the most contemporary period, focusing especially on the process by which it is 'constructed' and interpreted, and speculating on its possible repercussions for future political change.

5
MEDIA

> In fact, protest is a very indirect process in which the targets may be affected by the communications media and third parties. The media must play a key role in this process and their reportage is crucial.
>
> <u>Jim Spigelman, 1969</u>

November 1975.

The Whitlam Labor Government is dismissed by the Governor-General, John Kerr. Conservative leader Malcolm Fraser is installed as caretaker Prime Minister, and fresh elections are called. For those shocked by the dismissal, the rules of representative democracy seem to have been violated. Almost immediately, they express their outrage in rallies, demonstrations and marches. Perhaps democracy lies in the streets and city parks, not in gubernatorial antechambers and infernal constitutional disputes.

More than a thousand people gather outside the national parliament on successive days. Strikes and stop-work rallies are held. A 'memorial service for the death of democracy' is solemnly performed in Darling Street, Balmain, the birthplace of John Kerr. There are 'fun runs for Whitlam', concerts, and even strike action by journalists, anxious to challenge the apparent bias of the Murdoch-owned press.[1] Stages to contest and sometimes to laud the actions of the Governor-General are hastily erected. The political gimmick seems to merge into the very centre of established, electoral politics. But who will it benefit, and how will it relate to the battle at the ballot box?

On the afternoon of 13 November, these questions are posed with particular passion and physical urgency. The afternoon itself develops from quite prosaic beginnings. In Hyde Park, Sydney, the Australian

Union of Students call for a rally in support of the Whitlam Government. Around fifteen hundred attend, and federal ministers Tom Uren and James McClelland address the crowd. Restraint is urged from the platform, and the primacy of electoral politics is insisted on. Wrongs will be righted on election day. Little seems to have changed. But the confidence and the fluency of theatrical political performance will soon become apparent.

Around twenty Aboriginal activists demand the right to speak. Disputes break out. A young university student, Julie Bishop, clambers onto the podium and suggests more adventurous action. What about a march? Only the day before, Whitlam supporters had marched on the Stock Exchange. Why not take on the press today, and contest the editorial bias of Murdoch family newspapers?

Quickly agreeing with this suggestion, hundreds of marchers take off for the News Limited building, high-stepping through Sydney's cramped and crooked streets. At the Murdoch headquarters, police form a strong line of defence, and a struggle begins. Will they force their way into the building? Will the glass doors of the foyer continue to hold? What will the marchers do? Suddenly, an alternative whips the crowd around. If the protests move to the warehouse on Cowper Street, they can stop the Murdoch-owned *Daily Mirror* from spreading its apparent lies. Profits will be lost, distortions stymied, untruths countered. As the trucks lurch out on their delivery runs, quick hands pull papers from the tray. Bundles are hurled and sometimes ritually burnt. Somewhere, a smoke bomb goes off. There is a clamour of chaos, as the metal slats on the warehouse door are repeatedly struck and jammed. Police arrest four marchers, and fights break out. Is this 'adventurism' and romantic, revolutionary delusion, or is it a sincere and spontaneous assertion of democratic will? The crowd itself seems uncertain, fragmented.

It is now 2.40 p.m., and Bob Pringle, a former official in the Builders Labourers' Federation, climbs onto the bonnet of a ute. A sit-down demonstration is urged. If protesters simply sit down on Cowper Street, they may be able to prevent the afternoon edition of the *Daily Mirror* from getting out. The crowd expresses its assent, and the corner shop does a roaring trade in ice creams and soft drinks for the next hour. At 3 p.m. a delegate from the Printing and Kindred Industries Union (PKIU) emerges from inside to tell the protesters of the views of workers. News Limited printers have passed a resolution condemning the paper's editorial policies. Change has been demanded.

Half an hour, and then forty-five minutes, pass quickly. At 3.45 p.m. Pringle exclaims to those still present that 'We've achieved our point'. But the demonstration ends with a threat to News Limited. Unless the editorial direction of their coverage achieves a greater political balance, another crowd will gather in three days, this time attempting to halt the distribution of the *Sunday Mirror* and the *Sunday Telegraph*.

What, exactly, has happened on this passionate afternoon of argument and invention? Has a new form of political performance emerged? Will the representations of the media themselves become the object of contestation and regular collective challenge? Perhaps demonstrators are becoming more reflexive, targeting those who will report on and frame their public performances. Will we see demonstrations concerning the coverage of demonstrations (which may themselves provoke negative reporting and further demonstrations) — a kind of infinite doubling of performances and representations? Is a new form of media-oriented protest beginning to emerge — one that challenges the central role of the press and television in framing public debate?

Certainly, if the Murdoch press was threatened by these actions, this was not obvious to newspaper readers. The editorial line was not moderated. The conduct of protesters was excoriated. In the *Daily Mirror* on 14 November, the verities of liberal 'free speech' were stridently proclaimed, and the counterproductive impact of the demonstration confidently prophesied:

> Yesterday, a scruffy, screaming mob of young blockheads presented themselves at the *Daily Mirror* to light a few fires and disrupt our distribution. They objected to our right to form and publish our opinions. We don't object to their right to make their feelings known. What these professional protesters don't understand is that their march toward anarchy is putting parcels of votes into the pockets of the caretaker Prime Minister, Mr Fraser.

For the *Sunday Telegraph*, the political performance of 13 November was nothing more than a 'touch of blackmail'. The event was thoroughgoing in its violence and illiberalism. Not only that, but it was apparently due to the intemperate comments of elected Prime Minister, Gough Whitlam:

> Demonstrators smashed the windows of trucks, burnt papers and threatened unionists with violence ... This newspaper and the people of Australia will not be stood over by gangsters. The trouble is that Mr Whitlam is giving a lead in this type of statement by the emotional flavour of his speeches so far. They are turning what is an election basically on the economic state of the nation into a threatened bloodbath. If he cannot lead the country he should at least lead his own people in civilised behaviour.[2]

On the evening of Saturday, 15 November, Bob Pringle returned to loading bays at the corner of Cowper Street and Holt Street. But this time there were fewer angry protesters and a more prepared police force. Two hundred demonstrators faced off with around fifty officers.

Unionists criticised the gathering. Ken Owens, an engineer at the *Mirror* and a Communist, told the demonstrators that they were doing nothing more than attacking the workers. There would be no repeat of the Thursday action this time. There was an orderly retreat, and a quick march to Central Railway. Harry Kensell, the leading PKIU official or 'Father of the Chapel', expressed his hostility to earlier disruptions: 'I represent a thousand printers ... They have a democratic right to tell me what they want to do. I won't have people outside trying to coerce them'.

There would be no more demonstrations of this type at all. The press and the printers were now safe from 'coercion'. The Murdoch press continued to 'freely' enunciate its hostility to the Whitlam Government, and the Liberal-Country Party Coalition was soon elected. Dissent became a rare but, paradoxically, a devalued commodity. It was 1975, but it was the 'end of the sixties' in cultural and political terms. It seems apt to view this failed demonstration as the closing of an era.

What was at stake in this stillborn political intervention outside the News Limited offices? Why did it occur? What made the demonstration against the Murdoch press such a notable and yet such an ultimately ineffectual event? Undeniably, many ephemeral factors were at play: a passionate identification with the Whitlam Government; an anger at the perfidy of Murdoch; a recently established practice of pro-Labor rallies merging into marches. But other, more structural factors were also clearly relevant. The frustration at media bias was not at all a transitory characteristic of the political environment. It was, instead, a broader condition under which the political gimmick was regularly deployed. It expressed, in effect, the long-standing *centrality* of the press and television in the amplification of political contention to those not directly present. It expressed the *centrality of media representation* in the process of contemporary claim-making, and the practical dilemmas that political activists therefore routinely faced.

The horns of this dilemma are persistent and sharp: those performing moderate and sanctioned forms of contention are unlikely to attain 'newsworthiness', or to gain widespread political attention. Their performances are likely to be ineffectual. But if those performances contain the disruption or novelty to become newsworthy for the leading outlets of the commercial media, they are also likely to draw condemnation rather than approbation. The actions of protesters, rather than their fervently held aims, will become the key public issue. The wider cause will be sullied and trivialised. Either way, public claim-making will be unlikely to achieve its wider aims.

Of course, as Chapters 1 and 2 showed, in the mid-1960s contention was still a rare enough commodity to largely sidestep such dilemmas. Simply gathering in peaceful public protest was a novel enough occurrence to attain newsworthiness. It was only in the later 1960s that protesters faced difficult choices concerning the performance, likely publicity and public representation of their claim-making. While some retreated into relative quiescence, other actors pioneered novel forms of contestational and disruptive behaviour. Indeed, for a range of newly mobilised movements, the infamy and disorder of theatrical political performances was to be welcomed. It confirmed the challenge of protesters to the existing gender, sexual and racial order that seemed so burdensome and 'oppressive' (to use that now unfashionable term of the time). The disruption and outrage of elites accurately embodied the instability of the boundaries between the historically venerable 'public' and 'private' realms — to be disreputable was to be seriously 'political'.

By 1975, however, the challenge of the new movements had begun to ebb. The survival of an elected government was now at stake. The tools of political contention were now widely accepted. Indeed, even the sit-down and the violent affray had become relatively routinised. Journalist Bruce Hanford noted precisely this phenomenon in his report on the anti-Murdoch demonstration of 13 November:

> The demonstration has become normalised. There are definite rituals and conventions: for instance, police with their numbers on don't want to fight; and demonstrators with overwhelming superiority in numbers won't be denied the streets.
>
> In these circumstances, when the marchers feel they are supporting a party which has majority support in the electorate, and which is in their view conservative, they lack any trace of that uncertainty which sometimes gives rise to a compensatory viciousness. However frightening the demo may have appeared from inside the building, however anomalous a deviation from years of routine, it was for most marchers just something that happens.[3]

With the demonstration now 'normalised', the dilemmas of the demonstrator ironically became *more* rather than less pressing. As the leading opinion polls showed, the acceptance of the political gimmick was conditional and sharply demarcated. A 1969 Morgan Gallup Poll found widespread acceptance of the right to demonstrate — 70.5 per cent accepted this right across the population. But only 5.9 per cent agreed with the right to block traffic, and only 1.1 per cent with the right to behave in a violent fashion. A year later, little had changed. Although 72.8 per cent now accepted the right to demonstrate, and 8.1 per cent the right to block traffic, the right to take up violent behaviour was now only accepted by 0.6 per cent of those sampled. Even in the 1990s, the political culture had shifted only marginally. In 1996 a slightly greater proportion (79.3 per cent) agreed with the right to demonstrate 'even though there is a risk of violence'. But when asked about the actions of demonstrators who were involved in recent 'violence', only 3.9 per cent approved of their actions.[4]

In such circumstances political activists face an impossible set of choices. The staging of demands is now accepted as a routine part of democratic life. As a result, the demonstration, the march and the rally all lack the necessary 'charge' to attract widespread attention. At the same time, those actions most frequently associated with novelty and disruption — the blocking of traffic and the waging of 'violent' acts, are precisely those behaviours most strongly opposed. Even a hint of 'violence' will seriously damage the broader cause.

What can protesters do? How can they successfully negotiate this dilemma? How can a protest be disruptive enough to become newsworthy, careful enough to avoid interference with others, and yet peaceful enough to avoid any hint of violence? The continuing utility of the political gimmick seems to rest on an ability to negotiate this dilemma, and yet its resolution seems far off, even definitively impossible. In what directions are the most fruitful political improvisations evident?

THE MORATORIUM, THE PEACEFUL SPECTACLE AND THE DILEMMAS OF THE ACTIVIST

From the joint perspective of a number of contemporary media outlets, the answer to these questions is obvious. The ideal demonstration happened in May 1970: the first Vietnam Moratorium march. In replicating the Moratorium, protesters behave effectively; in departing from this ideal, they become violent, anti-democratic and inarticulate.

Indeed, the pre-eminent place of the Vietnam Moratorium in popular journalistic memory seems beyond doubt. When journalists examine the changing mores of Australian students, they are often quick to contrast the apparent conservatism and apathy of the contemporary mob with the idealism and devotion to the cause of their precursors. By 1979, the inability of students to draw large numbers to demonstrations had become frequently remarked on. Reporters asked, 'Why has the fire gone out of student politics?', and a kind of stock comparison had been installed: 'Then ... students readily supported causes. Now ... a student puts his feet up between classes'.

Many students themselves reached for comparisons with the Vietnam War campaign in order to locate and explain their own conservative position. For example, Deirdre Willmott, a conservative president of the University of Western Australia Students' Guild, was typically preoccupied with the anti-Vietnam movement in 1984: 'Ever since Vietnam students have been looking for another Vietnam ... They haven't found one. And now they are putting more time into their studies and they are looking for moderate representation'.[5] But if conservative students have been seen as pale, self-interested successors to their colourful, Moratorium-attending precursors, then the more radical students have also frequently been depicted as failing to climb the summit of the 1960s. When protesters mobilised against the Gulf War, historian Geoffrey Blainey worried that they lacked the respect or patriotism of the anti-Vietnam movement. He looked fearfully ahead to 'acts of political thuggery', and he felt sure that opposition 'could become very disruptive with tactics unlike those used against the Vietnam War'.

Similarly, the movement that opposed racism and that targeted the One Nation Party in the late 1990s was also seen as lacking in the sterling qualities of the anti-Vietnam resistance. Jim Cairns, a leading participant in the Vietnam Moratorium, felt sure that 'protesters have changed'. Others also saw them as more hostile and angry, more violent and less well organised than their canonised precursors.[6] Even the anti-globalisation protesters that targeted the World Economic Forum on 11 September 2000 found themselves unfavourably compared with the Moratorium. When the *Herald-Sun* editorialised on the subject, the 'S11' protest was seen as infinitely inferior to earlier, anti-Vietnam War campaigns:

> Australians enjoy a long tradition of publicly protesting legitimate complaints and expressing their support for worthwhile causes. It is a heritage that sparked a group of principled men to form the Australian Labor Party after the shearers' strikes late in the 19th century. The moratorium marches of the 1960s [sic], where thousands of Victorians protested peacefully against the war in South Vietnam, exemplified the same spirit of free expression. The moratorium protesters exercised their right to demonstrate a view different from that of the government. But those planning the September 11 protest show none of the character qualities evident in those who marched in the peace protests.[7]

The status of the Moratorium as the repository of all 'demonstrative' virtues extends beyond the precise nature of the activists. When contemporary protesters organise large and successful demonstrations, they are almost unfailingly compared with the (once feared, now canonised) Vietnam Moratorium marches. However large the numbers involved or however many years have elapsed since the 1970 mobilisations, the terms 'the biggest since the Vietnam War' seem inevitably to work themselves into newspaper accounts.

At times this defies common sense. According to movement accounts of the time, perhaps 120 000 people participated in the Vietnam Moratorium marches around Australia. But the Moratorium has retained the title of 'largest demonstration' despite vastly greater numbers participating in a cluster of later campaigns.

When the People For Nuclear Disarmament organised a 1982 protest in Melbourne against uranium mining, nuclear weapons and facilities, and the visitation of American warships to Australian ports, this was commonly (although perhaps inaccurately) seen as the 'return of the demo', the only significant action since 'the Moratoriums against the Vietnam War' more than ten years ago. When the marchers grew to number 250 000 around Australia and perhaps 130 000 in Sydney alone on Palm Sunday 1984, this was still seen as 'Australia's largest protest meeting since the anti-Vietnam days'. Paradoxically, when only 20 000 people marched in Melbourne against Australian and US participation in the Gulf War, January 1991, this was also described as the biggest local peace rally 'since the Vietnam era', or as 'reminiscent of anti-Vietnam War Moratoriums'. The intervening decade has not tarnished the Moratoriums' glow. When perhaps 250 000 people marched for reconciliation across Sydney Harbour Bridge on 28 May 2000, it should not be remarkable to learn that this, too, was apparently the biggest 'turnout for a political cause' since 'the Vietnam War moratorium marches 30 years ago'.[8]

Of course the historical ignorance of contemporary journalists should not be particularly surprising. However, something deeper is at stake than the glancing treatment of large protests in the 1980s and 1990s, the mere forgetting of a number of vibrant public demonstrations. This larger matter is what historians Robin Gerster and Jan Bassett have recently called the 'myth-making' that adheres to historical accounts of the 1960s. Survivors of that memorable decade continue to see themselves as those who 'saved the world from conservatism'. The protest actions that emerged at this time are inevitably depicted as the zenith of idealism, popularity, radical commitment, fun, seriousness, size and importance. Any subsequent actions exist only in (subordinate) dialogue with this earlier peak. They are the gawky, somewhat uncouth children of famous, well-loved parents.[9]

Even historians outside of the 'baby boomer' generation have been unable to shrug themselves free of this constricting cultural imaginary. The famously clear-eyed Donald Horne sees the first Moratorium as the apotheosis of popular radicalism: 'The crowds peacefully sitting in the streets during the first Moratorium represented the movement's peak; it was one of those moments when an ever-widening swell of peaceful protest that would not frighten off the respectable seemed almost possible ... But it was not to be'. According to this view, such broad coalitions would never again become manifest. The actions of small groups of 'pseudo-revolutionaries' would soon manage to alienate the progressive middle class. The movement was bound to decline into sectarian conflict and widespread irrelevance. The 'time of hope' was about to pass.[10]

Despite Gerster and Bassett's admonitions, they too see the May 1970 Moratorium in somewhat mythical terms — as the peak of radical protest activity, the glorious moment before the later decline. In

Seizures of Youth, they typify the first Moratorium as peaceable, congenial, good-humoured, broadly supported, and as a 'public relations triumph'. At the same time, they also see it as a moment of transition — marking the end of disruptive political tactics and the domestication of radical energies. There would be no later actions to match this initial flowering:

> The general success of the Moratorium meant that the old, violent, antiwar movement was on the wane; the street demonstration had, ironically, become depoliticised. The Moratorium was a 'day out', a place to see and be seen. Marching against war had become a popular fashion, and therefore, like all fashions, of a limited life: no wonder the Moratorium movement died an ignominious death in the two years following.[11]

Given the mythical and somewhat idealised evocation of the Moratorium, it should not be surprising to learn that even the *Moratorium itself* fails to measure up to its own mythical standards. Closer historical examination in fact reveals the Moratorium to be significantly more controversial, disruptive and challenging than contemporary nostalgia remembers it to be. The aims of the Moratorium were radical rather than moderate, challenging rather than accommodating. The family of actions staged represented an escalation of tactics. The nub of the campaign was to be a 'moratorium on business as usual', a refusal to go about normal activities, however briefly, while the war continued. Instead of merely demonstrating opposition in conventional fashion, the aim was to 'bring about a situation in which the establishment cannot continue the war without threatening its own continued occupation of the seats of power'.[12]

Citizens were encouraged to organise on a local level, conduct decentralised actions, leave work, and to attend a range of rallies, marches and demonstrations. Government attacks on the Moratorium were consistent and poisonous. The *Age* worried that there was a 'potential for violence', and claimed that 'responsibility' rested with the Moratorium organisers. The Melbourne *Herald* thought that a plan to occupy the streets of central Melbourne was 'astonishing'. The trade union movement was divided, and an extremely guarded motion of support was only narrowly passed by the ACTU Executive, and could not be ratified by a majority of the state-based Trades and Labour Councils. Federal Minister Billy Snedden expressed conservative outrage towards the Moratorium at its most vitriolic, claiming on the day before the marches, 'The organisers I can only think of as political bikies — political bikies pack-raping Australian democracy'.[13]

The mass occupation of the streets generated enormous controversy. Critics lambasted the disruption and deliberate violation of traffic laws. They feared that order had been kept by movement marshalls rather than by the police. They muttered darkly about the violation of liberal democracy and the use of 'the Leninist tactic of the establishment of a "counter-government"'. In Sydney two smoke bombs went off and a policeman was hospitalised. One newspaper alleged that a tomato had been thrown, another that a piece of television equipment had been dropped on his head.[14] Clearly, this was not a purely peaceful, widely welcomed form of collective action.

The achievements of the 8 May Moratorium march should not be trivialised. The campaign against the Vietnam War unquestionably demonstrated that it was a mass phenomenon. The range of taxi-drivers, high school students, poets, architects, nuns, unionists and merchants that attended was wider and more diverse than ever before. The peacefulness and warmth of the day offered a sharp riposte to government scaremongering.

But despite its achievements as a public performance, many in the movement felt that the emphasis on peacefulness and respectability was restrictive and bureaucratic. As John Murphy has persuasively argued in *Harvest of Fear*, the cultural energy of the Moratorium was primarily a product of the vagueness and ambiguity with which its aims were defined. Its political focus was weak and transitory. The large numbers of people who turned out were not always reported by the commercial media, and the issues themselves were often marginalised in newspaper and television reports. NSW Premier Bob Askin was quick to reduce the gathering to a typical crowd of sporting fans: 'The crowd in Sydney, including spectators, was no larger than the Sunday afternoon football attendance and there were fewer incidents than those that generally occur on the hill at the Sydney Cricket Ground'. The very fact that so many expressed their views openly was soon used as evidence that 'democracy works', and that Australian society was tolerant and robust. The movement began to divide over future tactics.[15]

On closer inspection, then, the Moratorium was no more dazzling, moderate, committed, peaceful or diverse than a range of later actions. Its dominating presence in popular memory is the product of widespread myth-making rather than an accurate reflection of its singular, marvellous historical status. Like other actions, it was sometimes radical, internally fractured, controversial, illegal, and punctuated by very rare moments of reported violence. It was, in short, a complex collective event, not the near unanimous channelling of sweetness and light that so many have deemed it to be.

Given this mythical historical status, it should now be obvious that the Moratorium does not represent a smooth, easily replicable means of negotiating the 'dilemmas of the activist'. It is very hard to replicate a myth. Only a handful of campaigns have attained the status of a mass, peaceful (Moratorium-like) spectacle — the Palm Sunday rallies of the early and mid-1980s, the rallies against French nuclear testing in 1995, and the reconciliation marches in major capital cities of 2000.

All of these events received an avalanche of support. Several hundred thousand attended the anti-nuclear rallies in successive years. Perhaps a quarter of a million attended the walk across the Sydney Harbour bridge, and hundreds of thousands also marched in Melbourne on 3 December 2000. Likewise, all of these events were able to attract a great diversity of supporters, and the leading media outlets were quick to concede the scale of such massive public spectacles. In 1984, the *Australian* saw the Palm Sunday rally as an event that included Christian surfers, anti-vivisectionists, Hare Krishnas, anarchists, Kurdish workers, and a range of other marchers proclaiming 'drinkers for disarmament', 'poofs for peace', 'archaeologists against the bomb' and 'surveyors against world levelling'. In a similar fashion, those attending the Sydney reconciliation walk were generally depicted as 'ordinary' people rather than as extremists, a happy family that included 'the toddlers, the elderly, those in wheelchairs, a one-legged man on crutches, a man with a purple mohawk, a little girl with cerebral palsy, parents pushing babies in prams, others leading dogs beribbonned with the Aboriginal colours of red, yellow and black'.[16]

Clearly, such an expansive range of peaceful supporters can together symbolise a powerful political mood. 'The people' can seem suddenly, unambiguously, to make their will evident. These events are a million miles from the simple burning of draft cards by three nervous youths in 1966, or even from the 'mass' student demonstrations of the late 1960s that typically involved no more than a few thousand committed activists. They are large, popular spectacles; concerted attempts to literally, peacefully, embody the popular will.

But if these events seem sometimes to represent a massive amplification of the political gimmick, they tend ultimately to remain as reliant on the representations of the media as any of their younger, less impressive siblings. If the very scale of these events can allow them to attract favourable media coverage, it can also lead to a kind of uncertainty as to their precise political meaning or implications.

Sniffing the political wind, politicians and government ministers can attend and embrace such large-scale, peaceful spectacles, smothering their critical aims and reducing them to vague outpourings of generalised sentiment. This was the complaint of some peace activists, for example, when the Federal Labor Government embraced and coopted the 1995 protests against French nuclear testing in the Pacific. For Greg Ogle, the 'sympathetic' media coverage was accompanied by a lack of attention to the precise issues at stake. The Australian Government rapidly proclaimed its diplomatic resolve to take on the French Government. The media 'rarely took up the political demands of the rallies which were often focused on the Australian Government', including the abandonment of uranium mining and export.[17] This is hardly atypical, either. The Australian experience is resembled by the cooption of the massive anti-nuclear campaigns that convulsed the United States in the early 1980s.[18]

Even when governments lack such political dexterity, the meaning of the large, peaceful spectacle can be open to dispute and disagreement. Why did so many march for reconciliation in 2000? What did they want to express? Their disquiet at Aboriginal disadvantage? The need to personally apologise for the enormous losses borne by indigenous people? Anger at the Howard Government's policies? A treaty? It was not entirely clear. While the *Sydney Morning Herald* thought that the walk across the bridge could promote the reconciliation of white and black Australians, it was still not entirely sure what reconciliation meant. It seemed 'drained of meaning', as the paper editorialised. For some correspondents, 'reconciliation' could be achieved by the establishment of a 'Council of Unity', and the abolition of 'taxpayer-funded' institutions dedicated to indigenous rights and representation. Others spoke hopefully of a treaty between Australia's original and later inhabitants. Others still were quick to contest alternative interpretations, and to affirm that the march *could not* be construed as any kind of support for a treaty. The bewildering array of interpretations and constructions of the march led some to worry over how this enormous political gesture could be converted into genuine social and political advance. Peter Yu of the Kimberley Land Council thought that 'the goodwill of those making the People's Walk will remain as unrewarded as that shown by those who have worked for and hoped for change in the past — unless it translates into real and lasting change'.[19]

Not only is the meaning of such events open to frequent disputation, but the very magnitude and scope of the gathering can itself become the subject of widespread argument. Precisely because these events are defined by their size, opponents and supporters alike can become preoccupied with estimating the number of participants. A kind of 'political auction' can develop. Some supporters of the reconciliation march in Sydney hazarded that up to 600 000 had attended the day's events. Others thought that only 100 000 had attended. Given the enormous size of contemporary cities, no matter how many thousands come out on the streets, opponents can insist that they do not represent a numerical majority of the population.[20] The issues at stake can be marginalised by an exercise in bean-counting and opinion polling. The force of the political gimmick can be reduced to a kind of poorly administered, questionably counted mass petition.

For these reasons alone, the peaceful spectacle represents a very doubtful saviour of the political gimmick. It is unable to sidestep the centrality of the media or the dilemmas that this raises for the activist. It remains a powerful political intervention, but one of by no means obvious impacts. Given the enormous organisational labour that such actions require, they cannot be quickly staged or easily held. Given their reliance on size to attain novelty and newsworthiness, they can easily become victims of past success. When 170 000 attended a Sydney Palm Sunday Rally in 1985 this seemed cause for celebration — the anti-nuclear movement had arrived as a mass phenomenon. But by 1986 this past success had become a kind of millstone. The 130 000 who attended became a disappointment. The media were comparatively uninterested, as peace activist Deborah Brooks soon recognised: 'It was more difficult to get pre-publicity for the rally this year — the media were not particularly interested (some commented that they could re-run previous years' articles and change the date because there were no "new angles")'.[21]

The dilemmas of the activist remain. While the size of political demonstrations is a good general guide to the likelihood of media coverage, it is no guarantee of sensitive news reporting or incipient political victory. The same complaints are consistently heard from concerned citizens who get involved in large-scale political campaigns: the media has ignored us; the aims of the demonstration have not been granted attention; the supporters who have gathered together have been depicted as an unintelligent mob; the arguments of the movement have not received a fair hearing. The peaceful spectacle is no solution to the dilemmas of the activist. If size matters, it is not enough.

How can concerned citizens find a way around this dilemma? How is it possible to consistently demonstrate your views to a wide public of media consumers without being depicted as part of an illiterate mob? While these questions have concerned social movements for many decades, they have unquestionably moved into the very centre of Australian political life since the late 1990s. With the emergence of a right-wing populist political movement around the personage of Queensland MP Pauline Hanson, the question of how to effectively oppose this movement became, for many, a matter of very real urgency. Should this be through rallies? Constestational gatherings? Institutional political manoeuvres? As concerned citizens grappled with these questions, the limitations of the repertoire of staging became starkly obvious. A crisis in the political gimmick seemed to break. In the process, many old tactics were reviewed and a variety of new and important political improvisations became evident. The methods of political contention showed signs of change and enlargement.

THE HANSON MOVEMENT AND THE (ELECTRONIC, DIRECTED) STAGING OF SUPPORT

On 10 September 1996 at 5.15 p.m., a new member of the House of Representatives in the Australian Federal Parliament rose to make her maiden parliamentary speech. The policy issues raised were voluminous — in order of reference: the apparent existence of 'reverse racism', welfare payments to Aboriginal Australians, multiculturalism, bureaucracy, immigration, unemployment, foreign debt, living standards, family law, privatisation of government assets, foreign aid, the United Nations, government investment in large-scale development projects, national military service, interest rates, and the (apparently threatening) status and size of Asian nations surrounding Australia. The speech was also characterised by a close examination of the member's personal history of single parenthood, ownership of a small business, and self-confessed 'ordinariness'.

The speaker's name was Pauline Hanson, and the speech was to have profound political repercussions. For Hanson's partisans, her maiden speech became a kind of declaration of independence. Sixteen thousand copies were apparently printed for distribution in the weeks after it was delivered, and it has invariably been reprinted in the subsequent publications of her supporters: *Pauline Hanson: The Truth*, *Pauline: The Hanson Phenomenon*, and *The Pauline Hanson Story*. The One Nation Party website proclaims 'Wake Up Australia!' in the text above the reproduced speech. Indeed, it is Hanson's maiden speech that her biographer, Helen Dodd, refers to as the moment prefigured in the messiah-like birth of her subject:

> On this day [27/5/54] was born a child, Pauline Lee Seccombe, who was to stand up in front of a nation forty-two years later and throw down a challenge to all politicians. She became the voice of the battlers and the hard workers of the country. For too long they had been suffocated by political correctness. They were unable, or reluctant to express, certain sentiments on issues close to their hearts. Their champion had been born! [22]

The speech itself was a halting, uncertain political performance, and it gained only glancing initial attention from the broadsheet press. But it was publicised and endorsed by a number of influential radio talkback hosts, and soon received wider coverage in the tabloid press and on soft-news television. Central to this process was the expression of support for Hanson's views by a wide variety of Australians. Indeed, the speech only became significant and newsworthy as apparent public support for it became obvious. The public embrace rather than the speech itself was the initial newsworthy fact. How, precisely, was this support expressed? It was not 'performed' with the conventional tools of claim-making — the convening of public rallies or demonstrations endorsing Hanson's comments, or even the rapid organisation of mass petitions that expressed specific agreement with her claims. The tools used instead were more immediate, novel, and electronic in nature. Two rather 'old-fashioned' but nonetheless 'electronic' means of communication were particularly important to this process: the telephone and the fax machine.

Research by the media-monitoring organisation 'Rehame Australia' suggests that reporters were generally condemnatory of Pauline Hanson's views during October 1996, only endorsing her views 13 per cent of the time, but that leading talkback hosts such as Alan Jones (66 per cent positive), Price (40 per cent) and Miller (44 per cent), were vastly more favourable. More than this, the possibility of supporting Pauline Hanson through phone calls and faxes was sometimes suggested by a number of talkback hosts, and, in the case of Alan Jones, Hanson's phone number was actually repeated on air. The phone calls flooded in, many undoubtedly from talkback listeners who had grown accustomed to using the telephone as a means of political self-expression. Hanson's fans would soon use these electronic communications as a sign of their leader's popular rapport. Indeed, in her biography of Hanson, Helen Dodd recalls the aftermath of the maiden speech this way: 'On the evening of 10 September 1996, the Parliamentary switchboard was inundated with telephone calls from people requesting a copy of her speech. Nothing like this had ever happened before'.[23] Within a day, the tabloid newspapers had also reported the emergence of public support for Hanson's comments and had used the electronic manifestation of that support as a sign that something extraordinary and popular was at play: 'As the three phones of her Parliament House office overloaded, sheets of faxes were unloaded on to her desk'.[24]

Through phone calls and faxes, the apparent significance of Hanson's constituency was soon widely accepted. The extent of that support was 'scientifically' confirmed over following days, as a series of voluntary, pseudo-democratic opinion polls proliferated on television and talkback radio. These phone polls were all rapidly held and reported on, and soon became fodder for a variety of news reports — apparent 'evidence' of the Australian public's embrace of 'the battler from Brisbane'. The public was summoned up and herded with astonishing rapidity, and the power of Hanson's maiden speech as a transformative, democratic event was thereby established. Leading Sydney talkback host Alan Jones was again the pacesetter. On 12 September, Jones founded a phone poll on Hanson's views, initiating it with a sympathetic interview with Ms Hanson herself, and encouraging phone calls with comments such as 'It's the chance for the majority to be heard, the people out there who no one listens to.' By 8 a.m., 22 190 phone calls had apparently been placed, indicating 98.7 per cent support for Hanson.

Further polls followed on television and radio. Pauline Hanson appeared on Channel Nine's *Midday Show*, and a phone poll posed the question 'Are Pauline Hanson's views racist?' Thousands of calls followed, with 94 per cent voting 'no'. Not to be outdone, Channel Seven held a survey in Hanson's own federal electorate, indicating 68 per cent prospective electoral support. From this survey, a highly 'scientific' calculation was made and reported: 'More than half — 54 per cent — said they had voted for Ms Hanson, indicating a 14 per cent increase in support'. A mania for testing the public's views developed — so much so that when a debate between Aboriginal leader Charles Perkins and Pauline Hanson occurred on television, the *Daily Telegraph* held its own poll of the studio audience: 'When asked by the *Daily Telegraph* after the show who the audience supported, 120 to 3 were in favour of Ms Hanson's views'.[25]

However, if these early forms of polling were of dubious authority, this did not prevent their frequent citation and interpretation. The radio poll held by Alan Jones eventually attracted some 37 000 phone calls, and this impressive number itself became the scientific figure, the poll's 'result', that political commentators and editorials took up and used to frame their stories on the aftermath of the maiden speech. The results of these early opinion polls justified the attention of the broadsheet media, and the formation of theories about the Hanson speech and the nature of her supporters soon followed. On 13 September, Geoff Kitney, chief political writer for the *Sydney Morning Herald*, noted the results of the Alan Jones poll in an article that detected a growing 'undercurrent' of support and that coined the term 'Hansonism'. Kitney's article was itself taken up to justify further broadsheet attention to a political speech that was becoming a genuine event, but that still needed a rationale for significant intellectual attention. Over the next two weeks, the Alan Jones phone poll and the Channel Seven survey would also be referred to by right-wing political commentators B. A. Santamaria and Tony Abbott, left-wing commentators Jim McClelland and Graham Richardson, and by editorial writers at the Melbourne *Age*.[26]

Interested social researchers came forward with their own findings and hypotheses. David Chalke, a figure who claimed to be a 'cultural analyst' with an organisation called AMR: Quantum Harris, developed the theory that Hanson's support was the product of disgust with 'ten years of political correctness'. His views were reported as a kind of scientific analysis, and generally grouped with the results of pseudo-democratic polls in the days after the Hanson speech. Similarly, when academic research in the journal *People and Place* found low support for current levels of immigration in Australia, this was integrated into the ongoing coverage of the aftermath of the maiden speech event, and received wide analysis and interpretation.[27]

When the national magazine the *Bulletin* published a poll conducted by the respected Morgan association in November 1996, it represented the first rigorous testing of public support for Hanson over the Australian polity. It found that a Hanson-led party in the Upper House of the Federal Parliament would gain 18 per cent of the national vote, and decisively hold the balance of power. This, in turn, provoked further commentary, polling and analysis from other news organisations. The poll was not received as the first of its kind, however. It came after a narrative of massive public support had already been established, and after the maiden speech of Pauline Hanson had already been constructed as an event of undeniable, founding significance. Other, earlier interventions had already manufactured the wave of public support that Morgan and the *Bulletin* would find and pronounce on. Everybody knew that the Hanson speech was supported by the public. They had already read about the phone calls and the faxes; they had already heard of the enormous polled support.[28]

Quickly taking advantage of this public clamour, Pauline Hanson launched a new political party in April 1997. Pauline Hanson's One Nation Party asserted itself with almost unprecedented political speed. In elections in the State of Queensland during June 1998, it won eleven seats in the Lower House and attained 22.7 per cent of the statewide vote. By 2000, it was represented in two State Parliaments and in the Federal Parliament. Since the zenith of 1998, electoral support for the organisation has clearly flagged, and earlier predictions that the party threatened the stability of the two-party system now appear grossly overstated. Nonetheless, to concerned citizens in 1997 and 1998, terrifying political events seemed to be unfolding. The Prime Minister, John Howard, was very slow to repudiate Hanson's views. The opinion polls continued to rise. Political commentators fearfully noted the re-emergence of the 'voice of our disreputable racist past' and members of Asian and Aboriginal communities identified the surge of a 'rising tide' of verbal and physical abuse. Public meetings featuring Hanson drew a thousand enthusiastic supporters in Hervey Bay, Rockhampton, and Gatton in rural Queensland. Would the inexorable rise ever stop?[29]

What could ordinary citizens who opposed Hanson do? How could they halt the torrent that political leaders seemed so unable to cope with? For many, the tools of staging seemed the most powerful political resource. Surely the political gimmick could stop the One Nation Party?

CONTESTING HANSONISM

Between October 1996 and October 1998, a variety of Australians came to demonstrate their opposition to the policies, views and sometimes presence of Pauline Hanson's One Nation Party. However, within this overall period of anti-Hanson mobilisation, the majority of contentious gatherings were concentrated within two comparatively brief moments: the period associated with the official formation of the One Nation Party, from 3 May 1997 until 27 July 1997; and the period associated with the aftermath of One Nation's success at the

Queensland state elections, from 20 June 1998 until 30 August 1998. Together, these two periods constitute more than two-thirds of total anti-Hanson contentious gatherings 1996–98.[30]

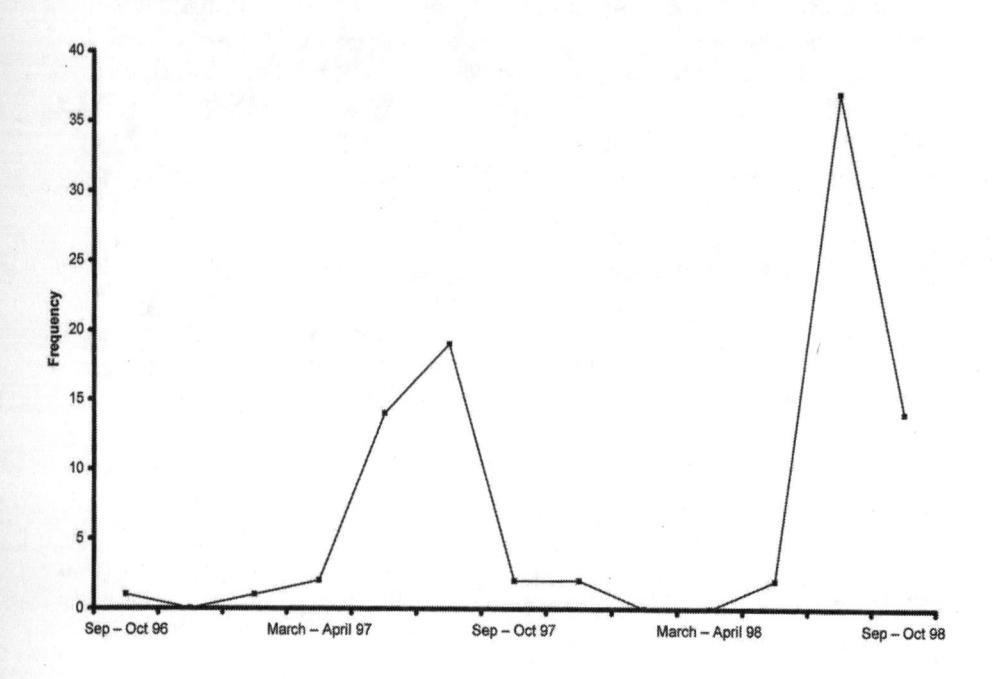

Figure 5.1
Anti-Hanson contentious gatherings, September 1996–October 1998

Clearly, this was an episodic and reactive movement. Both peaks of anti-Hanson mobilisation were also peaks of One Nation support, as reflected in the leading opinion polls. Demonstrations, rallies and marches against One Nation took off when the party was most popular, and fell away as the party's support declined. The presence of One Nation was not sufficient to promote mobilisation; only the possibility of the party's political triumph could stimulate contention on a wide scale.[31]

From its earliest moments, the anti-Hanson movement relied strongly on that great popular tool of the 1960s, the *contestational* gathering. From October 1996, anti-Hanson demonstrations were held at the site of important party functions, at inaugural meetings of party branches, and at scheduled appearances of Pauline Hanson. The very presence of Hanson and of her supporters was directly contested and problematised.

This form of action was clearly parasitic on the actions of the One Nation Party, and it shadowed the party's mobilisation around the country. Contestational demonstrations spanned the major metropolitan centres; suburban locations such as Hawthorn, Manly, Frankston, Richmond and Mortdale; provincial centres such as Newcastle, Geelong, Ipswich, Launceston, Werribee, Toowoomba and Bendigo; and smaller country towns such as Echuca and those in central-western New South Wales. As Hanson attempted to rally her own supporters and to begin the initial phases of party organisation, demonstrations followed her to a great variety of sites around Australia.

Contestational gatherings disrupted the public spectacle of Hansonism. Hanson's claim to represent the unspoken views of 'ordinary' Australians was exposed to critique when her supporters were outnumbered by demonstrators, sometimes by more than ten to one. When Hanson retreated from contact with 'the people', and sped away in a car, this was used to undermine her self-proclaimed 'ordinariness' and popular rapport. When Australians of all races entered public space in opposition to Hansonism, the existence of 'Asian', 'ethnic' and 'Aboriginal' protesters began to be reflected in the public sphere. The hurt, anger, and sometimes articulate refutation of One Nation by these Australians began to be granted rare attention, and the claims of protesters to be opposing racism were also frequently echoed on the pages of major newspapers. When Hanson was forced to flee, or when the smooth running of One Nation meetings was impeded, many demonstrators were jubilant. Their particular, local triumphs became metonymic of the broader contest between racism and anti-racism in Australian life. As Reihana Mohideen, an organiser of the demonstrations, put it:

> The views of genuine anti-racists have been getting very little publicity. It's only when we rally and demonstrate in large numbers that we get a hearing. So it's very important that these demonstrations against Hanson continue.
>
> During the course of mobilising this anti-racist support, if there is strong enough community sentiment against her expressing her views, then so be it. This sentiment should prevail.[32]

Gaining strength from a series of strong mobilisations in Geelong, Perth, Hobart and Launceston, contestational gatherings quickly became the key political tools of the emergent anti-Hanson campaign during 1997. Precisely because they violated the norms of liberal-rational discourse for those of direct contestation, they allowed dissident anti-racists to attain substantial public attention.[33]

FROM CONTESTATION TO DISRUPTION: THE DILEMMA OF ANTI-HANSON DEMONSTRATORS

However, the utility of these contestational gatherings was soon eroded. Because contestational gatherings were organised in direct opposition to the presence of Pauline Hanson and her supporters, they tended to involve 'disruptive' and violent behaviour. Although a large proportion of anti-Hanson demonstrations did not involve disruption, a range of violent, disruptive and norm-infringing actions were *reported to occur*, especially during the first peak of anti-Hanson contention. Among actions that were alleged to occur by the leading media outlets were the throwing of bottles, eggs and balloons, the forced closure or restriction of One Nation meetings, conflict with police, violent scuffles, and the arrest of demonstrators. Table 1 illustrates the strong presence of such disruptive gatherings between 3 May and 27 July 1997.

Table I
The character of Anti-Hanson gatherings, 3 May to 27 July, 1997

Interactivity	Normativity[a]	Frequency
Contestational	Sanctioned	6
Contestational	Disruptive	13
Autonomous	Sanctioned	6
Autonomous	Disruptive	0

NOTE a Normativity: degree of adherence to customary behaviour

The disruptive actions of May, June and July 1997 attracted substantial publicity. They also frequently led to the framing of demonstrators as hostile, intolerant, and atypical Australians. As a result, demonstrations characterised by such behaviour could be depicted as a threat to democratic freedom; as counterproductive; as likely to increase One Nation's public profile; as certain to drive more moderate demonstrators away; as the cause of upset and fear for One Nation supporters; and as an unfortunate drain on scarce police resources.[34]

In short, the tendency of contestational gatherings to also be characterised by disruption placed demonstrators in the jaws of a now familiar dilemma. When Pauline Hanson appeared at party functions without dissent or protest, this was taken as evidence of broad support for her policies and views. But if those functions were contested with large protests, the conduct of individual demonstrators could stigmatise the entire anti-Hanson campaign, and provoke apparent sympathy for the party's supporters. Contestational gatherings were often newsworthy, but only infrequently framed as successful political interventions.[35]

This dilemma that faced anti-Hanson demonstrators presented itself most starkly on 7 July 1997, when a One Nation party meeting was held in Dandenong, Victoria. A core of happenings in Dandenong on this date were uncontested: a One Nation meeting took place; a demonstration outside the meeting was organised; demonstrators outnumbered those attending by a substantial ratio; and one of those attending the One Nation function, 59-year-old Keith Warburton, was seriously injured and hospitalised after a violent incident.

In some senses, the precise happenings in Dandenong were in doubt. For example, the cause of Warburton's injuries was variously described as unknown, a push, a trip, an attack by three protesters, a hit over the head, and a 'king hit' from behind. However, if the causes of Warburton's injuries were the subject of dispute, the framing of the overall event within the mainstream press adhered to strikingly common dimensions across the major media outlets. Indeed, the political actions of all of those present at the Dandenong demonstration were framed in overwhelmingly violent, negative, and evocative terms.[36]

Table 2
Framing actions in Dandenong

Source	Actions of demonstrators
Beatrice Faust, 'Left Holding the Liability', *Australian*, 19–20 July 1997	'bashed' 'frustrated a peaceful celebration of diversity' 'I punch, therefore I am'
Stuart Honeysett and Jamie Walker, 'The Image of Unity Takes a Battering', *Australian*, 10 July 1997	'brutal beating' 'confronted' 'king hit'
Editorial, 'Violence Betrays Civil Society', *Weekend Australian*, 12–13 July 1997	'organised violence' 'violent acts of intolerance' 'mindless and sickening violence'
Mark Forbes, 'Shadowy Revolutionaries Behind the Hanson Violence', *Sunday Age*, 13 July 1997	'king hit' 'violent protests' 'trying to use any opportunity to create havoc'
Jamie Walker, 'Hanson Haters', *Weekend Australian*, 12–13 July 1997	'seemingly intent on causing damage' 'increasingly violent'
'Three held for assault of Hanson supporter', *Australian*, 15 July 1997	'near riot' 'wild demonstration'
Kimina Lyall and Ben Hutchings, 'Hanson supporter injured in rally clash', *Australian*, 8 July 1997	'lashed out with their feet and threw punches' 'turned on each other, calling each other "animals"'
Belinda Parsons, 'Loud cheers, angry jeers', *Age*, 8 July 1997	'became angrier and angrier' 'threw their rotten produce with more and more fury'
Editorial, 'The Politics of Hatred', *Age*, 9 July 1997	'they chose to chant "un-Australian" and to throw bottles, rotten eggs, and condoms full of urine'
'One Nation Attack: 3 to Trial', *Australian*, 22 January 1998	'pounced' 'kicking, elbowing and punching'
James Button, 'Blood and Circuses', *Age*, 21 July 1997	'angry, projectile-throwing crowd'

Along with a strongly negative framing of the actions at Dandenong, the anti-Hanson actors themselves were also constructed as hostile and unappealing subjects. Whereas opponents of Hanson had previously been described as 'ethnic' or as opponents of racism, in this case the motives of protesters were presented as more doubtful or even nefarious: the outright termination of One Nation meetings; the promotion of alternative political agendas; or blind, irrational anger. Equally, the ethnicity of protesters was now neglected. Demonstrators were comparatively colourless. They were framed simply as 'demonstrators' or 'protesters', or else they were depicted as the members of fringe or Far Left political parties. Indeed, after 7 July 1997, the racial or ethnic identity of demonstrators would not even be broached by the major media outlets until 1998. The racialised interactions of early 1997 were now supplanted by institutionalised interactions, in which the Far Left parties (Militant, Resistance, International Socialist Organization) squared off against One Nation. In the process, supporters of One Nation were framed as comparatively passive, 'ordinary', and assailed subjects.[37]

Table 3
Framing One Nation supporters after Dandenong

Source	Framing of One Nation supporters
Jamie Walker, 'Pauline puckers up for the nation', *Australian*, 19–20 July 1997	'ran the gauntlet' of protesters 'determined to hear for himself what Ms Hanson had to say'
'Protesters lay siege to Hanson Geelong meeting', *Sydney Morning Herald*, 19 July 1997	'forced to run the gauntlet' 'wearing rubbish bags to protect themselves from items being thrown'
Amanda Phelan and Adam Harvey, 'Party Poopers', *Sydney Morning Herald*, 10 July 1997	'people attending the meeting'
Gerard Henderson, 'Game of consequences', *Sydney Morning Herald*, 12 July 1997	'people too frightened to turn up' 'ran the gauntlet'
Jamie Walker, 'Hanson Haters', *Australian*, 12–13 July 1997	'come along to hear' 'was not even a member of One Nation'
Don Chipp, 'Stamp out this horror', *Sunday Telegraph*, 13 July 1997	'innocent people attending a public rally'
Greg Abbott, '14 arrested in fiery Hanson rally', *Sun-Herald*, 5 November 1997	'People attending ran a gauntlet'
Fiona Carruthers, 'Hanson-land: where the "little battler" feels big', *Australian*, 17 September 1997	'ran the usual gauntlet' 'bearing the chants of "racist scum" and other epithets'
Victoria Button, 'One Nation visit led to bashing, court told', *Age*, 22 January 1998	'abused as a racist and a Nazi before being bashed unconscious' 'remembered falling after telling them he did not know much about Pauline Hanson but was happy to hear what the One Nation party had to say'

Clearly, the public contestation of the One Nation Party in Dandenong on 7 July 1997 was a failure. The 'violence' associated with the staging of this action caused the leading media outlets to recast their framing of the anti-Hanson campaign. It was henceforth framed as a conflict between an assortment of violent and undemocratic protesters, often with alternative political agendas, and supported by Far Left parties, on the one hand, and on the other, a range of 'ordinary' Australians who simply wanted to hear what Hanson had to say and who faced violence and intimidation. In essence, this framing of interactions reproduced the self-understanding of One Nation party members: they were part of the mass of typical Australians, who had been neglected and suppressed, and who were being denied their democratic rights. Their opponents were outsiders or elites who didn't believe in a 'fair go'.[38]

Not only was the Dandenong protest framed as undemocratic and illiberal, it was repeatedly revisited as a metaphor for the entire anti-Hanson campaign over the following months. For some public intellectuals, it became a metaphor for the decline of democracy — the impossibility of open debate around Hansonism, and the stifling of free speech and assembly. For others, it was a metaphor for the changing forms of political protest, and the decline of rational, impassioned, well-disciplined dissidents. Others still revisited the event a year later as a metaphor for the failure of the media to deal with the One Nation Party fairly:

> When an elderly gentleman was bashed by protestors for merely attending a Pauline Hanson rally last year, many Australians who find her policies contemptible nonetheless realised an awful line had been crossed.
>
> Dreadful as it was, the event gave many in the media cause to consider how they had covered these often frightening anti-racism demonstrations. How did our unquestioning coverage of exhortations to kill Pauline Hanson sit with the fact that this was meant to be the voice of anti-racist tolerance?[39]

Unsurprisingly, the construction of the Dandenong protest within the public sphere altered the political methods and tactics of the anti-Hanson movement. Public opinion polls reflected both widespread public distaste for recent 'violent protests' and a widespread public expectation that they would increase political support for the One Nation Party. Moderate protesters now became concerned about both the political utility of their actions and about how they were perceived by others. The fear that they would be labelled as violent and illiberal was palpable. Even the more militant actors began to lament how One Nation had received a stream of positive publicity and had indirectly benefited from the demonstration. The idea that the Dandenong demonstration had directly fed support and even membership of One

Nation was widely reported. The fear that disruptive or violent behaviour would 'play into' the hands of the media was expressed. The strategy of contestation was now more circumscribed for many actors, and the need to avoid disruption was highlighted. As the socialist youth organisation Resistance put it in the aftermath of Dandenong:

> Attempting to close down all One Nation meetings simply means organising to have battles with the increasing numbers of police who are turning up to protect these meetings. Such futile attempts are more likely to demoralise anti-racist demonstrators than Hanson supporters. It will certainly prevent the movement from drawing in the much larger numbers of people it needs to defeat the racist resurgence.[40]

Reflecting this dissatisfaction with the public reception of contestation, those demonstrations that explicitly confronted Hanson henceforth became increasingly less disruptive and more moderate in character. Not only that, but contestational gatherings of all kinds fell away in the later half of 1997 and never retained their earlier centrality. When the anti-Hanson movement re-emerged in 1998, it would be characterised by quite different political methods.

However, the implications of the demonstrations that contested Hansonism were not restricted to the movement itself, or to the media's coverage of the so-called 'Hanson phenomenon'. They were also to have a quite substantial impact on the Hanson movement, and to result in the extension of its distinctive political methods. The most important form this extension would take involved the elaboration of those 'electronic' forms of staging that had so successfully underpinned the embrace of the maiden parliamentary speech.

CONTENTION ON THE NET: THE RISE OF THE CYBERBATTLE

For those who attended One Nation Party meetings, a sometimes horrifying experience awaited. The mostly middle-aged crowd were often shaken by the extent and depth of opposition. They claimed that they had been spat on, showered with rubbish, abused, assaulted. At times their meetings were abandoned after sustained demonstration, and a police escort was required to lead them from public halls. Unquestionably, this was a harrowing, intimidating political activity.[41]

Like the protesters who were often disappointed at the coverage of their actions, Hansonites were also frequently angered at the tenor and direction of news coverage. They claimed that reports of early demonstrations focused only on the articulate and respectable face of protest, and ignored the 'real goons' who physically threatened them. They complained that 'disgusting actions' had not been adequately reported, and that the violence they experienced would never be aired within the mainstream media. Pauline Hanson tried to insist that the contestational and disruptive rallies that opposed her were the direct product of 'elite' criticism of her policies and person. According to this view, Labor and Liberal politicians had declared 'open season' on her, and 'civil disobedience' was the result. When these claims were not widely accepted within the mainstream media, the suspicion of Hanson's supporters deepened. It became clear that this could not continue. Something needed to be done.[42]

It was the Internet that loomed as a possible solution to these strategic problems. The Hanson movement had attracted the support of successful Ipswich webmaster Scott Balson. Quickly, Balson became the webmaster of the official One Nation Party website, while his own Internet daily — *Australian National News of the Day* (*ANNOD*), became a key vehicle of party news, debate and information.

The importance of the Web to the ONP's success has often been emphasised. By September 1997, as the mainstream media continued to digest the impact of the Dandenong demonstration, the readership of *ANNOD* was alleged to top 100 000 hits in total for the first time. By September 1998, the One Nation website was registering 30 000 hits per day. As the federal election beckoned, the One Nation website had become one of Australia's most popular, garnering 45 000 hits per day.

In many ways, the uses of the Web were somewhat conventional. Advance publicity for party meetings was provided, and details on the organisation of future One Nation forums ardently espoused. Policies were launched. Updates were delivered on the sale of the movement's printed literature, and future publications disclosed. The *ANNOD* website detailed the future television appearances of Pauline Hanson and provided a running, critical commentary on the accuracy of the leading opinion polls. When media outlets as diverse as the *Courier-Mail*, the *Sunday Mail*, the *Australian*, SBS News, Four Corners, and *Sixty Minutes* attacked the One Nation Party, detailed, almost immediate refutations followed.[43]

However, the Internet was more than an alternative source of news commentary. It was also used to complicate and, eventually, to alter the public circulation of the anti-Hanson demonstrations. *Australian National News of the Day* became a site of provocative interpretations of One Nation rallies and of the demonstrations that contested them. First-person accounts of the violence and intimidation of Hansonites found a point of elucidation and exchange. Sound recordings of protester chants evoked the militancy of the anti-Hansonites. Through digital photography, images of leaders of the anti-Hanson movement were captured and publicised; through investigative journalism, their personal histories and institutional affiliations were uncovered. Photos of protesters in apparently violent poses helped to crystallise their depiction as 'violent', and even, on occasion, to lead to their arrest. When protests occurred on the Gold Coast, in Perth, Geelong, Hobart, Newcastle and Bulimba in mid-1997, detailed expositions of the 'One Nation' experience became available for members and web-surfers alike.[44]

This was more than a simple account of the experience of the party faithful, however. Balson used *ANNOD* to extend Hanson's claim that the political establishment was implicated in the violence of protesters. When the 31 May 1997 Newcastle Party meeting became violent, he alleged that a rally for multiculturalism, organised by the Australian Labor Party in nearby Civic Park, had been the cause. He highlighted the apparent fact that both the Liberal and Labor parties had been comparatively silent in the aftermath of the Dandenong protest. He trawled the Net itself in the search of direct ties between Labor and the 'violent protests'. In early July 1997, just a day after the Dandenong demonstration, he announced his discoveries.

Unsurprisingly, Balson discovered that there was a possible electronic connection between the Web presence of the ALP and that of a number of left-wing institutions involved in the Dandenong protest. That connection was mediated first through the ACTU, then through a generalised web-list for the Australian political Left, 'Left-Link', and on to organisations such as Militant Australia. The existence of this series of electronic connections or 'links' between Labor and such 'extremist' organisations was presented by Balson as 'five links to Labor's anarchy' and used to widen the debate around the Dandenong protest. As Balson put it himself in his investigative opus, 'Making the News':

> What we discovered through the Internet was *an undeniable link between the ALP and the extreme left wing radicals* who were using this new media as a key ploy to promote their un-Australian desire to '*shut down*' Pauline Hanson's One Nation Party's meetings amongst the promotion of a raft of other un-Australian activities …
>
> … In the weeks before the newspapers, television and radio stations countrywide had been hammering One Nation with baseless allegations of being hijacked by right wing radicals and here we had proof that the ALP *were in fact the bona-fide focus of the left wing extremists* …[45]

Both the *Queensland Times* and the *Courier-Mail* reported this apparent connection in the following days, and the Australian Labor Party was forced to release a press statement countering Balson's claims. Balson himself remained unhappy with the mainstream media's treatment of the issue. However, he drew a wider lesson on the role of the Internet and its connection to political mobilisation.[46]

It was apparent that a new arena of political action was emerging. Rather than the simple staging of the political gimmick for the interest of the mainstream media, it was becoming possible to intervene in the process and direction of media reporting itself. The interpretation of 'the protest event' was becoming the basis of its own, discrete political struggle, as important as the political mobilisation to generate 'the protest event' alone. News-making was becoming the object of intervention, news reporting the object of manipulation. As Balson saw it, the emergence of the Internet resulted in the decline of the 'mass media', and the rise of alternative interpretations. He called the process of intervention in media reporting the 'cyberbattle', and declared his adherence to its methods:

> the Internet is being used to force the mainstream media to take a more balanced approach in reporting on Pauline Hanson's One Nation. It is being used to confront and expose Pauline Hanson's political detractors in a daily ongoing cyber-battle. This feature is a *living, breathing frontline assault* on those who misquote, misrepresent and misreport Pauline Hanson's One Nation.[47]

Beyond the rhetoric, how could the Internet be used to shape the construction of media images? How, precisely, was a 'cyberbattle' waged? Clearly, the simple publication of material that offered a different interpretation was not enough. *Australian National News of the Day* also attempted to use the Internet to coordinate mass phone-in, fax and email campaigns, hoping thereby to raise policy issues, to ensure public acceptance of One Nation as a legitimate political party, and to frighten those media outlets that contemplated critical media coverage.

ANNOD promoted electronic petitions against policies such as timed local phone calls and the Multilateral Agreement on Investment. When Senator Mal Colston moved to oppose the full privatisation of Telstra, readers of the daily Internet publication were encouraged to participate in a campaign of phone-in support. When an electronic petition was circulated that urged the Liberal Party to place One Nation *last* on its list of electoral preferences, One Nation developed a counter-petition, and promoted it vigorously on the Internet. In a similar fashion, when Web administrators working for Telstra and for the Victorian State Library refused initially to establish links to the One Nation site, a campaign for 'fair' treatment of the party was powerfully waged.[48]

However, the tools of the phone-in and the email campaign were used more frequently and aggressively to pressure Hanson's opponents within the public sphere. The ABC was besieged by a plethora of complaints when interviewer Maxine McKew criticised Pauline Hanson on the *Lateline* program in May 1997. The Channel Nine program, *A Current Affair*, was similarly assailed after an interview in June 1998, and the station's switchboard was jammed. When the *Australia/Israel*

Review published a leaked list of 2000 One Nation members in July 1998, the journal's contact details were supplied by *ANNOD*. A few days later, the email address of its publisher, Mark Leibler, was also supplied, and contact was suggested. On the occasion of other attacks on One Nation, such as after the publication of a critical political cartoon in the *Australian*, readers of *ANNOD* were even urged to contact the Australian Press Council and lodge a formal complaint. When *Sixty Minutes* planned a critical profile of the party, readers of *ANNOD* were forewarned, and a 'call to arms' against the program was issued. An Internet poll on the program's website was highlighted and targeted for mass intervention. Its results were closely monitored. A petition against the program was organised, and individual letters of complaint suggested.[49]

At times, the phone-in campaign was complemented by an even more vigorous set of interventions on the part of Hanson's supporters. In an attempt to combat 'media bias', *ANNOD* began to organise and coordinate consumer boycotts of those businesses that attacked the One Nation Party in some way. This, for example, was the eventual response of One Nation partisans to the *Australia/Israel Review*'s publication of the personal details of 2000 One Nation party members. Jet Set Travel, the business of Mark Leibler, the magazine's publisher, was subsequently boycotted by One Nation supporters. The airline company Qantas also became the subject of a boycott, after Chief Executive Officer James Strong was critical of Hanson supporters and after Qantas briefly called on its in-flight news service to omit references to One Nation. Even Toyota motor vehicles were boycotted, in the hope that Toyota would exert pressure on the television program it sponsored, *Sixty Minutes*, to alter its coverage of party affairs.[50]

Of course, One Nation's attempts to get positive media coverage were not limited to Internet-based strategies. The party leadership also showed a willingness to learn the lessons of earlier party history and to adjust its political methods accordingly. Reflecting both the clamour of attention achieved by Hanson's maiden speech and the more positive coverage that followed in the wake of the Dandenong demonstrations, One Nation attempted to engineer a number of events calculated to achieve a similar representation in the media. At the core of these actions was an attempt to construct Pauline Hanson as an assailed figure — under violent political attack, denied the right to free speech, but battling on against the odds.

Despite the supposed violent threat to Hanson's supporters, the One Nation Party continued to organise large public meetings and to promote them widely. Indeed, there is some evidence to suggest that One Nation deliberately released detailed information on forthcoming party functions in the very hope of drawing disruptive opposition. If disruption occurred, the party's activities could expect widespread and sympathetic media coverage. If Hanson's individual supporters would have to bear direct, physical intimidation, the eventual victory in the media would be all the greater. The possibility that this strategy was being deployed by One Nation was even raised by *Herald* journalist Margo Kingston. In late 1998 she issued a critical report on Hanson's 'unusual' release of her full campaign itinerary in the first days of the federal election. Clearly, according to Kingston, deeper motives were at play.[51]

Even when violence did not materialise at One Nation meetings, the party attempted to use a range of electronic interventions in order to simulate its effects. In October 1997, Scott Balson claimed to possess and post photographs of leaders of an anti-Hanson protest calling others to violence. On 16 July 1997, *ANNOD* broke a story on an apparent conspiracy to assault Hanson by the 'Brisbane Anti-Racism Campaign'. It published an 'intelligence report' supposedly leaked from the campaign itself, in which the conspiracy was allegedly raised, and it quickly diffused the 'plot' to various media outlets. Howard Sattler, a sympathetic radio talkback host, gleefully took up the story, and television and newspapers rapidly followed suit. The *Queensland Times* newspaper even featured the conspiracy on its front page.[52]

In a similar fashion, One Nation was able to generate positive media coverage through the production and subsequent broadcast of a video recording that contained Hanson's 'political testament' and that began with the words 'Fellow Australians, if you are seeing me now, it means I have been murdered'. The video was aired to a substantial television audience on Channel Seven's *Witness* current affairs program on 25 November 1997. In one sense, it simply expressed the rampant paranoia of One Nation. In another, it was simply a 'contrived stunt' or political gimmick, as the *Sydney Morning Herald* noted: 'Her popularity is falling, and she needs such stunts to keep her alive politically'.[53] But this was an electronic political gimmick. No action in public space actually eventuated. The 'death' of Hanson, like her earlier 'assault', was purely imagined. The personal effects on Hanson were wholly simulated, while the public and positive implications were, ironically, very 'real' and beneficial.

The repertoire of staging, it seemed, had been outflanked. While anti-Hansonites attempted to contest Hanson's presence with a variety of protest actions, their most treasured political weapons appeared to be turning against them. For every contestational action, there was a negative headline. For every angry protest, there was concern expressed for Pauline Hanson's right to 'freedom of speech'. *For every demonstration in public space, there was an 'electronic' mobilisation that focused explicitly on the role of the mainstream media as reporter and publiciser.* What could Hanson's opponents do? Just as

One Nation partisans showed a commendable ability to adjust to the recent history of media representations, so anti-Hansonites also came to develop new tactics that reflected the quest for positive reporting of their cause. In the process, the dominant political performance moved from one of direct contestation to one of autonomous celebration.

FROM CONTESTATION TO AUTONOMY AND PARODY: THE CHANGING ANTI-HANSON CAMPAIGN

Autonomous gatherings held in alternative spaces to the One Nation Party could avoid the sharp, negative framing of the strategy of contestation. Beginning with a rally at the Ipswich Workers' Club to mourn the first anniversary of Hanson's election, on 2 March 1997, a variety of autonomous gatherings opposed the policies and impact of the One Nation Party over the next two years. At least to begin with, these actions offered a more moderate and respectable form of political dissent. They relied on the presence of official personages such as mayors, premiers, leaders of ethnic community institutions, MLCs and pastors, and they attempted to draw a broad coalition of citizens to civic celebrations, ceremonies and festivals. Such actions tended to be organised around a commitment to multiculturalism, rather than a direct opposition to Hanson as such. As one organiser put it, 'We are angry at the One Nation Party but we are not the type who will slam them for their beliefs'. Rather than violence or rebuke, Hanson was ignored as citizens participated in a variety of peaceful and symbolic actions — mass citizenship ceremonies, the lighting of candles and the singing peace songs, and sometimes even large, celebratory conga lines. These actions often received generous advance publicity, and a welcoming reception within the media.[54]

At least in the first phase of the anti-Hanson campaign, however, autonomous gatherings were often overshadowed by more conflictual and disruptive actions. In Geelong on 19 May, in Newcastle on 30 May, in Adelaide on 11 June, and in Werribee on 14 July 1997, autonomous anti-Hanson gatherings were held in deliberate competition with One Nation party meetings, and with the demonstrations that contested them.[55] In Newcastle, Adelaide, and Werribee, the autonomous gatherings were almost completely neglected in newspaper reports, and critical, negatively framed stories of contestational actions instead dominated media coverage.[56] Mobilising large numbers of Australians was not enough. Disruption was also necessary to attain newsworthiness.

When a new wave of anti-Hanson activity burst forth in the aftermath of One Nation's success at in the Queensland state elections of 1998, it began to reflect these crucial public dynamics. Both contestational gatherings that relied on disruption and autonomous gatherings that ignored Hansonism for a moderate celebration of multiculturalism were now equally eschewed: 'It was a mistake to think that racism would be pushed aside by small groups attempting to close down racist meetings or by ignoring it'.[57]

In their place emerged a coordinated campaign of actions that spurned contestation for autonomy, but that attained newsworthiness through their disruptive and norm-infringing character. Indeed, as Figure 5.2 shows, the reliance on contestation in the first phase of anti-Hanson action was now succeeded by an even greater reliance on autonomy in the second phase. (thus ironically reversing the comparative decline of 'autonomy' that occurred during the 1960s [see p. 56–57]).

The political activity of high school students was crucial to this second peak of anti-Hanson contention in 1998. One thousand Victorian students walked out of class and demonstrated their opposition to Hanson on 25 June. They were followed by students in Sydney and Canberra on 2 July, and in Brisbane on 28 July. The

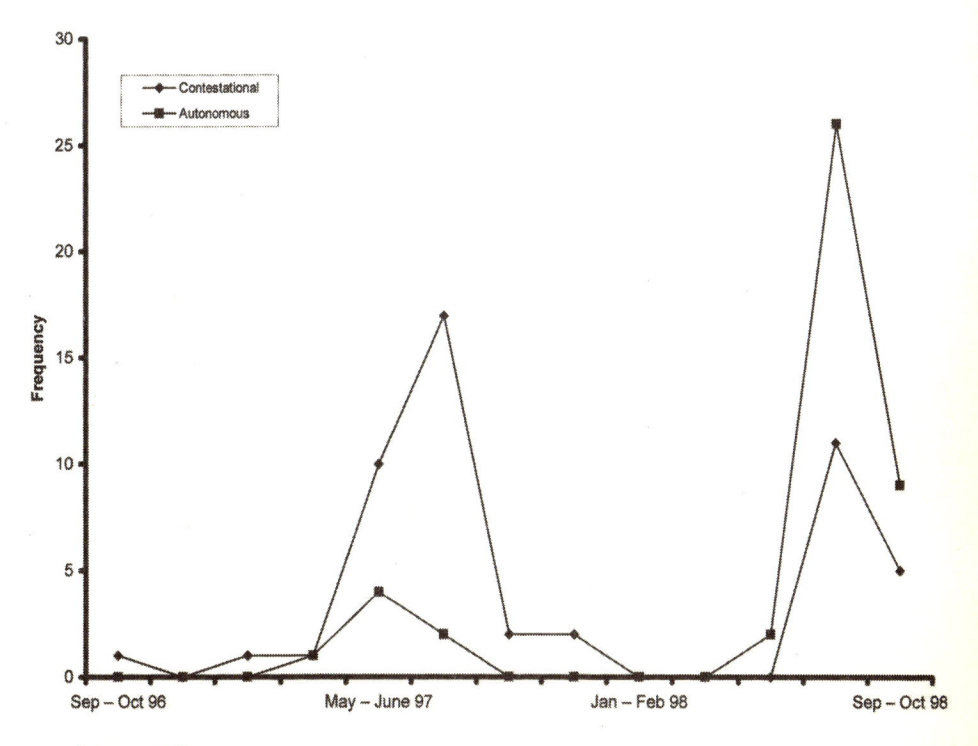

Figure 5.2
Changing balance of anti-Hanson actions, September 1996–October 1998

high point of anti-Hanson mobilisation was a coordinated series of national student 'walkouts', occurring in at least seven distinct locations on 24 July; in fourteen cities and towns around Australia on 28 August; and in a further nine locations on 30 September. These actions involved not only truancy or excused absence from school but a diverse range of marches, rallies, street theatre, and, in one case, the occupation of Prime Minister Howard's Sydney office. They sometimes led to arrests. They challenged both the adult depiction of youth as an 'innocent', apolitical time, and the direct authority of educational institutions, politicians, and sometimes parents. As a result, this cluster of actions can clearly be understood as a manifestation of 'disruptive' rather than 'sanctioned' political behaviour.[58]

Indeed, the mobilisation of so many young Australians and their willingness to flout both pedagogical and governmental authority was profoundly shocking to many. This was especially so because many walkouts divided educational authorities, and because some elite private schools were keen to support the actions. Like the mobilisation of high-school students against the Vietnam War, these actions therefore gained substantial publicity and waves of subsequent analysis and commentary. Despite sometimes hysterical criticisms, much of the news commentary was positive. Students were sometimes described as 'the conscience of the nation' or as a source of inspiration. They were supported by the Deputy Lord Mayor of Sydney, and, overall, compliments were estimated to outweigh criticisms of student action. In this way, *autonomous, disruptive* gatherings became the dominant form of collective action during the second wave of anti-Hanson contentious gatherings between 25 June 1998 and 30 August 1998. One enthusiastic student, 14-year-old Reuben Endean, explained why:

> We're doing it this way because we can't telephone or write a letter to John Howard saying he's being a racist. No one's going to hear that. And throwing a tomato at Pauline Hanson isn't going to do much either. But marching on the streets and chanting 'Hanson, Howard, racist cowards' got lots of people to look at us and hear our opinions.[59]

Table 4
The character of Anti-Hanson actions, 20 June to 30 August, 1998

Interactivity	Normativity	Frequency
Contestational	Sanctioned	6
Contestational	Disruptive	5
Autonomous	Sanctioned	3
Autonomous	Disruptive	25

In a remarkable example of reflexivity, anti-Hanson protesters adopted those forms of political performance most likely to achieve a positive representation in the media. In place of disruptive, sometimes violent actions that could be exploited by the One Nation Party, disruptive but celebratory actions emerged that did not interfere with One Nation's rights of 'free speech'. Indeed, the obsession with free speech on the part of One Nation and the mainstream media now became the object of parody and ironic inversion.

In 1998 the academic and performer Simon Hunt created the character of 'Pauline Pantsdown' as an apparition in drag. Hunt compiled a song from the cut-up and reassembled segments of Hanson's earlier speeches, set it to a dance beat, and released it as a single. The Pantsdown tune, 'I'm a Backdoor Man', offered a new kind of notable Hansonite speech, if still in her distinctive, flat delivery: 'I'm a backdoor man. I'm a homosexual ... I'm a backdoor man for the Ku Klux Klan, with very horrendous plans'. When the track was repeatedly broadcast on the ABC youth network, Triple J, Hanson took legal action. This time it was One Nation that was attempting to suppress the 'free speech' of others. Her position as the embattled outsider was now completely reversed, as a team of lawyers successfully argued for the imposition of an injunction in the Queensland Supreme Court.

By late 1998, Pantsdown had reappeared with another song, 'I Don't Like It'. It used the same cut-and-paste techniques, and this time included a film clip that showcased Pantsdown surrounded by a troupe of journalists and Asian dancers. It became a genuine popular success, and rose to number 13 on the ARIA music charts.

As the 1998 federal election was called, Hunt even adopted the name 'Pauline Pantsdown' by deed poll, and promptly stood as a candidate in the NSW Senate. Although she received less than 3000 votes, her mocking presence ironically restaged the earlier, contestational gatherings that had so controversially opposed Hanson and One Nation. On 24 September, Pantsdown and Hanson met each other at the Mortdale Bowling Club in Sydney. Rather than an intimidating mob tyrannising a lone battler, two cosmetically showered, red-headed media performers faced each other in debate. According to Hunt, 'she asked me to provide an example of a racist comment she had made. I proceeded to read over a page of them to her. She quickly scurried past without a word and the best that [One Nation official David] Oldfield could do was comment on my make-up'.

Camera crews captured the exchange for television, and respected journalist David Marr would later argue that the Pantsdown performance did 'real harm' to Hanson's cause. Clearly, the opponents of Hansonism were also learning their own lessons about the utility and nature of the political gimmick. Older performances were being reviewed. New interventions that focused more sharply on the mediating role of the press were emerging alongside them. The form of the political gimmick was changing again.[60]

EXTENDING THE POLITICAL GIMMICK

How do we make sense of the complex, shifting campaign that developed around Hanson and her use of the media? How important were its improvisations and performances? How useful its lessons for future politics? Clearly, it would be a mistake to overstate its epoch-defining qualities or its technologically determined characteristics. A new, Internet-based world of protest is not inevitable. As long ago as 1971, Australian activists were foretelling a technologically inspired transformation of political life. In terms strongly reminiscent of more contemporary discussions of the Internet, Albie Thoms then argued that the newly developed tools of 'portable video' offered nascent means of democratic advance and conversation:

> portable video opens up new areas, provides the possibilities of recording aspects of daily existence that often escape scrutiny. Feedback potential is infinite, with instant replay bringing time-past and time-present into a common time scale ... The one-way television at present on our screens can be replaced by dialogue, in which one person's tape can be followed by another's, in which a video letter can be erased and the reply sent back on the same tape ... [61]

This is a long way from the world of 'Blockbuster' megastores and 'Australia's Funniest Home Videos'. As Craig Calhoun has recently argued, it would constitute a similar error to equate the potential of the Internet for the revivification of democratic life with its likely political impact. Those already powerful are likely to shape the direction of the Internet's development and (at least partly) to capture its potential for change. Already, corporate advertising and mass entertainment dominate more classically political uses. Earlier claims that a new world of 'cyberdemocracy' beckons, in which the Internet becomes the means for the constitution of more 'fluid identities', for new forms of 'decentralised dialogue', and for the diminution of prevailing hierarchies of class, race and gender are all being hastily reviewed.[62]

'Old' public space is likely to coexist alongside 'cyberspace'; 'old' media alongside 'new' media; 'old' reality alongside 'virtual' reality; 'old' forms of the social movement activity alongside the new.[63] In this context, the new technologies will not create an autonomous arena for 'cyberdemocracy' (or cybertyranny, for that matter), but tools for an ongoing cyberbattle that connects with other forms of political contention. This is certainly the experience of political activists who have used the new technologies adroitly in Mexico, the United States and Japan. It reflects, too, Scott Balson's insistence that the Internet is a political tool used in opposition to the mainstream media, not as an alternative to it.[64]

But how, exactly, will contention change? How will the 'political gimmick' of the 1960s develop in the new century? The improvisations thrown up by the battle over Hansonism suggest what has been called a growing 'mediatisation' of politics, a term indicating a growing sensitivity to and engagement with the media's representation of public claim-making.[65] The quest to simply construct a public stage so as to perform demands is now being supplemented by attempts to influence the nature and form of media coverage received. It is as if the 'staging' explored in Chapter 2 is now being accompanied by the 'theorisation' discussed in Chapter 4 — as if the battle to construct the event in the public sphere is happening alongside the performance of the event in public space, with each impacting on the other. This presages a more reflexive politics, in which the mediating role of the press and television become the object of increasing political intervention. The range of the political gimmick is being extended and deepened.

As the demonstrations against the Murdoch press in 1975 showed, none of these issues are particularly new. However, as demonstrations succeeding the 'Hanson phenomenon' have also shown, the 'dilemmas of the activist' are likely to be tackled in increasingly novel, direct and effective ways.

When the so-called S11 protesters took on the World Economic Forum (WEF) in Melbourne in September 2000, they attempted to publicly raise a range of familiar issues: the power of multinational corporations; the need to regulate international capital flows; the rights of workers in the 'third world'; and so on. Similarly, many of their political techniques were long familiar: a contestational gathering at the Crown Casino where the Forum was held; a series of public meetings and action conferences; an effort to foster a range of decentralised, self-directed activities. This was a 'translated' action, like the 'Freedom Ride' explored in Chapter 1. Australian protests were directly inspired by actions that had targeted the meeting of the World Trade Organisation in Seattle in 1999. As the official S11 website put it: 'Seattle + Washington = Melbourne'.

Alongside these familiar processes, however, were a series of more innovative actions. While the press and the Victorian State Government attempted to portray the organisers of S11 as violent, un-Australian and threatening, members of the S11 Alliance were quickly prepared to meet and repudiate their charges. When they were interviewed by the mass media, they insisted on their non-violent orientation. Angered at misrepresentation by specific newspapers, they wrote letters outlining their peaceful, if militant aims. The S11 website carefully articulated the meaning and importance of non-violent direct action. A special electronic *indyBulletin* that covered S11 issues was produced by the Melbourne indymedia group. It emphasised that Melbourne protesters, like those in Seattle that inspired them, were non-violent in orientation. It emphasised the rights of protesters and urged preparation for arrest.[66]

Not only did supporters of the S11 action manage to use the alternative media to publicise an independent interpretation of the protests, they were also able to use the Web to gain advance publicity, even notoriety, both in Australia and overseas. In late June 2000, a still unknown group hacked into the official Nike website, and browsers were automatically redirected to the S11 Alliance site. Over the next nineteen hours, www.s11.org received almost 900 000 hits. The international and national media were astounded, fascinated. Both brief reports and sustained analyses followed. Less adventurously, but in a similar vein, 'cyberwarriors' supporting S11 set up a site using the name 'Melbourne Festival' as well as sites that aimed to attract those mistyping 'Olympics' — olympisc.com or searching for the 'Melbourne Trading Post' — melbournetradingpost.com over the following months. In all of these cases, surprised browsers were faced with announcements on the protest action, analysis, and links to further information. Both electronic browsers and newspaper readers soon learnt more about the anti-WEF actions.[67]

But perhaps the most complicated and abundant source of electronic and mainstream publicity for S11 derived from a quite remarkable dispute over an official 'protest anthem'. In late August 2000 it was announced that John Farnham's hit from the 1980s, 'You're the Voice', had been chosen as the official anthem of S11. A picture of Farnham and link to a recording of the song was posted at www.s11.org. The public attention was massive. Legal action was threatened unless the link was removed. S11 refused. Farnham's conservative manager, Glenn Wheatley, fretted over the impact on his client's reputation. Complaints from sincere fans flooded an affiliated website, while protesters defended the song as 'the people's anthem'. When Farnham's distaste for the protest became obvious, fellow rock veteran Ross Wilson offered his own song, 'No Soul', as an alternative.

The motives of S11 activists are open to question on this matter. Publicly, their commitment to the 'You're the Voice' was unwavering and seemingly ingenuous. Officially, the enormous media coverage that the issue aroused was only 'inadvertently' achieved. Perhaps this was the case. However, on 11 September itself the song was performed by many protesters with a kind of ironic glee and a knowing nod. The ruling tastes among most young participants were closer to European techno than to aged Australian rock. The entire incident may have been an elaborate 'publicity trap' — an engineered issue that was designed to provoke outrage, conflict, and the 'investigative' interest of commercial journalists.

Whatever the motives of protesters, the advance publicity for the 11 September demonstration became an avalanche. Net surfers barrelled to the S11 site. It became the 400th most popular website in the world over the first two weeks of September. As events unfolded on Melbourne's streets, they were eagerly observed around the globe. Demonstrators shouted 'The whole world is watching' with only faint hyperbole.[68]

And as this protest unfolded on the streets of Melbourne, 11–13 September, a battle over the precise meaning and nature of the protest event *also* continued apace. While the mainstream media and political leaders claimed that protesters had been violent and disruptive, adherents of S11 made and documented their own counter-charges. Legal observers were present throughout the three days, and dozens of protesters carried video and photographic equipment to capture evidence of police aggression. Video footage was distributed to mainstream television stations, and subsequently proffered as evidence of police harassment. When a police car ran over a protester on 13 September, a video camera and a photographer from the *Australian* newspaper captured the incident on film. When the commercial media alleged protester violence on 12 September, the indymedia site provided a different account — of 'creative and non-confrontational' actions overlooked; of a successful blockade of the Forum; and of police baton charges and provocation. Demonstrators themselves told their own stories: 'The only thing that I've seen that was violent today has been instigated by police'.

In the aftermath of the protest event, the indymedia site provided evidence of what appeared to be deliberate police attacks, and exerted strong pressure on Victorian Premier Steve Bracks to adopt a less strident advocacy of police actions. Video footage taken by roving camcordistas was also edited into a film — *Melbourne Rising* — and subsequently made available for sale. By 15 September, State Ombudsman Barry Perry had launched a major investigation into claims against police by protesters. The 'truth' of the event was subtly shifting. The notion that 'disruptive' protesters had behaved violently was becoming increasingly doubtful. The issue of 'globalisation' was being debated by a range of previously silent political actors. Suddenly the dilemmas of the demonstrator seemed less constant and oppressive.[69]

Who knows how the S11 protest will eventually be understood? Whether it is the protesters or the police who will be regarded as 'really' violent and provocative? Whether the claims of camera-wielding activists or uniformed officers will finally be believed? Whatever the eventual public consensus, it seems obvious that the 'dilemmas of the activist' are now weighing less heavily on well-organised and improvisational political demonstrators. Of course, routine and sanctioned forms of political claim-making cannot expect the slavish following of reporters. Equally, those who take up disruptive behaviour will continue to be attacked by the state, excoriated by media commentators, and pilloried on talkback radio. However, for those protesters intent on challenging and theatrical sorts of political performance, the resigned acceptance of negative media reception no longer appears as the only option.

In place of either wearied acceptance of media distortion or of intimidated political silence now looms a third possibility — 'mediatised politics', that is, politics in which the media's reporting practices become the object of direct struggle and intervention by protesters. This is a politics that focuses on the process of media framing, that attempts to intervene in that process, and that aims thereby to shape the public 'construction' of collective action. It represents a greater reflexivity on the part of political activists, an ability to complement 'public' claim-making with 'media-based' interactions, and a willingness to improvise in the cause of positive publicity. It is equally evident in the recent campaign around Pauline Hanson and the recent protests against the World Economic Forum. It seems a joint, groping creation of both the contemporary 'Right' and the contemporary 'Left'.

The politics of mediatisation represents an extension of the political gimmick, a widening of the interests of political activists. It does not promise political success, any more than the older forms of 'staging' or 'translation' guaranteed incipient triumph. It does, however, suggest a greater breadth and range of committed collective action. Amid political setback and triumph, across a range of venerable and newly minted movements, the ongoing, fascinating interaction between collective action and the media continues.

CONCLUSION

The political gimmick is not usually seen as worthy of detailed historical examination. The political performances and publicity stunts that have been analysed in this book are typically understood as too ephemeral, narrow and slight in their impacts to require serious attention. As individual events, they do not always involve the heroism and sacrifice that are associated with 'people's history'. As contributors to change, they do not inevitably result in the triumph of the social movement.

This doubtful status extends to the very definitional heart of the political gimmick. As a concept, it seems at first vague, slippery, muddy. It does not specify a particular behaviour or individual political strategy, such as 'revolution' or 'reform'. It is not associated with a single political cause, but cuts across a range of movements. It is not frozen in time, but historically supple. Indeed, thought of as an era of political change, the political gimmick involves a relation (between political actors and the contemporary media); an aim (publicity); a method (theatrical political performance); a dynamic (of constant invention to attain newsworthiness); and a dilemma (of routine performance and marginalisation or disruptive performance and depiction as unworthy).

Nevertheless, if the political gimmick is slippery, fuzzy and not always triumphant, I hope that I have also shown it to be historically coherent, intriguing and politically powerful. Since its revival in the 1960s, the political gimmick has had an incalculable impact on social movements, social change, and political culture. Through the self-production of publicity, a range of political actors have been able to stage their demands for a wide audience of fellow citizens. A wider range of political performances have been improvised. Public life has been invigorated. The political hierarchies of 'the Left' have been challenged, and new theories of the social structure and political transformation developed. While the contribution of the 'political gimmick' to these changes has seldom been acknowledged, the historical study pursued in this book allows us to venture an alternative interpretation — that at the root of democratic advance, social movement mobilisation and theoretical renewal lies a range of frustrating, variable, sometimes petty, publicity-seeking and theatrical political performances.

Contemporary commentators have often presented the political gimmick as intolerant and illiberal. This has sometimes been buttressed by a reference to past, apparently more peaceful and popular actions. In this way, the Vietnam Moratorium has often been contrasted favourably with recent actions against the Gulf War, Pauline Hanson's One Nation Party, and the World Economic Forum. The tendency of the political gimmick to shock and disrupt has been depicted as a quite recent change in the political culture.

From a longer historical view, however, this depiction seems narrow and tendentious. Theatrical political performances have been consistently lambasted, pilloried and criticised by political authorities. Their refusal to accept the existing boundaries between 'public' and 'private' interests has provoked outrage. Their tendency to disrupt has seemed self-defeating and anti-democratic. This challenging disruption is neither extraneous nor historically recent. It is evident in the mythical campaigns of the 1960s as it is in the assailed campaigns of the late 1990s. It does not reflect the degeneration of contemporary youth or the wilfulness of social movement activists. It lies at heart of the political gimmick and of its ability to generate publicity, debate and political change. Without the shock (and indeed the hysterical critique) gained by theatrical political performance, it would lose its ability to generate publicity and to stimulate the more measured and moderate political debate that leads to policy change.

Nonetheless, if the production of shock has remained at the centre of the political gimmick, a reflexivity, invention and self-consciousness about its deployment has also resulted in its ongoing development. Precisely because the political gimmick involves a relationship between activists and the media, political actors have continually reworked, refined and extended the range and the ambit of theatrical performance. In the pursuit of publicity, experiment and popular improvisation have both been evident. Since the observation and translation of theatrical political performance in the 1960s, Australian activists have introduced new performances, faced deadlock and decline, improvised contestation and disruption for publicity, applied contestation to 'movement space', developed theoretical propositions to explain the new moment, faced incorporation and retreat, and extended the range of performances to contest the media and to challenge its interpretive hegemony. They have shown sensitivity and intelligence. They have begun not only to stage events for the attention of the media but, in the most recent period, to act on and to attempt to influence the actions of the media themselves.

It seems doubtful that this process will reach its limit soon. Indeed, if the chapter on theory showed that the construction of 'the event' can be as politically important as its staging, then the lessons of the last chapter are that this construction is increasingly happening alongside the original performance. The cyberbattle is increasingly likely to supplement the political gimmick, the media intervention to complement the theatrical intervention. If this signals the continuing vitality and increasing complexity of popular political traditions, it also suggests an enlarged and politicised intellectual agenda.

In the 'mediatised' contemporary environment, the sustained analysis of the 'meaning', construction and staging of political events is likely to be a promising intellectual quest. But this theorisation and close study is unlikely to be politically innocent (if indeed it ever was). Tracing through and analysing particular combinations of collective action, media reporting and cultural production will not only extend our knowledge of contemporary political events but will influence and inflect the meaning of those events themselves. By taking up particular events, it will help to make them prominent and meaningful; by ignoring others, it will contribute to their marginalisation and historical irrelevance.

This book has itself been a self-conscious explication of this principle. It has attempted to rescue and rediscover a range of overlooked and sometimes long-forgotten collective acts. It has argued for their historical significance, contemporary resonance, and sometimes prophetic quality. It has aimed not only to install a new concept — 'the political gimmick', but to argue for its ongoing relevance to the quest for political change. In that sense, its aims have been both ambitious and humble. Ambitious, because it hopes to contribute to the re-emergence of a politicised theoretical practice that focuses on ongoing collective action events. Humble, because it hopes to be exceeded by new events which make its conceptual schemata redundant and fresh interpretations necessary.

ENDNOTES

INTRODUCTION

1. This account is drawn from 'Women Called and Kisch Jumped', *Telegraph*, 14 November 1934, p. 7; 'Kisch Jumps From Ship', *Workers' Weekly*, 16 November 1934, p. 1; 'A Flying Leap Over the Rail', *Labor Daily*, 14 November 1934, p. 5; 'Herr Kisch', *Sydney Morning Herald* (henceforth *SMH*), 14 November 1934, p. 13; 'Kisch Leaps Ashore from Liner', *Herald* (Melbourne), 14 November 1934, p. 1.
2. For synthetic accounts of Kisch's trip and political impact see: J Smith, *On the Pacific Front: The Adventures of Egon Kisch in Australia*, Australian Book Services Ltd, Sydney, 1936; C Rasmussen, *The Lesser Evil? Opposition to War and Fascism in Australia, 1920–1941*, History Dept, University of Melbourne, 1992; K Slater, 'Egon Kisch: a biographical outline', *Labour History*, 36, May 1979, pp. 94–103; D Rose, 'The Movement Against War and Fascism', *Labour History*, 38, May 1980, pp. 76–90; L Fox, 'The Movement Against War and Fascism: A View from Inside', *Labour History*, 39, November 1980, pp. 78–82.
3. Kisch's sense of the melodramatic is noted in 'Personal Items', *Bulletin*, 21 November 1934, p. 14; his place in a comedy-drama is remembered fondly in AF Howells, *Against the Stream: The Memoirs of a Philosophical Anarchist, 1927–1939*, Hyland House, Melbourne, 1983, p. 98; he is compared to a stage star in 'Society', *Bulletin*, 28 November 1934, p. 10.
4. K Slessor, 'Bertha Blither's Adventures in Czecho-slovakia', *Smith's Weekly*, 1 December 1934, p. 10.
5. For the reproduction of the speech and the Melbourne meeting see J Smith, *On the Pacific Front*, pp. 66, 37–38; Howells, *Against the Stream*, p. 106; 'Domain Meeting', *SMH*, 19 November 1934, p. 11; 'Cheering Thousands Greet Egon Kisch', *Workers' Weekly*, 23 November 1934, p. 1.
6. E Kisch, *Australian Landfall*, Australasian Book Society, Sydney, 1969, pp. 30–31.
7. J Smith, *On the Pacific Front*, pp. 161–62; for fear at Kisch's portrait see K Slater, 'Egon Kisch', p. 97.

8   This account is drawn from 'Youths Burn National Service Papers', *Daily Telegraph*, 3 February 1966; '3 Burn Draft Cards', *Australian*, 3 February 1966, p1; 'Three Burn National Service certificates' *SMH*, 3 February 1966, p. 1.
9   'Youths Burn National Service Papers', *Daily Telegraph*, 3 February 1966.
10 The resonance of self-immolation for Australian draft card burners is expressed in a political cartoon in the *SMH*, 4 February 1966, p. 2: as protesters burn their national service papers, many watch on. The caption reads: 'Some protest! They didn't pour petrol over themselves or anything!'.
11 For later draft card burnings see 'Student burned up over Army call-up', *Daily Telegraph*, 10 March 1966; 'Draft Card Burnt', *Australian*, 10 March 1966; 'Youth burns draft card', *SMH*, 10 March 1966, p. 5; 'Vietnam protest crowd cheers card-burners', *SMH*, 17 March 1966, p. 1; 'Vietnam protests in three States', *SMH*, 28 March 1966, p. 5; 'Anti-war march in Sydney', *SMH*, 8 August 1966, p. 7; 'Bid to Burn Flag Failed', *SMH*, 10 September 1966, p. 8.
12 For a critique of draft card burnings, see 'La Trobe', *National U*, 4 August 1969, p. 10. For an exploration of the multiple meanings of draft-card burning, 'How to beat the Draft', *National U*, 4 August 1969, p. 12. The quote is from 'Eureka!', Monash Resistance Pamphlet, in *Ian Turner Papers*, National Library of Australia (henceforth NLA), MS 6206, Box 41.
13 For the emphasis on social movements as worthy, unified, numerous and committed, see Charles Tilly, 'Social movements and (all sorts of) other political interactions — local, national, and international — including identities: Several divagations from a common path, beginning with British struggles over Catholic Emancipation, 1780–1829, and ending with contemporary nationalism', *Theory and Society*, 27, 4, 1998, p. 467.
14 This is recognised in relation to the US civil rights movement in D McAdam, 'The framing function of movement tactics', in D McAdam, J McCarthy and M Zald (eds), *Comparative Perspectives on Social Movements*, Cambridge University Press, 1996, p. 354. For a general analysis of social movements according to dramaturgical principles, see Robert D Benford and Scott A Hunt, 'Dramaturgy and Social Movements: The Social Construction and Communication of Power', *Sociological Inquiry*, 62, 1, 1992, pp. 36–55.
15 W Gamson, *The Strategy of Social Protest*, 2nd edn, Wadsworth Publishing, Belmont, 1990, p. 147.
16 M Lipsky, 'Protest as a Political Resource', *American Political Science Review*, 62, 40, 1968, p. 1145; Todd Gitlin, *The Whole World is Watching: Mass media in the making and unmaking of the new left*, University of California Press, Berkeley, Los Angeles and London, 1980, p. 3; R Clutterbuck, *The Media and Political Violence*, 2nd edn, Macmillan, London and Basingstoke, 1983, p. 53; S. J Ball-Rokeach and M DeFluer, 'A Dependency Model of Mass Media Effects', *Communication Research*, 3, 1, 1976, p. 17; H Molotch, 'Media and Movements', in MN Zald and JD McCarthy (eds), *The Dynamics of Social Movements*, Winthrop Publishers, Cambridge, Mass., 1979, p. 77.
17 S Hall, 'A World at One With Itself', and G Murdock, 'Political Deviance: The press coverage of militant mass demonstrations' in S Cohen and J Young (eds), *The Manufacture of News: A Reader*, Sage, Beverly Hills, 1973, pp. 89–94, 156-75; T Rochon, *Culture Moves: Ideas, Activism and Changing Values*, Princeton University Press, 1998, p. 180; Clutterbuck, *The Media and Political Violence*, p. 54; Gitlin, *The Whole World is Watching*, p. 182.
18 For a discussion of the Situationist International, see Greil Marcus, *Lipstick Traces:*

A Secret History of the Twentieth Century, Harvard University Press, Cambridge, Mass., 1989. For a history of the IWW, see the fine work of Verity Burgmann, *Revolutionary Industrial Unionism: The Industrial Workers of the World in Australia*, Cambridge University Press, 1995. For the actions of suffragettes, see the chapters 'Sex War' and 'Suffrage' in Susan Kingsley Kent, *Sex and Suffrage in Britain 1860–1914*, Routledge, London, 1990. On the theatre of American contention, see Charles Tilly, 'Repertoires of Contention in America and Britain, 1750–1830', in Mayer N Zald and John D McCarthy (eds), *The Dynamics of Social Movements: Resource Mobilization, Social Control and Tactics*, Winthrop Publishers, Cambridge, Mass., 1979, p. 129. For references to Roman non-violence, see Gene Sharp, *The Politics of Nonviolent Action*, vol. 1, Porter Sargent, Boston, 1973, pp. 75–76.

CHAPTER I TRANSLATION

1   Sidney Tarrow, *Power in Movement: Social Movements and Contentious Politics*, 2nd edn, Cambridge University Press, 1998, p. 103. For the leading account of the historical development of 'modular' collective action, see Charles Tilly, *Popular Contention in Great Britain, 1758–1834*, Harvard University Press, Cambridge, Mass., 1995. The recent critics are: Doug McAdam, '"Initiator" and "Spin-off" Movements: Diffusion Processes in Protest Cycles', in Mark Traugott (ed.), *Repertoires and Cycles of Collective Action*, Duke University Press, Durham and London, 1995, pp. 217–39; Sean Chabot, 'Transnational Diffusion and the African American Reinvention of Gandhian Repertoire', *Mobilization*, 5, 2, 2000, pp. 201–216.
2   The quote is Michael Kirby's 'A Call to Action by the President of the S.R.C.', *Honi Soit*, 5 March 1963, supplement p. 4. The impact of the restrictions and their lifting is referred to in Bob McDonald, 'Student Politics — by a participant', *Honi Soit*, 19 March 1963, p. 5; Peter Wilenski, 'Wilenski on South Africa', *Honi Soit*, 23 July 1963, p. 4.
3   On the American New Left, see Todd Gitlin, *The Sixties: Years of Hope, Days of Rage*, Bantam Books, New York, 1987. On the British New Left see Michael Kenny, *The First New Left: British Intellectuals After Stalin*, Lawrence & Wishart, London, 1995; Lin Chun, *The British New Left*, Edinburgh University Press, 1993; Paul Byrne, *The Campaign for Nuclear Disarmament*, Routledge, London, 1988.
4   Leyden's comments and search are in 'An analysis of protest movements', *Honi Soit*, 21 July 1964, p. 4. See also Bob McDonald 'Student Politics — by a participant' and Peter Wilenski, 'Wilenski on South Africa'.
5   For protest history: JP Magnus, 'Le Peuple Emu …', *Honi Soit*, 16 March 1963, p. 7; for the failure of the CND in Sydney: Dennis Strangman, 'The university Right wing — flapping weakly', *Honi Soit*, 17 March 1964, p. 5.
6   Derek Evans, 'Anti-Apartheid', *Crux*, 67, 1, 1964, p. 20; Peter D Bakalor, 'Comments on Apartheid', *Tharunka*, 14 June 1963, p. 2; 'Government Ban on Student Body', *Tharunka*, 23 April 1964, p. 1.
7   On the history of Australian comics, see J Ryan, *Panel by Panel*, Cassell, Sydney, 1979. On Australia–USA Relations, see P Bell and R Bell, *Implicated: the United States in Australia*, Oxford University Press, Melbourne, 1993. For the copying of pranks, see for example ME, 'The Case for some Awards', *Tharunka*, 19 April 1963, p. 1. For the singing of folk songs on public occasions, see 'Commem Park protest climaxes in "Wynyard Riots" 28 students arrested and police go right off',

Honi Soit, 12 May 1964, p. 1; Patrick Dawson in 'The Student Bus: SAFA Interviewed', *Outlook*, 9, 2, 1965, p. 5.

8   For a reference to the evils of racial segregation, see RJKE, 'A minor apocalypse', *Honi Soit*, 9 July 1963, p. 2. A first-person account of heroism of those integrating buses is: n.a. 'Golden Rule for Negroes', *Honi Soit*, 25 June 1963, p. 4. An example of a story lifted from the 'Forum News Service' is Herbert Krosnev, 'Change and the Negro Way down South in Dixie', *Honi Soit*, 12 May 1964, p. 4. The sit-in is recalled as an inspiration for students in Derek Evans, 'Anti-Apartheid', *Crux*, 67, 1, 1964, p. 20. The American 'freedom summer' is explored in Doug McAdam, *Freedom* Summer, New York and Oxford, 1988. Its inspiration for Australians will be explored in detail later in this chapter. A picture of the tribute 'freedom ride' from the UNSW Foundation Day procession is in *Tharunka*, 14 June 1963, p. 6.

9   On the translation of rock'n'roll, dance and subcultural groupings such as surfies, see Peter Cox and Louise Douglas, *Teen Riots to Generation X: the Australian rock audience*, Powerhouse Publishing, Sydney, 1994, pp. 6–10 and Michael Sturma, *Australian Rock'N'Roll: The First Wave*, Kangaroo Press, Sydney, 1991, p. 65. Protesting students were dubbed as 'beatniks' (in a typical 'translation') in 'Minister Refused Beds to Color Bar Pickets', *Australian*, 16 February 1965, p. 4.

10 Bob McDonald 'Student Politics — by a participant'.

11 WF Connell et al., *Australia's First: A History of the University of Sydney*, vol. 2, University of Sydney in association with Hale & Iremonger, 1995, p. 30.

12 *Honi Soit*, 28 April 1964, p. 3.

13 Victor Turner, *The Ritual Process: Structure and Anti-Structure*, Cornell University Press, Ithaca, 1977.

14 'US Civil Rights: protest from Uni Students?', *Honi Soit*, 28 April 1964, p. 1; 'Council hears Directors' report on Commem Day: "hundreds have entered the marathon march"', *Honi Soit*, 28 April 1964, p. 8.

15 'Commem Park protest climaxes in "Wynyard Riots"'.

16 A wide range of newspapers and figures are quoted on the affair in *Honi Soit*, 12 May 1964, p. 5.

17 'Commem Park protest climaxes in "Wynyard Riots"'.

18 JS Baker, 'Letter of Protest', *Honi Soit*, 9 June 1964.

19 'Voice of America?', *Honi Soit*, 9 June 1964, 'The Grand Festive' supplement, p. 1.

20 The quote is cited in a letter from Charlie Pyatt II, 'Negro Thanks on Protest', *Honi Soit*, 30 June 1964, p. 2.

21 Ibid.

22 Lynette Nightingale, '"If you're black, get back ..."', *Honi Soit*, 9 June 1964, p. 2.

23 Heather Meredith, 'Tasmanian Racial Problem: Cape Barren Island', *Honi Soit*, 23 June 1964, p. 7; 'Aborigines', *Honi Soit*, 4 August 1964, p. 1; Gillian Harrison, 'The Hypocrisy of National Aborigines Day', *Honi Soit*, 30 June 1964, p. 5.

24 Harrison, 'The Hypocrisy of National Aborigines Day', p. 5.

25 Lin Morison, review of 'The Fire Next Time', *Crux*, 67, 5, 1964, p. 17.

26 'Aboriginal protest Wed.', *Honi Soit*, 7 July 1964, p. 1.

27 'Demonstration for Aborigines', *Tharunka*, 17 July 1964, p. 9; 'March for Aboriginal Rights', *Honi Soit*, 14 July 1964, p. 1.

28 Jim Spigelman, 'Student Action for Aborigines', *Honi Soit*, 23 September 1964, p. 9.
29 For example, see Charles Perkins, *A Bastard Like Me*, Ure Smith, Sydney, 1975; Peter Read, *Charles Perkins: A Biography*, Viking, Melbourne, 1990; Ann Curthoys, 'Sex and Racism: Australia in the 1960s', in Jane Long, Jan Gothard and Helen Brash (eds), *Forging Identities: Bodies, Gender and Feminist History*, University of Western Australia Press, Perth, 1997, pp. 11–28.
30 Heather Goodall, *Invasion to Embassy: Land in Aboriginal Politics in New South Wales, 1770–1972*, Allen & Unwin, Sydney, 1996, p. 320; Ann Curthoys, 'Sex and Racism', p. 12. The prayers of Ted Noffs sent the trip on its way: Peter Read, 'Darce Cassidy's Freedom Ride', *Australian Aboriginal Studies*, 1, 1988, p. 46.
31 Jim Spigelman, 'Student Action for Aborigines', p. 9.
32 Jim Spigelman, *SAFA Talkabout*, 2, December 1964, p. 1.
33 Sam Lipski, 'The Freedom Riders: "I wish I was jet-black"', *Bulletin*, 20 February 1965, p. 21; 'SAFA Comes to NSW', *Tharunka*, 3 May 1965, p. 4.
34 The leaflet is entitled 'Our Struggle', and the passages mentioned are underlined — see a surviving copy in the folder 'Student Action for Aborigines', *Aboriginal Australian Fellowship Records, 1956–1978*, Mitchell Library, ML MSS 4057, Box 15.
35 For the emphasis on tactical rather than ethical non-violence, see an illuminating critique of spiritual non-violence by a freedom summer participant: Sally Belfrage, *Freedom Summer*, New York, 1965, p. 16.
36 Bill Ford cited in Sam Lipski, 'The Freedom Riders', p. 21.
37 Spigelman's statement is in a letter to J. Horner 24 January 1965, to be found in the folder 'Student Action for Aborigines', *Aboriginal Australian Fellowship Records, 1956–1978*, Mitchell Library, ML MSS 4057, Box 15.
38 Jim Spigelman cited in Peter Read, 'Darce Cassidy's Freedom Ride', p. 51.
39 The picket of the Walgett RSL Club is related in 'Minister Refused Beds to Color Bar Pickets', *Australian*, 16 February 1965, p. 4; the initial demonstration at Moree baths is reported in 'Students Crack Pool Color Bar at Moree', *Australian*, 18 February 1965, p. 2; publicity for reserve conditions includes: 'Reserve Disgusts Student Group', *Australian*, 20 February 1965, p. 4; publicity for segregation of retail includes 'Race Bar Students in Angry Scenes', *SMH*, 16 February 1965, p. 1; for segregation in hotels, see: 'Students Will Check on Hotel Discrimination', *SMH*, 19 February 1965, p. 1; for segregation in picture theatres, see 'Close Theatre Picketed by Touring Students', *SMH*, 25 February 1965, p. 4.
40 Heather Goodall focuses on the importance of land in *Invasion to Embassy*. She notes that civil rights is an interruption to this concern on pp. 312–13. Whites at the time who admitted the importance of 'land' include Colin Tatz, 'Some Aboriginal Thoughts', *Dissent*, 15, Spring 1965, p. 14; Ian Spalding, 'No Genteel Silence', *Crux*, 68, 3, 1965, p. 3. For a measured reassertion of the existence of some struggles for civil and political rights in Aboriginal mobilisations, see Peter Read's review of *Invasion to Embassy*, *Aboriginal Law Bulletin*, 3, 86, 1996, p. 15.
41 A copy of the handbill SAFA, 'Aborigines' is in the folder 'Student Action for Aborigines', *Aboriginal Australian Fellowship Records, 1956–1978*, Mitchell Library, ML MSS 4057, Box 15.
42 Freedom rides are compared in the radio broadcast of Darce Cassidy, reproduced in Peter Read, 'Darce Cassidy's Freedom Ride', p. 46; the towns are referred to in Sam Lipski, 'The Freedom Riders', p. 21. The student comparisons are made by the interviewer in 'The Student Bus: SAFA Interviewed', *Outlook*, 9, 2, 1965, p. 5; the white stronghold comparison is in Jim Spigelman, 'Reactions to the SAFA

Tour', *Dissent*, 14, Winter 1965, p. 48; the ubiquity of the Perkins–King comparison is noted in Sam Lipski, 'Alien Son: The Dark World of Charles Perkins', *Bulletin*, 24 September 1966, p. 28.

43 The argument that the term 'freedom ride' was mistaken is in Jim Spigelman, 'Reactions to the SAFA Tour', p. 44. Typical uses of 'color bar' are Graham Williams, 'Color Bar', *Australian*, 6 January 1965, p. 7; 'Renshaw: "No Color Bar in My Seat"', *Australian*, 17 February 1965, p. 2; 'Students Crack Color Bar at Moree', *Australian*, 18 February 1965, p. 2. The poor white and Uncle Tom references are made by the interviewer in 'The Student Bus', pp. 6–7.

44 See McAdam, 'The framing function of movement tactics', in McAdam et al., *Comparative Perspectives on Social Movements*. A typical juxtaposition of country and city is Graham Williams, 'Brown Men in a White World', *Australian*, 11 January 1965, p. 7; a critique of blindness to racial inequalities in the city is BEK, 'A Case for the Whites', *Tharunka*, 22 February 1965, p. 3.

45 'Color-Bar Crisis At Moree Today', *Australian*, 20 February 1965, p. 1; 'Race Tour Bus Driver Walks Out', *Australian*, 22 February 1965, p. 1.

46 For Perkins' assessment: Sam Lipski, 'Alien Son', p. 28. For his inspiration and the impact on Aboriginal people: Lyall Munroe cited in Peter Read, 'Darce Cassidy's Freedom Ride', p. 52; 'To Walgett', *Honi Soit*, 30 June 1965, p. 10; Ann Curthoys, 'Sex and Racism', p. 12

47 Elite and city-press support is noted in Alex Mills, 'SAFA Trip', *Honi Soit*, 31 March 1965, p. 4; Jim Spigelman, 'Reactions to the SAFA Tour', p. 44; Patrick Dawson in 'The Student Bus: SAFA Interviewed', p. 10. For SAFA as antidote to indifference see: Editorial, 'Aborigines have right to full life', *Australian*, 24 February 1965, p. 8; Ian Spalding, 'No Genteel Silence', *Crux*, 68, 3, 1965, pp. 2–3.

48 The BBC's presence is in: 'Color Ban 'for health'', *Australian*, 26 February 1965, p. 1. The editorial commentary is 'Facing up to Facts', *Australian*, 18 February 1965, p. 8. Letters are by BC Stevens and Raymond Atchison, *Australian*, 24 February 1965, p. 4. For the persistence of the production of white political dominance in Australian discourse around race, see Ghassan Hage, *White Nation*, Pluto Press, Sydney, 1998.

49 The poll data is from *Australian Public Opinion Polls*, 1787, survey 171, September–October 1964; *Australian Public Opinion Polls*, 1864, survey 176, September–December 1965. The Western Australian data from 1965 is published in Ronald Taft, 'Attitudes of Western Australians to Aborigines', in Ronald Taft, John LM Dawson and Pamela Beasley, *Attitudes and Social Conditions*, Australian National University Press, Canberra, 1970. The history of polling on these matters is explored in Murray Goot, A New Enlightenment? Polled Opinion on Aborigines Prior to the 1967 Referendum, unpublished paper, Department of Politics, Macquarie University.

50 'Renshaw: 'No Color Bar in My Seat', *Australian*, 17 February 1965, p. 2.

51 The latter sit-ins in Sydney hotels are reported in 'Sit-in Backs Drink Demand', *Sun-Herald*, 21 March 1965, p. 7; 'Women Chained in Hotel', *SMH*, 1 April 1965, p. 6; *Courier-Mail*, 1 April 1965, p. 1. The positive editorial is in *Courier-Mail*, 2 April 1965, p. 2.

52 Each of these actions was reported in the *Herald*: 'Three Held in Vietnam Demonstration', *SMH*, 4 May 1965, p. 10; 'Many Protests on Vietnam', *SMH*, 5 May 1965, p. 1; 'Four Youths Arrested in Student Stunts', *SMH*, 6 May 1965, p. 1; 'Hasluck Warning on Vietnam War', *SMH*, 26 May 1965, p. 1.

53 For reports of these actions, see: 'Students' Protest Roadblock', *SMH*, 6 August 1965, p. 4; 'Just Sitting', *SMH*, 12 May 1966, p. 4; 'City Protest', *Sun-Herald*, 11 April 1965, p. 23. The quote is from '"Strike War" Over Prices', *Sun-Herald*, 20 May 1965, p. 26.

CHAPTER 2 STAGING

1 'Paint is smeared on march leader', *SMH*, 9 June 1966, p. 5; 'Paint protest girl is fined £, gets bond', *SMH*, 10 June 1966, p. 6; 'Bombs of dye in pool as protest', *SMH*, 28 February 1970, p. 1; 'Police asked to leave', *SMH*, 5 April 1969, p. 1; John Tapp, 'Watch those women', *National U*, 23 March 1970, p. 3; Rod Noble in Don Beer (ed.), *A Serious Attempt to Change Society: The Socialist Action Movement and Student Radicalism at the University of New England, 1969–75*, Kardoorair Press, Armidale, 1998, p. 12; Ian Langman, 'Land Rights Vigil', *National U*, 12 May 1969, p. 14; 'Hippies Cooler in Hyde Park', *Sun-Herald*, 18 January 1970, p. 22.
2 The Romeril play is advertised in *Print*, 16 July 1970, *Ian Turner Papers*, NLA, MS 6206, Box 41; 'Guerilla Theatre got a "moving" welcome", *SMH*, 18 September 1968, p. 12.
3 Ian Channel, 'Soul Power and Fun Powder', *Tharunka*, 9 July 1968, p. 14. On 'living theatre' see Ian Channel, 'ALF Living Theatre is Crap', *Tharunka*, 28 November 1969, p. 10.
4 'In the Deepest Dark of Night', *Tharunka*, 9 April 1968, p. 9.
5 Julie Stephens, *Anti-Disciplinary Protest: Sixties Radicalism and Postmodernism*, Cambridge University Press, 1998.
6 Erving Goffman, *The Presentation of Self in Everyday Life*, Anchor Books, New York, 1959.
7 Nancy Fraser, 'Politics, Culture, and the Public Sphere: Toward a Postmodern Conception', in Linda Nicholson and Steven Seidman (eds), *Social Postmodernism: Beyond Identity Politics*, Cambridge University Press, 1995, p. 287.
8 David I Kertzer, *Ritual, Politics and Power*, Yale University Press, New Haven and London, 1988; Don Handelman, *Models and Mirrors: Toward an Anthropology of Public Events*, Cambridge University Press, 1990; Eric W Rothenbuhler, 'The Liminal Fight: Mass strikes as ritual and interpretation', in Jeffrey C Alexander (ed.), *Durkheimian Sociology: Cultural Studies*, Cambridge University Press, 1988, pp. 66–89.
9 Charles Tilly, *Popular Contention in Great Britain, 1758–1834*, Harvard University Press, Cambridge, Mass., 1995, pp. 46–47.
10 Cumulatively, over the whole of 1965, political actors performed staging as a proportion of non-industrial contention 67.9 per cent of the time; by 1971 they performed staging as a proportion of non-industrial contention 90.1 per cent of the time. This is a measure of staging as a proportion of non-industrial contention. Clearly, the percentages do not express the probability of performing staging over representation. They are not perfectly substitutable actions.
11 Sidney Tarrow, *Democracy and Disorder: Protest and Politics in Italy 1965–1975*, Clarendon Press, Oxford, 1989. The citation is from p. 8.
12 Daniel Dayan and Elihu Katz, *Media Events: The Live Broadcasting of History*, Harvard University Press, Cambridge, Mass. and London, 1992, pp. 118, 210.
13 These principles are variously enunciated in Joshua Meyrowitz, *No Sense of Place*, Oxford University Press, New York, 1985, p. 90; M Lipsky, 'Protest as a Political Resource', *American Political Science Review*, 62, 4, 1968, p. 1151; S. Iyengar

and D Kinder, *News That Matters*, University of Chicago Press, 1987, p. 33; Zald and McCarthy, 'Introduction', in *The Dynamics of Social Movements*, p. 3; Bert Klandermans, 'The Formation and Mobilization of Consensus', in Bert Klandermans, Hanspeter Kriesi and Sidney Tarrow (eds), *From Structure to Action*, JAI Press, Greenwich, Connecticut, 1988, p. 174; S Barkan, 'Strategic, Tactical and Organizational Dilemmas of the Protest Movement Against Nuclear Power', *Social Problems*, 27, 1, 1979, p. 33; D Snyder and W Kelly, 'Conflict Intensity, Media Sensitivity and the Validity of Newspaper Data', *American Sociological Review*, 42, February 1977, p. 110; Stuart Hall, 'A World At One With Itself', in S Cohen and J Young (eds), *The Manufacture of News*, Sage, Beverly Hills, 1973, p. 86; TR Rochon, *Culture Moves: Ideas, Activism, and Changing Values*, Princeton University Press, 1998, p. 180; William Gamson and D. Meyer, 'Framing Political Opportunity', in McAdam et al., *Comparative Perspectives on Social Movements*, p. 288; James D Halloran, Philip Elliot and Graham Murdock, *Demonstrations and Communications: A Case Study*, Penguin Books, London, Baltimore and Melbourne, 1970, pp. 80–81.

14 Dorothy Dalton cited in Greg Langley, *A Decade of Dissent: Vietnam and Conflict on the Australian Homefront*, Allen & Unwin, Sydney, 1992, p. 21
15 'Parade Near Court', *SMH*, 26 November 1965, p. 4.
16 'Protests to Dr Gough', *SMH*, 9 November 1965, p. 1; 'Move to include migrant youths in Army call-up', *SMH*, 12 March 1966, p. 1; '100 Police in Street Protest Struggle', *SMH*, 25 March 1966, p. 1; 'Hasluck Warning on Vietnam War', *SMH*, 26 May 1965, pp. 1, 5; 'Silent 300 Protest on Vietnam', *SMH*, 21 May 1965, p. 1.
17 'Race Bar Students in Angry Scenes', *SMH*, 16 February 1965, p. 1; 'Students in Wild Moree Scenes', *Sun-Herald*, 21 February 1965, pp. 2, 28. The positive appraisal is from the editorial 'Students and the Aborigines', *SMH*, 23 February 1965, p. 2.
18 Peter Edwards, *A Nation at War: Australian Politics, Society and Diplomacy during the Vietnam War, 1965–1975*, Allen & Unwin, Sydney, 1997, pp. 67–70; Ann Mari Jordens, 'Conscription and Dissent: The genesis of anti-war protest', in Gregory Pemberton (ed.), *Vietnam Remembered*, Weldon, Sydney and London, 1990, p. 75.
19 Bob Gould in Langley, *A Decade of Dissent*, p. 40; '60 Arrested as Demonstrators and Police Clash in Street', *SMH*, 23 October 1965, p. 1.
20 'Sit-down at Moomba, 40 on road', *SMH*, 15 March 1966, p. 8; 'Demonstrators mob Holt: besiege car at noisy meeting', *SMH*, 29 March 1966, p. 1; 'Man protests on rooftop', *SMH*, 16 April 1966, p. 1; 'Bid to Burn Flag Failed', *SMH*, 10 September 1966, p. 8; 'Students Burn Flag Outside P.M.'s Residence', *SMH*, 6 November 1966, p. 1
21 'The Johnsons Go Visiting', *SMH*, 21 November 1966, p. 1; 'Wild Greeting for Johnson in Melbourne', *SMH*, 22 November 1966, pp. 1, 8; 'Violent Brawl involves 3,000', *SMH*, 22 November 1966, p. 6; 'Vietnam Hunger Strikers Arrested', *SMH*, 22 November 1966, p. 12; 'Gaiety and Drama in a Visit to Remember', *Sun-Herald*, 23 November 1966, pp. 2–3; 'Police Charge 13: wild scenes', *Sun-Herald*, 23 November 1966, p. 3. For the short story referred to, see Frank Moorhouse, *The Americans, Baby*, Sydney 1996 (first published in 1972), especially pp. 122–23.
22 The citation is from: Harry Robinson, 'Surfers' encounter', *SMH*, 23 November 1966, p. 14. The *Herald*'s assessment is in: 'Limits of Protest', *SMH*, 29

November 1966, p. 2. Complaints by Victorian protesters are expressed in: *Facts About the ANTI LBJ Demonstration*, Monash University, 1966. An inquiry is flagged in 'State Inquiry into Rowdy Demonstrations', *SMH*, 25 November 1966, p. 9.

23 On the difficulties of 'performing sincerity' for media consumers, see Paddy Scannell, *Radio, Television and Modern Life: A Phenomenological Approach*, Blackwell, Oxford and Cambridge, Mass., 1996, p. 58.

24 Edwards, *A Nation at War*, pp. 129, 167–68; Peter McIntyre, 'Demonstrations and Police', *National U*, 31 March 1967, p. 2; Brian Laver, 'Behind Student Action', *Australian Left Review*, 3, June–July 1968, pp. 22–25; 'Police Repression', *National U*, 8 July 1968, p. 3; 'Comment', *Australian Left Review*, 4, August–September 1968, p. 7.

25 Askin's view is analysed in Max Teichmann, 'After Vietnam — What?', *Australian Left Review*, 5, October–November 1968, p. 14. Whitlam emphasised that protest should not become 'the private luxury of irresponsibles': 'Stopping war is main Vietnam goal', *SMH*, 10 June 1967, p. 4. The liberal critique of students as uninterested in debate: 'The Demonstrators', *SMH*, 26 November 1966, p. 2; as betrayers of the university: 'The Wrong Place', *SMH*, 2 August 1967, p. 2; as exceeding legitimate criticism: 'Beyond the Fringe', *SMH*, 19 August 1967, p. 2.

26 Many of these criticisms redoubled into 1968: Edwina Bremer and Michael Powell, 'The Canberra Demonstration — a little ludicrous', *Tharunka*, 4 June 1968, p. 2; Mr J Wilson Hogg, Headmaster of Trinity Grammar, cited in 'A Caution on some points of Protest', *SMH*, 5 December 1968, p. 7; Ann Mari Jordens, 'Conscription and Dissent', p. 78; Warren Osmond, 'Australia Too?', *National U*, 24 June 1968, p. 2; Christopher Opie, 'Crucifixion in Retrospect', *National U*, 8 July 1968, p. 2. The negative framing of student protesters in the late 1960s is surveyed in: Rob Watts, '"Revolting, lewd, disgusting and indecent": Australian press representations of student protesters, 1965–1969', in Judith Besant and Richard Hill (eds), *Youth, Crime and Media: Media Representations of and Reaction to Young People in Relation to Law and Order*, National Clearinghouse for Youth Studies, Hobart, 1997, pp. 191–200.

27 Peter Middleton, 'Demonstration', *Tharunka*, 16 July 1968, p. 12; T. Drake-Brockman, 'Student Political Action — An Assessment of the Idea', *Tharunka*, 26 March 1968, p. 5; Edwina Bremer, 'On Demonstrations', *Tharunka*, 9 July 1968, p. 5; Nick Spartalis, 'An Alternative to Demonstrations', *Tharunka*, 16 July 1968, p. 13.

28 Pat Ryan, 'Vietnam Vigil', *Tharunka*, 11 April 1967, p. 8; Christopher A Rootes, 'Queensland Civil Liberties Support Overstated', *National U*, 22 July 1968, p. 4; 'Tame Demo in Melb.', *National U*, 24 March 1969, p. 3; Peter McIntyre, 'Demonstrations and Police', *National U*, 31 March 1967, p. 2; Humphrey McQueen, 'A Single Spark', *Arena*, 16, 1968, p. 56.

29 MC, 'Match for Stars and Stripes?', *Arena*, 14, 1967, p. 15; Goffman, *The Presentation of Self in Everyday Life*, p. 86.

30 Bill Bottomley, 'The Demo Bandwaggon', *Tharunka*, 22 April 1969, p. 5.

31 For example, Michael Hamel-Green, 'Vietnam — Beyond Pity', *Australian Left Review*, 24, April–May 1970, p. 55. The ability of the election defeat to fragment the peace movement is dexterously surveyed in John Murphy, *Harvest of Fear: A History of Australia's Vietnam War*, Allen & Unwin, Sydney, 1993, p. 211.

32 The critique of moderation is made by Humphrey McQueen, 'A Single Spark', p. 52. The power of threats of violence is noted by Rowan Cahill cited in 'Student

Activism', *Australian Left Review*, 4, August–September 1968, p. 33. A typical critique of the ALP is MC, 'Match for the Stars and Stripes?', p. 15, and this is combined with a plea for the extension of past, successful militant actions on p. 17. Michael Hamel-Green's praise for direct action is in his 'Vietnam: Beyond Pity', p. 57.

33 The survey of the European scene is: 'Europe's revolting students', *National U*, 10 June 1968, p. 12. The need to learn from American experience is noted by Helen Palmer, 'Beyond Debate?', *Outlook*, 2, April 1968, p. 24. Brian Aarons notes the motivating power of the Vietnamese people in the joint interview 'Student Action', *Australian Left Review*, 4, August–September 1968, pp. 35–36. Michael Hamel-Green relates his study in 'Vietnam — Beyond Pity', p. 56. The historian Bob Gollan informs readers of the actions of British students in 'America's No. 1 Ally', *Outlook*, 2, April 1968, p. 4.

34 The action is reported in 'Students defy ban on NLF Aid', *SMH*, 3 October 1967, p. 12. Langer expresses his motivations in a citation from Louis Matheson, *Still Learning*, Macmillan, Melbourne, 1980, p. 29. Thanks to Megan Jones for assistance on this point.

35 For 'tremendous publicity', see: 'Student Aid for NLF', *Tribune*, 2 August 1967, p. 12. For the *Arena* assessment: Doug White, 'Fifty Years On', *Arena*, 15, 1968, p. 5.

36 Editors, 'A Single Spark', *Arena*, no. 16, 1968, p. 50.

37 'Anti-Vietnam demonstrators protest over call-up', *SMH*, 8 February 1968, p. 5.

38 'Wild Gorton Meeting: 12 arrested', *SMH*, 14 February 1968, p. 1.

39 '69 Arrests at Protest Sit-down', *SMH*, 20 May, 1968, p. 1. The background is sketched in Hamel-Green, 'Vietnam: Beyond Pity', p. 56. The actions are praised in the editorial, *SMH*, 21 May 1968, p. 2.

40 For the Holsworthy Protest, see: 'Service protest — 22 held', *Sun-Herald*, 21 April 1968, p. 18 and 'O'Donnell Protest Mounts', *National U*, 22 April 1968, p. 1. On the 4 July action see: 'Mounted charge ends mass student riot', *SMH*, 5 July 1968, p. 1. The Queensland action is reported in: 'Noose Held Over Envoy', *SMH*, 20 July 1968, p. 11.

41 'Students take police hostage, win a point', *SMH*, 3 August 1968, p. 1.

42 Donatella della Porta, *Social Movements, Political Violence and the State: A Comparative Analysis of Italy and Germany*, Cambridge University Press, 1995; Donatella della Porta and Herbert Reiter (eds), *Policing Protest: The Control of Mass Demonstrations in Western Democracies*, University of Minnesota Press, Minneapolis and London, 1998.

43 Both Melbourne and Brisbane actions are reported in: 'Police Film War Protest', *SMH*, 26 November 1968, p. 5.

44 The notion of the 'revolutionary thrust' is developed by Humphrey McQueen in 'A Single Spark', *Arena*, 16, 1968, p. 51. Goffman's views on dramatic dominance are in *The Presentation of Self in Everyday Life*, pp. 101–102.

45 The notion of contest as a scripted performance is developed in Dayan and Katz, *Media Events*, p. 26.

46 Kertzer, *Ritual, Politics and Power*, pp. 119–20.

47 Don Mitchell analyses the conflict between liberalism and political contest in American public space in his excellent article 'Political Violence, Order, and the Legal Construction of Public Space: Power and the Public Forum Doctrine', *Urban Geography*, 17, 2, 1996, pp. 152–78.

48 The reliance of the liberal model of the public sphere on self-evident boundaries

between publicity and privacy is critically analysed in Nancy Fraser, 'Sex, Lies and the Public Sphere: Reflections on the Confirmation of Clarence Thomas', in Nancy Fraser (ed.), *Justus Interruptus: Critical Reflections on the 'Postsocialist' Condition*, Routledge, New York and London, 1997, p. 101.

49 The United Front, 'Discipline in a University Community', Leaflet authorised by Graham Ihlein, *Ian Turner Papers*, NLA MS 6206, Box 41, p. 1.

50 Ian Morrison, 'Film', *Outlook*, 3, June 1968, pp. 20–23.

51 Warren Osmond, 'Australia Too?', *National U*, 24 June 1968, p. 2. Another typical use of the concept of 'repressive tolerance' is in Craig Johnston, 'The false premise of protest politics', *Tharunka*, 3 August 1971, p. 4.

52 Charles Tilly, 'Parliamentarization of Popular Contention in Great Britain, 1758–1834', in his *Roads From Past to Future*, Rowman & Littlefield, Lanham and Oxford, 1997, pp. 217–44.

53 Examples abound of all of these forms of contest. For Parliament Houses, see: '400 striking nurses in strike on parliament', *SMH*, 20 May 1970, p. 5. On office blocks: 'Railmen's signs for higher pay', *SMH*, 10 June 1970, p. 9; 'Uni Sit-In', *SMH*, 21 July 1970, p. 5. On post offices: 'Protesters Close Port Kembla P.O.', *SMH*, 18 January 1970, p. 9; 'Vietnam Protesters Rampage', *SMH*, 25 July 1970, p. 1. On offices: 'Students invade Minister's office', *SMH*, 27 May 1969, p. 8; 'Demonstration Violence: 103 Charged', *SMH*, 12 April 1969, p. 1. On embassies and consulates, see e.g.: 'Flag Burnt at Rally on Apartheid', *SMH*, 21 March 1970, p. 5; 'Marchers Protest at N-Tests', *SMH*, 21 May 1970, p. 6; 'A Little Opposition', *SMH*, 16 December 1970, p. 12; 'Australian Churchmen ask Russia to Spare Jews', *SMH*, 30 December 1970, p. 5; 'Police and Protesters Clash at Consulate', *SMH*, 31 December 1970, p. 6; 'Croations Stage Big Anti-Tito Protest', *SMH*, 29 December 1971, p. 9.

54 For courts, see e.g.: 'Court incidents as protest cases are heard', *SMH*, 20 August 1970, p. 9. For gaols: 'Peace Groups in Gaol Rally', *SMH*, 22 June 1970, p. 5. The police headquarters protest is reported in 'Unionists Stop Work for Funeral', *SMH*, 2 April 1971, p. 2.

55 'Protest over censorship', *SMH*, 21 February 1970, p. 8; 'Campaign on Film Cuts', *Sun-Herald*, 1 March 1970, p. 52; 'Protest by Jews', *SMH*, 4 March 1971, p. 3; 'Jews put out fake russian ballet programs', *SMH*, 15 June 1971, p. 11.

56 'Wild Sydney Racist Brawls', *Sun-Herald*, 14 June 1970, pp. 1–2; 'Vic. tennis held up by brawls', *Sun-Herald*, 21 January 1971, p. 3; 'Group's noisy retreat', *SMH*, 12 January 1971, p. 5; '49 arrests at rowdy game', *SMH*, 22 July 1971, p. 1; 'Protestors block the Springbok game twice', *SMH*, 7 July 1971, p. 1; 'Police Arrest 65 at Match', *SMH*, 1 July 1971, p. 1; '139 arrested as violence breaks out at anti-apartheid demonstration: police batons crash down: unruly crowd', *Sun-Herald*, 4 July 1971, pp. 1–3; 'Police Break Up Surf Protest', *Sun-Herald*, 28 March 1971, pp. 1–2; 'Protestors, police clash at carnival', *SMH*, 5 April 1971, p. 2; 'Quiet Protest To Dynamos', *SMH*, 1 March 1971, p. 2.

57 'Minister uses bat to ward off gang', *SMH*, 17 August 1970, pp. 1, 3; 'Midnight March on Hughes' Home', *SMH*, 18 August 1970, p. 1; 'Quiet Protest at Hughes' Home', *SMH*, 24 August 1970, p. 4.

58 'Askin Attacks Student March', *SMH*, 25 January 1969, p. 5; 'Students protest', *SMH*, 27 January 1969, p. 5.

59 'PM stayed put while artist's son was evicted', *SMH*, 2 April 1971, p. 2; 'Police Hunt Fire Vandals', *SMH*, 3 September 1971, p. 1.

60 For Australian Portland Cement: 'Colong protesters vocal at APCM meeting',

SMH, 29 April 1971, p. 1. For Boral: 'Concrete plant protest', *SMH*, 13 November 1970, p. 11. For Mobil: 'Petrol runs low', *SMH*, 15 July 1970, p. 12. For Vestey's: 'Protest on Gurindjis: 40 arrested', *SMH*, 1 August 1970, p. 10. For Angliss & Co.: 'Police and students clash over land issue', *SMH*, 17 July 1970, p. 5. For supermarket actions: 'Gurindji Land: Sharp Support', *Tribune*, 22 July 1970, p. 1. For Honeywell and General Electric: 'Police in Victoria ready for rioters', *SMH*, 3 July 1970, p. 1.

61 Denis Freney, A *Map of Days: Life on the Left*, Heinemann, Melbourne, 1991, p. 272. The Melbourne Stock Exchange raid is reported in: 'Exchange "bombed" in Vic. protest', *SMH*, 2 July 1970, p. 4. The Sydney action: 'Shouting Group Invades Exchange', *SMH*, 3 July 1970, p. 1.

62 Michel de Certeau, *The Practice of Everyday Life*, University of California Press, Berkeley, Los Angeles and London, 1984, p. 36.

63 Ibid., p. xix.

64 Ronald Aminzade, 'Between Movement and Party: The transformation of mid-nineteenth-century French republicanism', in Craig Jenkins and Bert Klandermans (eds), *The Politics of Social Protest: Comparative Perspectives on States and Social Movements*, University of Minnesota Press, Minneapolis, 1995, p. 39; Frances Fox Piven and Richard A. Cloward, *Poor People's Movements: Why They Succeed, How They Fail*, Pantheon Books, New York, 1977.

65 Tarrow, *Democracy and Disorder*, p. 60.

66 Tim Cresswell, *In Place/Out of Place: Geography, Ideology, and Transgression*, University of Minnesota Press, Minneapolis and London, 1996. The discussion of space and norms (including the example of the library) is on p. 16. The emphasis on the response of the press, the law and government as a marker of transgression is on p. 23. For Da Matta's views: Roberto Da Matta, 'Carnival in Multiple Planes', in John J MacAloon (ed.), *Rite, Drama, Festival, Spectacle: Rehearsals Toward a Theory of Cultural Performance*, Institute for the Study of Human Issues, Philadelphia, 1984, pp. 213–14. For the Czechoslovakian protest: 'Sydney Czechs in protest', *Sun-Herald*, 25 August 1968, p. 7. For the La Trobe action: 'Vic. students battle police', *SMH*, 17 September 1970, p. 5; Newsletter *Repression*, 24 September 1970 in *Ian Turner Papers*, NLA MS 6206, Box 41.

67 This is reflected in the 'mean level' of disruptive staging. It increases from 17.4 per cent of all staging in early 1967 to 40.2 per cent of all staging in late 1969 to 55 per cent of all staging in late 1970. As this clearly shows, although the new performance of disruption was becoming increasingly important over the period 1967–71, it only became dominant in 1970–71. The disruptiveness of staging increased over time.

68 The quote is from a spokesperson of SDS, cited in 'Our Own Army?', *National U*, 14 July 1969, p. 3. The use of police violence to justify student violence is in John Jenkins, 'The Sixth Republic?', *National U*, 24 June 1968, p. 11. The attempt to prove 'oneself' after brutality is expressed in 'The Sydney Demos', *National U*, 28 April 1969, p. 3. The impetus gained from television coverage of police violence is in 'Adelaide Also', *National U*, 28 April 1969, p. 3. The pleasure at outwitting police is clearly evident in the remembrances of Hamel-Green in *A Decade of Dissent*, p. 177.

69 Frank Moorhouse, *The Americans, Baby*, Picador, Sydney, 1996 (first published 1972), pp. 102–103.

70 The quote is from: Silas Grass, 'Stop the War to Stop the Moratorium', *Tharunka*, 20 July 1971, p. 5. The theoretical connections forged between Australian activists

and overseas actions will be explored in detail in Chapter 4. The presence of police is used to confirm the radical credentials of actors in *Print*, 16 July 1970 — the leaflet of the Monash Labor Club. Copy held in *Ian Turner Papers*, NLA MS 6206, Box 41.
71 Cited in Hamel-Green, *A Decade of Dissent*, p. 177.
72 Geoff Mullen, 'Draft Resister Speaks', *National U*, 22 March 1971, p. 7.
73 The importance of the My Lai massacre as a metaphor of the Vietnam War and as a spur to increased opposition is explored in Murphy, *Harvest of Fear*, p. 229. The account of the student invasion is reported in a column by 'Plain Australian', entitled 'Girlies', *Tribune*, 2 July 1969, p. 2. For the Cabinet discussion on a new bill to restrict and more firmly penalise the demonstrations on Commonwealth property, see the recently declassified records: Australian Archives, Series numbers: A5882, A5869, A5619, A5869.
74 'Occupation X', 1 October 1970, published by Monash Association of Students Discipline Committee, in *Ian Turner Papers*, NLA MS 6206, Box 41.
75 The threat posed to conscription by Draft Resistance is claimed in 'Draft Resister Speaks', *National U*, 22 March 1971, p. 7. The ability of the anti-Springbok actions to successfully destroy the spectacle of the Rugby matches was emphasised by John Wentworth, 'Pigskin's but tough', *Tharunka*, 11 May 1971, p. 4.
76 Kertzer, *Ritual, Politics and Power*. For the importance of rituals to popular movements, p. 92; for the definition of rituals, p. 9; for the release of communitas, pp. 72–73. The relationship between the crossing of spatial and normative boundaries and the intensity of symbolisation is related in Da Matta, 'Carnival in Multiple Planes', pp. 213–14.
77 For a (critical) reference to the growth of 'fancy dress' in demonstrations: Richard Amery, Sandra Lowery, John Miller, Grazina Bagdonas, Erika Pater, H Pryor and Jan Hartman, 'Protests', *On Dit*, 5 September 1968, p. 10. On shocking middle-class shits: Andrew Martin, 'Inadequacies of the Left Here at Sydney', *Honi Soit*, 2 November 1969, p. 2. On warmth for others during Moratorium: Brian Aarons, 'Wider Still and Wider …', *Tribune*, 20 May 1970, p. 7. Victor Turner describes liminal behaviour as existing across the threshold between stable phases of the social process in *Dramas, Fields, and Metaphors: Symbolic Action in Human Society*, Cornell University Press, Ithaca and London, 1974, p. 39. For the extension of 'liminal' to embrace the normative cracks in a social order, see Eric W Rothenbuhler, 'The Liminal Fight: Mass strikes as ritual and interpretation', in Jeffrey C Alexander (ed.), *Durkheimian Sociology: Cultural studies*, Cambridge University Press, 1988, pp. 66–89.
78 For the transcendence of police: 'Moratorium Friday', *Tribune*, 13 May 1970, p. 3. For the ability of the crowd to determine its own form: Mavis Robertson, 'The myth of manipulation', *Tribune*, 20 May 1970, p. 5. For the decision to participate in the Moratorium leading to a break with normal family life, see 'A Moratorium Every Day', *On Dit*, 30 April 1971, p. 9. The entire Moratorium campaign was depicted as a 'Moratorium on business as usual'; see the later discussion in Chapter 5. For the questioning of 'normal life' after the Moratorium: Dave Davies, 'Melbourne: Why 'we couldn't believe our eyes'', *Tribune*, 20 May 1970, pp. 6–7.
79 For the opposition between bus rides and street walking, television watching and chanting, see the anonymous 'Thoughts on a demo', *On Dit*, 16 April 1970, pp. 12–13. This is also the source of the quote concerning the bourgeoisie and their Valiants. For the reference to behaviour not tolerated in the 'official community'

and the extended block quote, see Frank Starrs, 'Poem: Demos', *On Dit*, 9 July 1969, p. 2.
80 The description as 'authoritarian' is in: Editorial, 'The Cricket Tour', *SMH*, 9 September 1971, p. 6; as 'anti-intellectual' in: Editorial, 'The Anti-Intellectuals', *SMH*, 9 September 1970, p. 2.
81 Dennis Altman, 'Don't Shoot, We Are Your Children' (1971) in *Coming Out in the Seventies*, Wilde & Woolley, Sydney and Eugene, 1979, pp. 193–94.
82 Jim Spigelman, 'The Politics of Confrontation', *Honi Soit*, 4 March 1969, p. 11. For the discussion of the American New Left, see Gitlin, *The Whole World is Watching*.
83 Editorial, 'The Cricket Tour', *SMH*, 9 September 1971, p. 6.
84 For the contraction of the public realm through the Cold War, and the embrace of private commitments see John Murphy, *Imagining the Fifties: Private Sentiment and Political Culture in Menzies' Australia*, UNSW Press, Sydney, 2000, esp. pp. 28–29. The denial of permission to Communists and peace activists was common, e.g. 'Charges against union officials', *SMH*, 17 September 1966, p. 8. The views of Cutler are paraphrased in: 'Uni. protests criticised by Governor', *SMH*, 22 March 1969, p. 14. Leaflet distribution was restricted to the point of banned under Melbourne City Council By-Law 418 (24) 1, as reported in 'Dr Cairns prepared for gaol if ...', *SMH*, 4 April 1969, p. 1. The Queensland Anti-Marching legislation is discussed and opposed in 'Students put off march in Brisbane', *SMH*, 12 July 1967, p. 14.
85 Rosalyn Deutsche, *Evictions: Art and Spatial Politics*, MIT Press, Cambridge, Mass., 1996, pp. 267, 288.
86 Jean McLean, *A Decade of Dissent*, p. 206.

CHAPTER 3 DIFFUSION

1 'Exam Resisters' Manifesto', *National U*, 10 April 1972, p. 16.
2 Geoff Sharp, 'Notes on the Gaoling of Clarrie O'Shea', *Arena*, 19, 1969, p. 92.
3 'Tree Liberation at Geelong', *National U*, 1 April 1974, p. 2.
4 'End the Australian war now', *National U*, Black Moratorium Liftout, 10 July 1972.
5 'Why we're not marching', leaflet distributed 6 May 1973, in Craig Johnston, *A Sydney Gaze: The Making of Gay Liberation*, Schiltron Press, Sydney, 1999, pp. 2–3.
6 Patrick Morgan, 'Where Have All the Issues Gone?', *National U*, 13 November 1969, p. 7
7 The 'running out of steam' reference is from: Editorial, 'Target — South Africa', *SMH*, 4 March 1971, p. 6. The larger quote is from: Editorial, 'The Spoilers', *SMH*, 10 July 1971, p. 6.
8 Patricia Giffney, 'Woman's Angle on the Week', *Sun*, 22 June 1973, p. 51.
9 A typical hierarchy of needs is enunciated by former male student radical Bob Cavanagh, in Beer, *A Serious Attempt to Change Society*, p. 64. The Women's Lib. critique is from Glorfindal Eunuchwarbler, 'Shit-Pouring Time', *Honi Soit*, 19 July 1973, p. 6.
10 See Patrick Morgan, 'Where Have All the Issues Gone?', *National U*, 13 November 1969, p. 7; Silas Grass, 'Stop the War to Stop the Moratorium', *Tharunka*, 20 July 1971, p. 5.
11 See Tarrow, *Power in Movement*, ch. 5.
12 For Toomaleh Reserve: 'Students will check on hotel discrimination', *SMH*,

19 February 1965, p. 1. For Brunette Downs: 'Natives refused drinks at race meeting', *SMH*, 21 June 1965, p. 6. For Newcastle Waters: no title, *SMH*, 31 May 1966, p. 3.

13 For Moree: 'Tension grows at Moree over Baths Ban on Aboriginals', *SMH*, 20 February 1965, p. 1. For Arbitration Court: 'Cattle Station Seen as 'Starting Point' in Aboriginal Assimilation', *SMH*, 8 July 1965, p. 5. For Walgett and Coonamble: 'Students, Aborigines charged at Walgett', *SMH*, 9 August 1965, p. 1; 'Aboriginal Aims to Sue the Walgett Hotel Licensee', *SMH*, 30 August 1965, p. 5; 'Student Hit in Cinema Showdown', *SMH*, 13 September 1965, p. 5. For Parliament House: 'Aborigines Need Less than cost of a Jet', *SMH*, 1 December 1965, p. 1. The Bandler quote is from 'Data: People, Ideas, Action', *SMH*, 1 December 1965, p. 6

14 'Protests to Dr Gough', *SMH*, 9 November 1965, p. 1; 'Women Shake Their Fists at Ship', *Sun-Herald*, 2 May 1965, p. 21.

15 On respectability: Jean McLean cited in Langley, *A Decade of Dissent*, p. 32. On genteel use of public space: Murphy, *Harvest of Fear*, p. 143. For examples of 'repertoire of representation' by SOS: 'Silent 300 in Protest on Vietnam', *SMH*, 21 May 1965, p. 1. For increasing contestation: 'Eight arrests in clash at consulate', *SMH*, 1 July 1966, p. 1; 'Women picket call up centre', *SMH*, 13 July 1967, p. 11; 'Anti-Vietnam demonstrators protest over call-up', *SMH*, 8 February 1968, p. 5. For disruption and arrest: 'Mother is in jail', *SMH*, 10 April 1971, p. 1; 'Fairlea five out of jail', *SMH*, 19 April 1971, p. 1.

16 For chainings with a suffragette influence: 'Women chained in hotel', *SMH*, 1 April 1965, p. 6; 'Man protests in rooftop', *SMH*, 16 April 1966, p. 1; 'Women who stopped parliament', *SMH*, 12 June 1970, p. 1. For antics on car bonnets: 'Police charge 13: wild scenes', *Sun-Herald*, 23 October 1966, p. 3. For abuse: 'Court told of "fascist" cry by girl', *SMH*, 12 September 1970, p. 10. For anti-Springbok disruption: 'Police break up surf protest', *Sun-Herald*, 28 March 1971, pp. 1–2. For protest over clothing: 'Student walkout in dress protest', *SMH*, 5 May 1967, p. 7. The *Pix* claim and the *Herald* description are both in: 'Explanation of picture', *SMH*, 22 May 1967, p. 4.

17 The citation on priorities is from Mavis Robertson, 'Will History Ever Include Her Story?', *Tharunka*, 6 April 1971, p. 7. On attempts by Men to dominate in 'New Left': Kaye Shumack, 'Behind the News', *National U*, 3 July 1974, p. 4; on the 'Old': Mavis Robertson, 'Victims of Double Oppression', *Australian Left Review*, 28, December–January 1971, pp. 5–6. On unpaid labour: Ann Curthoys, '"Shut up, you bourgeois bitch": Sexual identity and political action in the anti-Vietnam war movement', in Joy Damousi and Marilyn Lake (eds), *Gender and War: Australians at War in the Twentieth Century*, Cambridge University Press, 1995, p. 332. On sexism of male leaders: Ann Curthoys in Langley, *A Decade of Dissent*, p. 96.

18 The 'liberate' claim is in Tony Morgan's interview of David Taylor, 'Why we are Revolting', *Tharunka*, 29 October 1968, p. 13. The 'diversionary' claim is in Chris Dale, 'Student Union's Tied to the State', *Labour Press: Organ of the Socialist Labour League*, 16 July 1973. The complaint concerning publications is made in EB Wilson, 'Where Have All the Women Gone?', *Australian Left Review*, 5, October–November 1969, p. 36. The caricature is in: *National U*, 16 March 1972, p. 3.

19 On economic determinants of racism, see: Monash Labour Club, *Print*, 18, 16 April 1970. The attempts by white Marxists to 'correct' Aborigines are recalled and critiqued by Warren Osmond, 'Black Militancy and the White Left', *Arena*,

28, 1972, p. 15. On homophobia in AUS: Laurie Bebbington, interviewed in '"Women have very little to celebrate"', *National U*, 24 March 1974, p. 9. The quote concerning the culture of left politics, the specific complaints concerning SYA and CPA, and the citation from Leonard Amos in 1974 are all in Graeme Tubbenhauer, 'Gayness and Marxism: Are they compatible?', *Gay Liberation Press*, 1, June 1974, pp. 4–6.

20 Graeme Dunstan, 'Got dem Moratorium blues', *Tharunka*, 4 May 1971, p. 6.
21 Wendy Bacon, 'Intercourse without Orgasm', *Tharunka*, 14 May 1970, p. 2. On the gender breakdown of conference speakers, see 'Women and the Anti-War Conference', *Mejane*, 1, March 1971, p. 10. Elizabeth Jacka complained of male attempts to control the Sydney University action in: 'Women scab in this Lib struggle', *Australian*, 21 July 1973. The marginalisation of the 'sexist aspect' is noted in Henry Mayer, 'Making Sense of the University Strike', *Australian*, 11 July 1973, p. 10. The quote is from: Deirdre Black, 'Child Care: occupation at Melbourne', *National U*, 26 May 1974.
22 Kate Jennings, cited in Ann Curthoys, 'Mobilizing Dissent: The Later Stages of Protest', in Gregory Pemberton (ed.), *Vietnam Remembered*, Weldon, Sydney and London, 1990, p. 159.
23 Freney, *A Map of Days*, p. 267.
24 John Tapp, 'Watch those women', *National U*, 23 March 1970.
25 'Miss Bovine Robbed of Title', *Mejane*, 3, July 1971, p. 3.
26 Craig Johnston, 'The homosexual movement in Australia 1970–1975' (1976), reprinted in his *A Sydney Gaze*, p. 20.
27 The *Honi* burning is reported in: Barbie, 'Sydney University Feminists', *Sydney Women's Liberation Newsletter*, June 1974, p. 16. For the feminist attack on *National U*, see Felicity Clarke, 'Greer Sneer', *National U*, 27 March 1972, p. 4. The gay liberation critique is Craig Johnston, 'Sexism', *National U*, 29 April 1974, p. 2.
28 A critique of the peace movement from a feminist perspective is Joyce Stevens, 'The Radicalisation of Women', *Mejane*, 1, March 1971, p. 10. The changes to the official strategy statement of the Moratorium are noted in Peter Edwards, *A Nation at War: Australian Politics, Society and Diplomacy during the Vietnam War 1965–1975*, Allen & Unwin, Sydney, 1997, p. 301. For the critique of the CPA: Mavis Robertson, 'Victims of Double Oppression', *Australian Left Review*, 28, December–January 1971, pp. 5–6, and specifically of 'Women's Committees': Judy Gillett and Betty Fisher, 'Paternalism and the CPA', ibid., p. 42. For theoretical examination of women/sex: Anna Yeatman, 'The Liberation of Women', *Arena*, 21, 1970, p. 21; Anna Yeatman, 'The Marriage-Family Institution', *Australian Left Review*, 28, December–January 1971, pp. 36–37; Ann Curthoys, 'Historiography and Women's Liberation', *Arena*, 22, 1970, p. 36. For women's status in social theory: Mia Campioni, Liz Jacka, Paul Patton, Pat Skenridge, Margo Moore and David Wells, 'Opening the Floodgates Domestic Labour and Capitalist Production', *Refractory Girl*, 7, November 1974, pp. 10–14. On 'racism' of AUS: Gary Foley, 'Blacks', *National U*, 9 July 1973, p. 12. On homophobia: Bill Morley, 'La Trobe Gay-iety', *National U*, 15 July 1974, p. 2.
29 For an early example of Black Power rhetoric within Aboriginal institutions: AB Pittock, 'Report on Aboriginal and European Leadership in FCAATSI', in FCAATSI, *Reports and Proceedings of the 11th Annual Conference on Aboriginal Affairs*, Canberra, 12–14 April 1968, p. 13. For the November and December 1971 actions: 'Rowdy night as Aborigines vote', *SMH*, 27 November 1971, p. 3;

'Anti-race march ends in violence', *SMH*, 4 December 1971, p. 3; 'Black Power Hits Victoria', *SMH*, 16 December 1971, p. 8.

30 The FCAATSI actions are discussed in: Verity Burgmann, *Power and Protest: Movements for Change in Australian Society*, Allen & Unwin, Sydney, 1993, p. 34. On Len Watson's actions: 'Outburst by Aboriginal', *SMH*, 23 August 1973. On the critique of the Institute: 'Open Letter', *National U*, 6 May 1974, p. 3.

31 See 'Women and the Anti-War Conference' and Martha, 'Anti-Imperialist Practice', *Mejane*, 1, March 1971, p. 10; Freney, *A Map of Days*, p. 327. The ACTU action is reported in: 'Hawke Jostled', *SMH*, 31 August 1971, p. 2. The feminist appraisal is Narien Gale, 'The Melbourne Story', *Mejane*, 5, November 1971, p. 4. The novel referred to is Frank Moorhouse, *Conference-Ville*, Angus & Robertson, Sydney, 1976.

32 The quote is from Hobart Women's Action Group, 'Sexism and the Women's Liberation Movement', *Refractory Girl*, 5, Summer 1974, p. 30. For criticisms of the sexism of Gay Lib. see 'A Radicalesbian Lifestyle', *Refractory Girl*, 5, Summer 1974, p. 15, and the account of a 1972 Conference: Lesley Lynch, 'Mythmaking in the Women's Movement', *Refractory Girl*, 5, Summer 1974, p. 36.

33 On the later performance of the 'movement dissident' by Aborigines and migrants see the account of Bronwen Levy, 'Sisterhood in Trouble: the Fourth Women and Labour Conference, Brisbane 1984', *Hecate*, 10, 2, 1984, pp. 105–109 and Jackie Huggins, 'Black Women and Women's Liberation', *Hecate*, 13, 1, 1987, pp. 77–82. Later performances by lesbians include Gill, 'Lesbian Purges', *Sydney Women's Liberation Newsletter*, January 1976, p. 13. A lesbian occupation of a conference is described in 'Lesbians on Liberation', *Gay Liberation Press*, 4, October 1974, p. 10. Bisexuals founded their first national conference in Australia with a critique of the existing gay and lesbian movement. See Graham Willett, *Living Out Loud: A History of Gay and Lesbian Activism in Australia*, Allen & Unwin, Sydney, 2000, p. 257. On the rise of the demands of the periphery, and the centrality of this phenomenon to 'postmodern thinking and politics', see Steven Seidman, 'Identity and Politics in a 'Postmodern' Gay Culture: Some Historical and Conceptual Notes', in Michael Warner (ed.), *Fear of a Queer Planet: Queer Politics and Social Theory*, University of Minnesota Press, Minneapolis and London, 1993, pp. 109–110. An influential attempt to rethink 'the Left' in terms of difference is Ernesto Laclau and Chantal Mouffe, *Hegemony and Socialist Strategy*, Verso, London, 1985.

34 Dennis Altman, 'Redefining Sexuality', *Arena*, 29, 1972, p. 50.

35 The importance and variety of the abortion campaign is stressed by: Syliva Kinder, 'Adelaide Women's Liberation: The first five years, 1969–1974', in Margaret Bevege, Margaret James and Carmel Shute (eds), *Worth Her Salt*, Hale & Iremonger, Sydney, 1982, p. 371. Demonstrations outside courts: 'Demonstrators at court call for legalised abortion', *SMH*, 3 June 1970, p. 8 and 'Demonstration by 20 women', *SMH*, 16 December 1970, p. 7. On NSW Parliament: 'Abortion protest — uproar in house', *SMH*, 21 April 1971, p. 2 and 'Abortion reformers disrupt parlt.', *SMH*, 26 November 1971, p. 3. On 'street theatre': 'Abortion reformers protest at parlt.', *SMH*, 7 May 1971, p. 13. Later demonstrations in NSW are reported in: 'Women's Abortion Action Campaign Report', *Sydney Women's Liberation Newsletter*, June 1974, p. 11 and 'Women's Abortion Action Campaign December 6 Demonstration', *Sydney Women's Liberation Newsletter*, January 1976, p. 11. The quote is from: Deb Shnookal, 'Abortion Campaign', *National U*, 18 March 1974, p. 1.

36 'Pill Ban Produces Mass Debate', *National U*, 2 September 1968, p. 3. On sex education: 'Women's Lib Rebuffed', *SMH*, 5 November 1971, p. 3 and 'Principal 'right' on sex booklet', *SMH*, 21 November 1971, p. 2. On 'rape vigilantes': 'Feminist Action Front', *Sydney Women's Liberation Newsletter*, June 1974, p. 1.

37 The origins of this protest in Canberra in 1978 and the campaign for the abolition of Anzac Day are suggested in: Adrian Howe, 'Anzac Day — who owns the means of resistance?', *Scarlet Woman*, 19, Spring 1984, pp. 22–26. The rationale is from: 'Women Against Rape' pamphlet (1984), *Women's Electoral Lobby Papers*, National Library of Australia (henceforth NLA), MS 3683, Series 14, Folder 33. For the history of arrests, legislative and police responses in Canberra, see: 'Women Against Rape' Leaflet (1983), *Women's Electoral Lobby Papers*, NLA, MS 3683, Series 14, Folder 98. The comments of the magistrate are in: 'Wimmin Against Rape' (1981), *Women's Electoral Lobby Papers*, NLA, MS 3683, Series 14, Folder 33. A copy of the legislation is in: *Women's Electoral Lobby Papers*, NLA, MS 3683, Series 14, Folder 33. The assessment by Marilyn Lake is in her *Getting Equal: the History of Australian Feminism*, Allen & Unwin, Sydney, 1999, p. 247.

38 The 'Regatta' action is reviewed in Chapter 1. For Canberra: 'ANU', *National U*, 14 July 1969, p. 17. For Sydney: 'Women's Liberation Invades a Hotel', *SMH*, 21 November 1970, p. 5; 'Girls Fail at Desegregation', *SMH*, 27 February 1971, p. 3. The rallying cry to liberation is Susan Wyatt, 'Tossed out because I'm female', *Sydney Women's Liberation Newsletter*, September 1975, p. 2.

39 The threat to invade the educational institution: Stanley Joseph, 'Octopus Dei', *Tharunka*, 6 April 1971, p. 5. An invasion occurred later: 'Students besiege uni. college', *SMH*, 10 August 1971, p. 1. On supermarkets: 'Working Women's Group Report', *Mejane*, 1, March 1971, p. 15. For stickers: 'Glebe Group Report', *Mejane*, 2, May 1971, p. 15. For fare payment: Lake, *Getting Equal*, p. 224. On the need for constant challenge: Gale, 'Male Supremacy, or a Good Belt in the Head', *Mejane*, 2, May 1971, p. 11. The challenge of feminism to the mores of student parties is recalled by Alan McClure in Beer, *A Serious Attempt to Change Society*, p. 156.

40 On the valuing of homosexuality: Dennis Altman, *Homosexual: Oppression and Liberation*, Outerbridge & Dienstfrey, Sydney, 1972, p. 49. The book draws from Marcuse to argue for the inherent bisexuality of all humans, and the ability of gay liberation to liberate all from existing sex roles. On the failure to report political action: Dennis Altman, *Coming Out in the Seventies*, Wilde & Woolley, Sydney and Eugene, 1979, pp. 18, 59.

41 On Penny Short actions: 'Victimisation by Ed. Dept.', *Refractory Girl*, 5, Summer 1974, p. 11. On Peter Bonsall-Boone, see the reference in *Gay Liberation Press*, 2, August 1974. On 'zapping' bars: 'A radicalesbian lifestyle', *Refractory Girl*, 5, Summer 1974, p. 14. On the ability of 'zapping' to increase gay self-confidence and provide positive models: Altman, *Homosexual*, p. 119.

42 The demonstration and Hughes' puzzlement is reported in: 'Gay Lib. Demonstrates', *Mejane*, 5, November 1971, p. 3. See also Colin Gray, 'A Man's View', *Mejane*, 7, 1972, p. 11.

43 Graham Willett, *Living Out Loud: A History of Gay and Lesbian Activism in Australia*, Allen & Unwin, Sydney, 2000, pp. 84–85, 105.

44 On Gay Pride: Terry Bell, 'Gay Pride Done in', *Gay Liberation Press*, 1, June 1974, p. 8. The quote is from Terry Bell, 'Massive retrenchments: pooftas get the axe!', *Gay Liberation Press*, 5, November–December 1974, p. 32.

45 On the early history of Mardi Gras, see Johnson, *A Sydney Gaze*, pp. 25, 88–90. The description of the 1981 marchers is his, from p. 89.
46 On land: Goodall, *Invasion to Embassy*. The civil rights focus of SAFA is explored in Chapter 1.
47 'Fifth Column', *National U*, 22 March 1971, p. 3
48 The student claim concerning new legislation: 'Fifth Column', *National U*, 22 March 1971, p. 3. On the Gurindji walk-off: 'Land fight: tribe holds rally', *SMH*, 26 July 1968, p. 4. On marches, petitions and fasts: Dulcie Flower, 'Land Rights', in FCAATSI, *Report and Proceedings of the 14th Annual Conference on Aboriginal Affairs*, Townsville, 9–11 April 1971, p. 2. The Bandler quote is from 'President Report', ibid., p. C2. On Langton and Poynton actions: Ian Langman, 'Land Rights Vigil', *National U*, 14 July 1969, p. 14. On Vestey's action: 'Protest on Gurindjis: 40 arrested', *SMH*, 1 August 1970, p. 10. On Angliss & Co.: 'Police and students clash over land issue', *SMH*, 17 July 1970, p. 5.
49 The demonstration is reported in Alec Robertson, 'Black and White Join in Demonstration for Gurindji Land', *Tribune*, 5 August 1970, p. 12
50 On representation: Roberta Sykes, *Snake Dancing*, Allen & Unwin, Sydney, 1998, p. 145. On the history of the Embassy, including its establishment, early statements, the ministry and media interest, see Scott Robinson, 'The Aboriginal Embassy: An Account of the Protests of 1972', *Aboriginal History*, 18, 1, 1994, pp. 49–64.
51 The 'unsightly' comment and response was to a later version of the Embassy: 'Unsightly Black Embassy', *National U*, 22 April 1974. On the comparison with 'squalid' reserves: FCAATSI press release, 12 May 1972 in *Gordon Bryant Papers*, NLA, MS 8256, Series 11, Box 173, Folder entitled 'FCAATSI Annual Conference Alice Springs'.
52 The first public statement is cited in Goodall, *Invasion to Embassy*, p. 339. The decision to remain until demands were met is described in Robinson, 'The Aboriginal Embassy', p. 51. Bryant's views are in a letter to Hon. RJ Hunt, Minister for the Interior, 9 June 1972, *Gordon Bryant Papers*, NLA, MS 8256, Series 11, Box 173, Folder entitled '1972 Annual Conference, Alice Springs Report'.
53 On the history of final days of the Embassy: Scott Robinson, 'The Aboriginal Embassy', pp. 56–62. On the subsequent reuse by Aboriginal protesters, see p. 63. On the Western Australian Consulate: 'Natives threaten squat at airport', *Sunday Times*, 18 June 1972 and 'Prepared for a long wait', *West Australian*, 19 June 1972. On the 'Forest Embassy': *Canberra Times*, 5 November 1994, p. 5. On the Gay Rights Embassy: Bob Beatty, 'Gays Abandoned by Sydney Press', *New Journalist*, 43, April 1984, pp. 38–39. On later union actions at Federal Parliament as well as the 'Workers Embassy': Janis Bailey and Kurt Iveson, '"The Parliaments Call Them Thugs": Public Space, Identity, and Union Protest', *Journal of Industrial Relations*, 42, 4, 2000, pp. 517–34.
54 From a rich history of the green bans and the union see Meredith Burgmann and Verity Burgmann, *Green Bans, Red Union: Environmental Activism and the New South Wales Builders Labourers' Federation*, UNSW Press, Sydney, 1998.

CHAPTER 4 THEORY

1 Douglas Kirsner, 'Reform or Revolution', *National U*, 14 April 1969, p. 12. For the critique of the 'fetish' for demonstrations, see Kelvin Rowley and Terry Counihan, 'Radical Student Politics', *National U*, 17 March 1969, pp. 6–7.

2   Rowley and Counihan, 'Radical Student Politics', p. 6–7. For the need for a new start, see Terry Counihan and Kelvin Rowley, 'Pipedream Revolutionaries', *National U*, 12 May 1969, p. 16.
3   Rowley and Counihan, 'Radical Student Politics', pp. 6–7.
4   For well-known representatives of these propositions, see Alain Touraine, *The Post-Industrial Society: Tomorrow's Social History: Classes, Conflicts and Culture in the Programmed Society*, Random House, New York, 1971; Alvin Gouldner, *The Future of the Intellectuals and the Rise of the New Class*, Seabury Press, New York, 1979; Andre Gorz, *Farewell to the Working Class: An Essay on Post-Industrial Socialism*, Pluto Press, London, 1982. For a recognition of the decline of Marxism: Frederic Jameson, *Postmodernism, or, The Cultural Logic of Late Capitalism*, Verso, London and New York, 1991; for the decline of politics and the rise of culture: Meaghan Morris, 'Politics Now (Anxieties of a Petty-Bourgeois Intellectual)', in *The Pirate's Fiancee*, Verso, London and New York, pp. 173–86; for intellectual circulation: Michele Lamont, 'How to Become a Dominant French Philosopher: The Case of Jacques Derrida', *American Journal of Sociology*, 93, 3, 1987, pp. 584–622 and Pierre Bourdieu and Loic Wacquant, 'On the Cunning of Imperialist Reason', *Theory, Culture and Society*, 16, 1, 1999, pp. 41–58.
5   For articulate examples of each position, see Andrew Milner, 'Cultural Studies and Cultural Hegemony', *Arena*, 9, 1997, pp. 133–54; Judith Allen and Paul Patton (eds), *Beyond Marxism? Interventions After Marx*, Intervention Publications, Sydney, 1983.
6   For map analysis: Kathleen Carley, 'Extracting Culture through textual analysis', *Poetics*, 22, 1994, p. 293.
7   The treatment of political and discursive interventions as events of the same order reflects recent critiques of the thought/action distinction; see Michael Freeden, *Ideologies and Political Theory: A Conceptual Approach*, Clarendon Press, Oxford 1996, p. 43
8   The quote concerning Marxism is from S. Moston, 'Party Education — Marx House', *Communist Review*, 22, June 1942, p. 74. On Marxism as a master discourse, see Sean Scalmer, 'Marxist Ideology inside the Communist Party of Australia, 1942–1956', *Journal of Political Ideologies*, 3, 1, 1998, pp. 45–61.
9   For the citation of these texts, among others, see Doug Kirsner, 'The Impossibility of Philosophy', *Arena*, 13, Winter 1967, pp. 46–49; Vin Bourke, 'Why Blame Marx?', *Arena*, 9, Autumn 1966, p. 20; Lloyd Churchward, 'Theories of Totalitarianism', *Arena*, 12, Autumn 1967, p. 42; Rex Mortimer, 'The Sociology of C. Wright Mills', *Arena*, 2, 1963, p. 19; Geoff Sharp, 'Class, Education, Politics', *Arena*, 4, 1964, p. 5; Eric Aarons, 'Lenin's Philosophical Notebooks', *Arena*, 3, Autumn 1964, pp. 26–27.
10 For the exploration of these concepts, sequentially, see P-G, 'Artists and Reality', *Arena*, 11, Summer 1966, pp. 5–6; Ian Turner, 'Socialist History and the Socialist Historian', *Arena*, 11, Summer 1966, p. 13; Alan Roberts, 'The Mechanist Conception of History', *Arena*, 7, Winter 1965, p. 19; Doug Kirsner, 'Is Sartre a Marxist?', *Arena*, 10, Winter 1966, p. 11; Jack Blake, 'Sartre, Marx and Humanism', *Arena*, 12, Autumn 1967, p. 25; Churchward, 'Theories of Totatitarianism', p. 42; Geoff Sharp, 'Sociologists and the New Strata', *Arena*, 1, September 1963, pp. 14–15.
11 On the diminishing working class, Turner, 'Socialist History and the Socialist Historian', p. 8; on the need for higher consciousness, Blake, 'Sartre, Marx and Humanism', p. 34. On the transformation of the employed strata, Sharp, 'Class,

Education, Politics', p. 5. On the need to take account of social changes, Doug White, 'The New Right', *Arena*, 9, Autumn 1966, p. 6.

12 On the analysis of intermediate classes, Bob Gollan, 'Class in the Social Consciousness', *Arena*, 7, Winter 1965, pp. 5–6. A definition of the intelligentsia that was claimed as 'objective' was Lloyd Churchward, 'Structure of the Intelligentsia', *Arena*, 5, Spring 1964, p. 5; for a 'cultural' definition, Ian Turner, 'Culture of the Intelligentsia', *Arena*, 5, Spring 1964, pp. 8–9; for a definition in terms of social function, Bob Gollan, 'The Professionals', *Arena*, 5, Spring 1964, p. 3. For the intelligentsia as left-wing, John M. Legge, Rex Mortimer, Geoff Sharp and Henry Zimmerman, 'Why *Arena*?', *Arena*, 1, September 1963, p. 6; as radical and testing ideas, Geoff Sharp, 'Sociologists and the New Strata', *Arena*, 1, September 1963, pp. 18–19; for transitional consciousness, Rex Mortimer, 'The Folk Wave', *Arena*, 4, Winter 1964, p. 14; for understanding the technical-scientific revolution, Geoff Sharp, 'Out of Tribalism', *Arena*, 8, Summer 1965, p. 3; for adherence to the values of rationality, universalism and communality, and ethically motivated political action, Doug White, 'Education and Ethics', *Arena*, 10, Winter 1966, p. 5–6. For the place of the 'new strata' in humanistic culture, Doug White, 'Skills Without Learning', *Arena*, 14, Spring 1967, p. 32.

13 On the rise of the multiversity, Geoff Sharp, 'Editorial', *Arena*, 12, Autumn 1967, pp. 3–4. On the growth of credentialist orientation, Doug White, 'Service Station Academies', *Arena*, 9, Autumn 1966, p. 29; on the hegemony of human capital theory, White, 'Skills Without Learning', p. 25.

14 These claims concerning French events are found in Geoff Sharp, 'A Revolutionary Culture', *Arena*, 16, 1968, pp. 2–11; Doug White, 'Czechoslovakia', *Arena*, 17, 1968, pp. 2–6; David Hudson, 'Provocateur or Detonateur?', *Arena*, 17, 1968, p. 15.

15 For an emphasis on the persistent theoretical interest in France, May 1968, see Julie Stephens, *Anti-Disciplinary Protest: Sixties Radicalism and Postmodernism*, Cambridge University Press, 1998, p. 1. For the views of Sewell, see William H. Sewell Jr, 'Historical Events as Transformations of Structures: Inventing Revolution at the Bastille', *Theory and Society*, 25, 6, 1996, pp. 841–81.

16 For a citation of the Cohn-Bendits: Doug White, 'Shadows in the Long Reaches of Bureaucracies?', *Arena*, 18, 1969, p. 8; for banner-hangers, White, 'Czechoslovakia', p. 2. For the need for French writing, Hudson, 'Provocateur or Detonateur?', p. 15. The quote on the availability of French journal duplications is from 'The Events in France', *Arena*, 16, 1968, p. 56.

17 For the citation of Sartre: Warren Osmond, 'Marxists and the Changing Communist Party', *Arena*, 20, 1969, p. 64; Peter O'Brien, 'Culture and Revolution', *Arena*, 24, 1971, p. 26; Anna Yeatman, 'The Liberation of Women', *Arena*, 21, 1970, p. 23. For Althusser: Humphrey McQueen, 'The Hegemony of Dead Generations', *Arena*, 18, 1969, p. 38; John Playford, 'Davidson Defended', *Arena*, 18, 1969, p. 44. For Lefebvre: Ron King, 'The Sociology in Marx', *Arena*, 18, 1969, p. 72. For the Cohn-Bendits and Quattrachi and Nairn: Dennis Altman, 'Students in the Electric Age', *Arena*, 21, 1970, p. 13. For Poulantzas: Michael Goddard, 'Critiques of Mainstream Economics', *Arena*, 25, 1971, p. 24. For anonymous students: White, 'Czechoslovakia', p. 2. For anonymous leading Marxists: Playford, 'Davidson Defended', p. 46. For Mandel: Ian Lennie, 'English Studies in Australia', *Arena*, 20, 1969, p. 41. For the *New Statesman*: Geoff Sharp, 'A Revolutionary Culture', *Arena*, 16, 1968, pp. 5–6.

18 For acceptance of his view of the history of Marxism: Zawar Hanfi, Translation

and Introduction to Feuerbach's 'Preliminary Theses on the Reform of Philosophy', *Arena*, 19, 1969, p. 6. On acceptance of his reworking of base-superstructure model: Humphrey McQueen, 'The Hegemony of Dead Generations', *Arena*, 8, 1969, pp. 38–40. For expository articles: Alistair Davidson, 'Althusser: Marxism Old and New', *Arena*, 19, 1969; for polemics: John Playford, 'Davidson Defended', *Arena*, 18, 1969. For uses of Marcuse to justify other propositions: Kelvin Rowley, 'Ideology in the Electric Age', *Arena*, 22, 1970, pp. 25–34; Douglas Kirsner, 'Misinterpreting Marcuse', *Arena*, 21, 1970, p. 80; John Playford, 'Big Business and the Australian University', *Arena*, 17, 1968, pp. 34–47; Alan Roberts, 'A Preliminary to the Reading of Marcuse', *Arena*, 18, 1969, pp. 27–36. For uses of Gramsci to justify other propositions: Humphrey McQueen, 'Labor Versus the Unions', *Arena*, 20, 1969, pp. 22–34; Humphrey McQueen, 'Three Tactics for Student Power', *Arena*, 18, 1969, pp. 17–22; Davidson, 'Althusser: Marxism Old and New', pp. 28–61.

19   For a questioning of the determining power of the 'base': McQueen, 'The Hegemony of Dead Generations', p. 40. For rethinking the role of the party, Alistair Davidson, 'Gramsci's Marxism', *Australian Left Review*, 3, June–July 1968, pp. 42–51; Playford, 'Davidson Defended', p. 45. For the use of Perry Anderson as a 'referent': Ian Lennie, 'A Language for Cultural Politics', *Arena*, 28, 1972, p. 42; Michael Goddard, 'Critiques of Mainstream Economics', *Arena*, 25, 1971, p. 21; for Gareth Stedman Jones: Altman, 'Students in the Electric Age', p. 17; McQueen, 'Three Tactics For Student Power', pp. 21–22; for Fred Halliday: Kelvin Rowley, 'Marxism and Asia', *Arena*, 25, 1971, p. 86; for Juliet Mitchell: Anna Yeatman, 'The Liberation of Women', *Arena*, 21, 1970, p. 19.

20   For a comparison of US and Australian anti-Vietnam War campaigns: Geoff Sharp, 'Redeye Missile', *Arena*, 15, 1968, p. 11. For the comparison of Australian students with those elsewhere: Geoff Sharp, 'A Revolutionary Culture', *Arena*, 16, 1968, p. 2. For a comparison of O'Shea and Paris actions: Geoff Sharp, 'Notes on the Gaoling of Clarrie O'Shea', *Arena*, 19, 1969, p. 92. For a comparison of Monash and Columbia students: Doug White, 'Czechoslovakia', *Arena*, 17, 1968, p. 6. For a comparison of Berkeley and Monash: Warren Osmond, 'A 'Monash' At Monash', *Arena*, 16, 1968, p. 12.

21   For a description of Monash actions as the 'first challenge': Doug White, 'Fifty Years On', *Arena*, 15, 1968, p. 6. For its ability to stand out over others: Editors, 'A Single Spark', *Arena*, 16, 1968, p. 50. For a detailed description and endorsement of actions at Monash see Osmond, 'A "Monash" At Monash', pp. 12–13; Hamish Boyne-Anderson, 'The New Left — Vita Nuova?', *Arena*, 17, 1968, p. 12.

22   For the 'revolutionary thrust': Humphrey McQueen, 'A Single Spark', *Arena*, 16, 1968, pp. 50–56. For its extension to Melbourne and Brisbane demonstrations: McQueen, 'Three Tactics For Student Power', p. 18. For student actions as presenting lessons for the Left; Doug White, 'Shadows in the Long Reaches of Bureaucracies?', *Arena*, 18, 1969, pp. 7–9. The plea for analyses of Monash actions is in Editors, 'A Single Spark', p. 50.

23   Alec Robertson, 'A Weakness in *Arena* 15', *Arena*, 16, 1968, p. 75.

24   Geoff Sharp, 'Sociologists and the New Strata', *Arena*, 1, September 1963, pp. 18–19; Doug White, 'The New Right', *Arena*, 9, Autumn 1966, pp. 5–6.

25   Geoff Sharp and Doug White, 'Features of the Intellectually Trained', *Arena*, 15, 1968, pp. 30–33.

26   Geoff Sharp, 'One Dimensional Civilization', *Arena*, 8, 1969, p. 15.

27 On conflict with class relations and the need for fuller understanding: Geoff Sharp, 'Beginnings of a New Practice', *Arena*, 23, 1970, pp. 2–3. On the scientific culture: Doug White, 'In a Liberated Society Creative Science Would Be Reincorporated Within the Practice of Everyday Life', *Arena*, 29, 1972, p. 23. On intellectual culture and conventional society and the ability to act as an independent base for socialism: Geoff Sharp, 'A Revolutionary Culture', *Arena*, 16, 1968, pp. 3, 7. On the ability to detonate or lead workers, Doug White, 'Czechoslovakia', *Arena*, 17, 1968, p. 6; Humphrey McQueen, 'Three Tactics for Student Power', *Arena*, 18, 1969, p. 20.
28 Sharp, 'A Revolutionary Culture', p. 7.
29 On 'intellectual rationality' and Vietnam: Geoff Sharp, 'Redeye Missile', *Arena*, 15, 1968, p. 11. On campus dissent and the importance of intellectuals: Sharp and White, 'Features of the Intellectually Trained', p. 33. On campus actions as a trigger, White, 'Czechoslovakia', p. 6. On the coining of the 'Arena thesis': Warren Osmond, 'Towards Self-Awareness', in Richard Gordon (ed.), *The Australian New Left: Critical Essays and Strategy*, Heinemann, Melbourne, 1970, pp. 166–216.
30 On communist inability to accept criticism: Sharp and White, 'Features of the Intellectually Trained', pp. 75–76. On poor leadership, Kelvin Rowley, 'Introduction', *Arena*, 22, 1970, p. 42. For a critique of the factions: Kelvin Rowley and Warren Osmond, 'Whither the Communist Party?', *Arena*, 22, 1970, p. 44. For absence of theoretical renewal and need for intensive discussion outside the party: Geoff Sharp, 'Hegemony, Theory, Programme', *Arena*, 20, 1969, pp. 2–3. For a critique of party renewal and the need for a 'New Left' approach, Warren Osmond, 'Student Revolutionary Left', *Arena*, 19, 1969, p. 26.
31 For the critique of Australian Communists and their reception of the French events, see David Hudson, 'Provocateur or Detonateur?', *Arena*, 17, 1968, pp. 16–19; Doug White, 'Shadows in the Long Reaches of Bureaucracies?', *Arena*, 18, 1969, p. 8.
32 For the first take-up of the '*Arena* thesis': Rex Mortimer, 'Democracy and the New Capitalism', *Arena* 15, 1968, p. 49. For Sharp's first take-up; 'A Revolutionary Culture', p. 8. For White's: 'Czechoslovakia', p. 6. For the extensions of Blake and Nonie Sharp: Jack Blake, 'Bureaucracy of Democracy?', *Arena*, 17, 1968, p. 64; Nonie Sharp, 'Integrating Farmers', *Arena*, 20, 1968, p. 15.
33 For *Arena*'s recognition of Women's Liberation: Leonie Campbell, 'Women's Liberation', *Arena*, 27, 1971, pp. 33–34, 36. For indigenous mobilisation: Don Atkinson, 'Aboriginal Project', *Arena*, 30, 1972, p. 5; Warren Osmond, 'Black Militancy and the White Left', *Arena*, 28, 1972, p. 16; White, 'In a Liberated Society', p. 18. For educational movements: Doug White, 'Set Up Your Own School', *Arena*, 28, 1972, p. 9. For gay liberation: Dennis Altman, 'Redefining Sexuality', *Arena*, 29, 1972, pp. 50–55. For ecological movements: White, 'In a Liberated Society', p. 23. For prisoners and builders' labourers: Doug White, 'A Politics of Culture', *Arena*, 25, 1971, p. 6; Geoff Sharp, 'A Problem of Perspective', *Arena*, 29, 1972, p. 1.
34 For these descriptions see, sequentially, Geoff Sharp and Doug White, 'In This Arena ...', *Arena*, 30, 1972, p. 2; Sharp, 'A Problem of Perspective', p. 1; Ian Lennie, 'A Language for Cultural Politics', *Arena*, 28, 1972, p. 56; Doug White, 'A Politics of Culture', *Arena*, 25, 1971, p. 6.
35 For their cultural focus: Geoff Sharp, 'Armed Insurrection', *Arena*, 27, 1971, pp. 9–10. For the struggle to recognise oppression: Sharp and White, 'In this Arena

...', p. 2. For the taking up of 'self-development': Sharp, 'A Problem of Perspective', p. 2. For the disruption of the traditional cultural framework of the Left: White, 'A Politics of Culture', p. 7. For the need for a thorough renovation of the language of culture and politics: Gerald Gill, 'In this Arena ...', *Arena*, 27, 1971, pp. 1–2; Lennie, 'A Language for Cultural Politics', p. 56. Altman's admission of difficult relations between the movements is in his 'Redefining Sexuality', p. 50.

36 Sharp's claims concerning the role of intellectuals in the reordering of culture are in his 'Armed Insurrection', p. 2. For the rise of the intellectual culture as the universal human culture, see White, 'A Politics of Culture', p. 6. For the roots of the newer movements in the cultural forms of the intellectuals: Geoff Sharp, 'Liberation Incorporated?', *Arena*, 32–33, 1973, p. 3. For the muted but distinctive interest in a politics of culture: Geoff Sharp, 'In Coming Arenas?', *Arena*, 26, 1971, p. 2. For the cultural politics no one had anticipated, Sharp, 'A Problem of Perspective', p. 2.

37 Sharp, 'A Problem of Perspective', pp. 1–3.

38 The Habermas translation is Jurgen Habermas, 'Historical Materialism Reconsidered', *Arena*, 38, 1975, pp. 69–79. The introduction is John Keane, 'Work and Interaction in Habermas', *Arena*, 38, 1975, pp. 51–68.

39 For intellectuals as a new petit bourgeoisie, see Nicos Poulantzas, *Classes in Contemporary Capitalism*, New Left Books, London, 1975. For Eyerman's more historical account, Ron Eyerman, *Between Culture and Politics: Intellectuals in Modern Society*, Polity Press, Cambridge, 1994. A later move from Marxism to post-Marxism is Allen and Patton, *Beyond Marxism?*. An exhilarating later example of linking international events and new theory is Meaghan Morris, 'Eurocommunism vs. Semiological Delinquency?', in Paul Foss and Meaghan Morris (eds), *Language, Sexuality and Subversion*, Feral Publications, Sydney, 1978 pp. 47–76. The same collection contains both European contributors (such as Eco and Baudrillard) alongside young Australian scholars. For emphases on the importance of understanding European events and/or languages in the development of radical Australian intellectual practice, see Alistair Davidson, 'Althusser: Marxism Old and New', *Arena*, 19, 1969, p. 28; Paul Patton in George Alexander, 'Introduction: On Editorial Strategies', in Foss and Morris, *Language, Sexuality and Subversion*, pp. 15–43. For Australian Cultural Studies, see John Frow and Meaghan Morris (eds), *Australian Cultural Studies: A Reader*, Allen & Unwin, Sydney, 1993. For Australian feminism, Barbara Caine et al. (eds), *Australian Feminism: A Companion*, Oxford University Press, Melbourne, 1998; Moira Gatens and Alison Mackinnon (eds), *Gender and Institutions: Welfare, Work and Citizenship*, Cambridge University Press, 1998.

40 This emphasis on the language and construction of events in their 'actualisation' is recently evident in Paul Patton, *Deleuze and the Political*, Routledge, London and New York, 2000, pp. 27–28, and strongly associated with Murray Edelman, *Constructing the Political Spectacle*, Chicago University Press, 1988, p. 104.

41 For a trenchant critique of the ranking of 'new' social movements over 'old', and of the marginalisation of class, see Burgmann, *Power and Protest*, esp. the Introduction and Conclusion.

CHAPTER 5 MEDIA

1 On Parliament House rallies: 'Darmody in Canberra', *Daily Mirror*, 13 November 1975, p. 4. For strikes and stop-work rallies on 14 November, see 'Four held as

protest stops papers', *SMH*, 14 November 1975, p. 8. On the memorial service, run and concert, see 'Rallies round-up', *The National Citizen*, 1 December 1975, p. 2. On strikes by journalists, see 'Strike at 3 papers: 'Bias' Protest', *SMH*, 9 December 1975.

2   The citations are from Editorial, 'No Place For Violence', *Daily Mirror*, 14 November 1975, p. 2 and Editorial, 'A Touch of Blackmail', *Sunday Telegraph*, 16 November 1975. The account of the demonstration is drawn from Bruce Hanford, 'Politics Comes Out of the House — and Into the Streets', *National Times*, 24–29 November 1975, pp. 30–32; 'Four Held as Protest Stops Papers', *SMH*, 14 November 1975, p. 8 and 'Censorship Is Not the Way!', *Australian Spartacist*, 25 November 1975, p. 4.
3   Bruce Hanford, 'Politics Comes Out of the House — and Into the Streets', *National Times*, 24–29 November 1975, pp. 30–32
4   Morgan Gallup Poll 205, 15 August 1969, pp. 4–8; Morgan Gallup Poll 213, 3 October 1970, pp. 42–46; Morgan Poll 1380, 22 August 1996.
5   On declining numbers at demonstrations: David Wilson, 'Radicals gain influence as moderates move out', *Australian*, 27 September 1979, p. 9. See also John Hanscombe, 'Why has the fire gone out of student politics', *Australian*, 9 March 1982, p. 7; and for the student comparison: Helen Trincia, 'New Right Now in Vogue on the Campus', *Australian*, 6 April 1984, p. 7. The Willmott quote is from Susan Wyndham, 'Students are marching — to a Tory drum', *SMH*, 4 August 1984, p. 39.
6   Geoffrey Blainey, 'The Place of the Peace Movement', *Bulletin*, 12 February 1991, p. 38. Tony Stephens, 'Dr Cairns recalls how it was done in the 70s', *SMH*, 9 July 1997. On hostility and organisation: Beatrice Faust, 'Left holding the liability', *Australian*, 19–20 July 1997 and Jamie Walker, 'Hanson Haters', *Australian*, 12–13 July 1997.
7   'Editorial', *Herald-Sun*, 28 August 2000, p. 18.
8   For a movement estimate of 120 000: JF Cairns, *Silence Kills*, The Vietnam Moratorium Committee, Richmond North, 1970, p. 9. On the 1982 action: Martin Armiger, 'The return of the demo', *National Times*, 18–24 April 1982, p. 24. The assessment's inaccuracy lies in the existence of quite large Palm Sunday rallies in earlier years. On 1984: '250,000 turn out in march for peace', *Australian*, 16 April 1984, pp. 1–2. On the Gulf action: Kevin Childs, 'Thousands at anti-war protests', *SMH*, 19 January 1991, p. 6 and Mark Forbes, 'Thousands march to give peace a chance', *Age*, 20 January 1991, p. 5. On reconciliation march, Mike Steketee and Megan Saunders, 'PM Stays Home On Historic Day', *Australian*, 29 May 2000, p. 1.
9   Robin Gerster and Jan Bassett, *Seizures of Youth: The Sixties and Australia*, Hyland House, Melbourne, 1991. On myth-making, p. 3, on saving the world, p. 190.
10 Donald Horne, *Time of Hope: Australia 1966–72*, Angus & Robertson, London and Sydney, 1980, pp. 56–57, 179.
11 Gerster and Bassett, *Seizures of Youth*, p. 77.
12 The quote is from Brian Aarons, 'Vietnam Moratorium', *National U*, 24 February 1970, p. 4. See also David Armstrong, 'Moratorium: Two Opinions', *Annals*, 83, 4, 1970, p. 30.
13 On government attacks, Malcolm Saunders and Ralph Summy, *The Australian Peace Movement: A Short History*, Peace Research Centre, ANU, Canberra, 1986, p. 42. For newspaper views: Editorial, 'To Moratorium Day', *Age*, 8 May 1970; Editorial, 'Dr Cairns on a Perilous Path', *Melbourne Herald*, 26 March 1970. On

trade union actions: MJ Saunders, 'The Trade Unions in Australia and Opposition to Vietnam and Conscription: 1965–73', *Labour History*, 43, November 1982, pp. 64–82. The Snedden quote is in 'Political Bikies Raping Democracy', *SMH*, 8 May 1970, p. 1.

14 For a conservative critique: NE Lauritz, *The Vietnam Moratorium*, Hawthorn Press, Melbourne, 1970, p. 33. For newspaper reports, 'Peaceful call for peace', *Australian*, 9 May 1970, p. 1; 'M-Day Draws 20,000 to City', *SMH*, 9 May 1970, p. 1.

15 For an account of the range of attendees see David Martin, 'On a Melbourne Pavement', in Shirley Cass, Ros Cheney, David Malouf and Michael Wilding (eds), *We Took Their Orders And Are Dead*, Ure Smith, Sydney, 1971, p. 93. For critics of bureaucracy: Graeme Dunstan, 'Got Dem Moratorium Blues', *Tharunka*, 11 May 1971, p. 6; Silas Grass, 'Stop the War to Stop the Moratorium', *Tharunka*, 1 June 1971, p. 5. On distortive media coverage: Richard Giles and Jim Hart, 'Two weeks of fun and games across the nation', *National U*, 14 July 1971, p. 2. The Askin quote is from 'M-Day Draws 20,000 to City', *SMH*, 9 May 1970, p. 1. The use of the Moratorium to defend Australian democracy is noted in *Print*, 11 June 1970, p. 1 in *Ian Turner Papers*, NLA MS 2606, Box 41. For John Murphy's acute analysis, see his *Harvest of Fear*, especially p. 233.

16 On Palm Sunday: '250,000 turn out in march for peace', *Australian*, 16 April 1984, pp. 1–2. On the Sydney Reconciliation Walk: Sian Powell, 'Thousands walk to bridge the racial divide', *Australian*, 29 May 2000, p. 3. The Melbourne walk is reported in: Alison Crossweller and Bronwyn Daly, 'Reconciliation Marches On', *Australian*, 4 December 2000, p. 3.

17 Greg Ogle, 'An Official Peace Movement: The Australian Reaction to French Nuclear Testing', *Social Alternatives*, 15, 3, July 1996, pp. 31-34.

18 Andrew Rojecki, *Silencing the Opposition: Antinuclear Movements and the Cold War*, University of Illinois Press, Urbana and Chicago, 1999.

19 Adele Horin speculates on the range of unclear motives for marching in her 'How the city of success has hardened its heart', *SMH*, 3 July 2000, p. 43. On the meaning of reconciliation: Editorial, 'A walk across the bridge', *SMH*, 27 May 2000, p. 48. On the suggestions concerning a 'Council of Unity', see the letter of Margaret Gunter, *SMH*, 27 May 2000, p. 48. On the view that the march did not embody support for a treaty: Editorial, 'Treaty is the hard edge reconciliation', *Australian*, 31 May 2000, p. 12. The quote is from Peter Yu, 'Walk to show we can bridge differences', *SMH*, 25 May 2000, p. 21.

20 The political auction metaphor and the reference to an estimate of 100 000 is in Malcolm Knox, 'The madding crowd', *SMH*, 3 June 2000, p. 34. For the citation of a supporter estimate of 600 000 and an argument that this does not represent the 'majority of Australians', see Padriac P McGuinness, 'Failing to bridge the gap', *SMH*, 1 June 2000, p. 19.

21 Deborah Brooks, '300,000 Australians say, "We Care"', *Peace Action*, 50, April 1986, p. 8. On the massive organisational labour required for Moratorium-like events, see Beverly Symons, 'Australian Action for Peace: the challenge ahead', *Social Alternatives*, 1, 6–7, June 1980, pp. 113-17.

22 Helen J Dodd, *Pauline: The Hanson Phenomenon*, Boolarong Press, Moorooka, Qld, 1997, p. 1. On the reprinting of the speech: John Pasquarelli, *The Pauline Hanson Story: by the Man Who Knows*, New Holland, Sydney, 1998, p. 134.

23 The quote is from Dodd, *Pauline*, p. 50. On media coverage statistics, see: 'Appendix A', Phillip Adams and Lee Burton (eds), *Talkback: Emperors of the Air:*

A Snapshot of Australian Society, Allen & Unwin, Sydney, 1997, and on Alan Jones solicitation of phone calls, see p. 220–21.
24 Malcolm Farr, '800 callers back Hanson', *Daily Telegraph*, 12 September 1996, p. 9.
25 On the role of opinion polls in creating the appearance of media dialogue, see McKenzie Wark, *Virtual Geography: Living with Global Media Events*, Indiana University Press, Bloomington and Indianapolis, 1994, p. 25. On the Jones poll: Adams and Burton, *Talkback*, p. 227. On the 'Midday Show' poll: Pasquarelli, *The Pauline Hanson Story*, p. 153. On the Channel 7 poll: 'Support Rises', *Daily Telegraph*, 17 September 1996, p. 7. For the 'post-debate' poll: Jonathan Porter, 'Black, white and blue rinse backlash', *Daily Telegraph*, 17 September 1996, p. 7.
26 The Geoff Kitney article is 'The lesson in Pauline's perils', *SMH*, 13 September 1996, p. 11. It is cited in: Wayne Smith, 'My Secret Life', *Daily Telegraph*, 28 September 1996, p. 11; BA Santamaria, 'Beware the mass revolt', *Weekend Australian*, 21–22 September 1996, p. 22. The 'poll' is cited in: Tony Abbott, 'Free Speech: A Test of Leadership', *Weekend Australian*, 28–29 September 1996, p. 28; Jim McClelland, 'Trapped in a talkback time-warp', *SMH*, 23 September 1996, p. 13; Graham Richardson, 'It's a long way from sanctimonious to saintly', *Bulletin*, 24 September 1996, p. 37; Editorial, 'The battle for tolerance', *Age*, 16 September 1996, p. 10.
27 For example, Chalke's comments were cited favourably in 'Nation in revolt against political correctness', *Daily Telegraph*, 17 September 1996, p. 7; PP McGuinness, 'Intolerance of the enlightened', *Age*, 18 September 1996, p. 17; Marcus Priest and Jonathan Porter, 'Hanson support up amid bitter TV feud', *Courier-Mail*, 17 September 1996, p. 2.
28 The poll is cited in: Kerry-Anne Walsh, 'The Power of One', *Bulletin*, 5 November 1996, p. 24.
29 Premature predictions of One Nation dominance include Anthony Green, 'Elections become a new numbers game', *SMH*, 30 July 1998, p. 13; Pilita Clark, 'The party pooper', *SMH*, 1 August 1998, p. 41. On the re-emergence of racism: Jim McClelland, 'Trapped in a talkback time-warp', *SMH*, 23 September 1996, p. 13. On racist abuse: Nigel Vincent, 'Asian leaders brace for racist groundswell', *Daily Telegraph*, 14 October 1996, p. 4; Michael Millett and Greg Roberts, 'PM unable to deliver knockout to Hanson', *SMH*, 8 May 1997, p. 7; Marcia Langton, 'Pauline as the thin end of the wedge' in Phillip Adams (ed.), *The Retreat from Tolerance*, ABC Books, Sydney, 1997, p. 103. On the importance of these meetings, see Peter Boyle, 'Who is behind Pauline Hanson's racist offensive?', *Green-Left Weekly*, 30 April 1997.
30 The data on anti-Hanson contention are drawn from reports in various newspapers: *SMH*, *Age*, *Australian*, and *Green-Left Weekly* were read comprehensively. Supplementary searches were carried out in *Daily Telegraph*, *Canberra Times*, *West Australian*, *Adelaide Advertiser*, *Canberra Times*, *Illawarra Mercury* and *Courier-Mail*. Reports of contention were catalogued, entered on a database, and coded. I would not claim total comprehensiveness. The sources used are likely to contain a bias towards the major cities, especially along the East Coast, and to those more newsworthy events that involve disruption of some kind. Events in non-metropolitan locations, or events that did not involve disruption, are likely to be under-represented to some extent. This is only partly countered by the selective use of the *West Australian* and the *Adelaide Advertiser*. The comprehensive use of *Green-Left Weekly* is likely to counter the political selection of the mainstream

newspapers, but, conversely, to overselect those events that involve the Democratic Socialist Party or Resistance. Even given such bias, I would still claim that the variety of sources mean that the data represent a reasonably faithful reflection of the overall pattern of anti-Hanson contention. They contain, furthermore, a very faithful reflection of the 'mediatised', constructed anti-Hanson campaign that readers of the press would have received.

31 See Murray Goot's tabular representation of party support as measured in opinion polls: M Goot, 'Hanson's Heartland: Who's for One Nation and Why'. In Nadine Davidoff (ed.), *Two Nations: The Causes and Effects of the Rise of the One Nation Party in Australia*, Melbourne, 1998, p. 56.

32 The quote is from Reihana Mohideen, interviewed in 'Hanson, racism and the far right', *Green-Left Weekly*, 14 May 1997. On the ability of protesters to outnumber Hansonites as a vindication of such political action, see protest organiser, Guenter Sahr — 'Protesters lay siege to Hanson Geelong Meeting', *SMH*, 19 July 1997; Iggy Kim, 'Hanson protesters outnumber supporters', *Green-Left Weekly*, 14 May 1997. Jim Remedio of the Dja Dja Wrung Aboriginal Association claimed that Hanson's popular rapport had been undermined after she sped away from a demonstration in Bendigo: Fegus Shiel, 'Hanson makes a run for it', *Age*, 22 July 1998. On the presence of non-Anglo-Australians at protests: David Langsam, 'Students to rally against "racist" views on campus', *SMH*, 12 October 1996; Greg Roberts, 'Hanson movement's national launch sunk', *SMH*, 9 January 1997; 'Hanson bucketed', *Sunday Telegraph*, 4 May 1997; 'They're out to get me: Hanson', *Australian Financial Review*, 6 May 1997; Tim Pegler, 'One Nation, Two Sets of Voices', *Age*, 6 May 1997; Belinda Parsons, 'Geelong Host to Rival Rallies With Hansonites the Losers', *Age*, 20 May 1997; 'Scheme to Swamp Hanson', *Sun-Herald*, 15 June 1997. The views of non-Anglo Australians on One Nation are cited in: Tim Pegler, 'One Nation, two sets of voices', *Age*, 6 May 1997; 'Violence feared at Hanson launch', *SMH*, 18 December 1996; Robyn Dixon, 'Leader flees as police and protesters fight', *SMH*, 23 July 1998; Fergus Shiel, 'Hanson makes run for it', *Age*, 22 July 1998. The idea that the demonstrations opposed racism is reproduced in such reports as: Judy Hughes, 'Tomatoes fly in the wild West', *Australian*, 5 May 1997; Tim Pegler, 'One Nation, two sets of voices', *Age*, 6 May 1997; Belinda Parsons, 'Geelong Host to Rival Rallies With Hansonites the Losers', *Age*, 20 May 1997; Elisabeth Wynhausen, 'Festival of diversity rejects Hanson', *Australian*, 19 May 1997. The idea that the forced closure of a One Nation meeting represented a victory for anti-racism over racism was expressed by a member of the International Socialist Organisation, cited in Amanda Phelan and Adam Harvey, 'Party Poopers', *SMH*, 10 July 1997.

33 This reflects Don Mitchell's claim that dissident groups often need to violate the norms of rational discourse in order to attain public representation: Don Mitchell, 'Political Violence, Order, and the Legal Construction of Public Space: Power and the Public Forum Doctrine', *Urban Geography*, 17, 2, 1996, pp. 152–78.

34 To take a by no means exhaustive case of each claim in turn: Editorial, 'Time for a fair go?', *Sunday Telegraph*, 1 June 1997; Don Chipp, 'Compo claims help Hanson', *Sunday Telegraph*, 22 June 1997; David McNicoll, 'Softly, softly catches One Nation monkey', *Bulletin*, 18 August 1998; Sushila Das, 'Fringe group behind Hanson meeting trouble, say Asians', *Age*, 11 July 1997; Scott Emerson and David Fagan, 'Protesters disrupt One Nation launch', *Australian*, 12–13 April 1997; 'Premier appeals for Hanson calm', *Age*, 2 June 1997.

35 On the case of the absence of demonstrations as a barometer of local support, see Nicholas Rothwell, 'Hanson finds not town quite like Cobar', *Australian*, 8 October 1997. The tendency of isolated actions to damage the overall anti-Hanson movement is mourned by a protest organiser, Maurice Sibelle, in Letter, *Age*, 9 July 1997.
36 For alternative accounts of Warburton's attack, see Kimina Lyall and Ben Hutchings, 'Hanson supporter injured in rally clash', *Australian*, 8 July 1997; Belinda Parsons, 'Violence erupts over One Nation', *Age*, 8 July 1997; Fergus Shiel, 'One Nation backers blame "criminals" for street attack', *Age*, 9 July 1997; Tim Hilferty, 'What a disgrace', *Daily Telegraph*, 8 July 1997; Claire Miller, 'I just wanted a few facts, says protest bash victim', *Age*, 10 July 1997; Mark Forbes, 'Shadowy revolutionaries behind the Hanson violence', *Sunday Age*, 13 July 1997.
37 On the doubtful motivations of protesters: Amanda Phelan and Adam Harvey, 'Party Poopers', *SMH*, 10 July 1997; Mark Forbes, 'Shadowy revolutionaries behind the Hanson violence', *Sunday Age*, 13 July 1997; Don Chipp, 'Stamp out this horror', *Sunday Telegraph*, 13 July 1997. On their framing as simply 'demonstrators' or 'protesters': 'Hanson supporters bombarded', *SMH*, 8 July 1997; 'Police arrest five in Hanson protest', *Australian Financial Review*, 8 July 1997; Kimina Lyall and Ben Hutchings, 'Hanson supporter injured in rally clash', *Australian*, 8 July 1997; Karen Middleton, 'Hanson's advice is to turn the other cheek', *Age*, 9 July 1997. Accounts that emphasise the role of "far-left" political parties include: Beatrice Faust, 'Left holding the liability', *Weekend Australian*, 19–20 July 1997; Gerard Henderson, 'Game of Consequences', *SMH*, 12 July 1997; Mark Forbes, 'Shadowy Revolutionaries Behind the Hanson Violence', *Sunday Age*, 13 July 1997; Miranda Devine, 'Not so spontaneous combustion', *Daily Telegraph*, 10 July 1997; Jamie Walker, 'Hanson Haters', *Weekend Australian*, 12–13 July 1997; Amanda Phelan and Adam Harvey, 'Party Poopers', *SMH*, 10 July 1997.
38 For an interesting account of the construction of Hanson and her supporters, focusing on her maiden parliamentary speech, see: Mark Rapley, "Just an ordinary Australian': self-categorization and the discursive construction of facticity in 'new racist' political doctrine', *British Journal of Social Psychology*, 37, 3, 1998, pp. 325–44.
39 The direct quote is from: Ross Couthart, 'Pauline Hanson and the Media', transcript of Sunday program at www.sunday.ninemsn.com.au/sun_covtrans.asp?id=409, viewed July 1998, page 1 of 11. A metaphorical account of the demonstration that emphasises the damage to democracy is James Button, 'Blood and Circuses', *Age*, 21 July 1997; Claire Miller, 'I just wanted a few facts, says protest bash victim', *Age*, 10 July 1997. An account that emphasises the decline of protest is Beatrice Faust, 'Left holding the liability', *Weekend Australian*, 19–20 July 1997.
40 The direct quote is from 'How we can defeat the racists', in *Resist*, 6, August 1997. An opinion poll indicating distaste for such demonstrations is *Morgan Poll* no. 1445, held 16/17 July 1997. A typical enunciation of fear by a moderate protester is Mr Phong Nguyen, in Sushila Das, 'Fringe group behind Hanson meeting trouble, say Asians', *Age*, 11 July 1997. More militant actors who admitted possible negative impacts include Paul True, former editor of *Militant*: Letter, 'Wrong to blame hard left for rally bashing', *Age*, 4 August 1998. Claims that such demonstrations fed support for One Nation were never proven, but were frequently made, e.g. Ron Boswell (Leader of National Party in Senate), Letter,

Australian, 16 July 1997; Mark Forbes, 'Shadowy Revolutionaries Behind the Hanson Violence', *Sunday Age*, 13 July 1997. The fear that disruption would 'play into the hands' of Hansonites was expressed by Emma Webb, 'How can we defeat Hanson?', *Green-Left Weekly*, 21 May 1997.

41 For claims concerning such events, see Judy Hughes, 'Tomatoes fly in wild west', *Australian*, 5 May 1997; 'Protesters lay siege to Hanson Geelong meeting', *SMH*, 19 July 1997; Claire Miller, 'Stay away call on Hanson meeting', *Age*, 14 July 1997; Julie Delvecchio, 'Two arrested at Hanson protest', *SMH*, 17 September 1997; Fiona Carruthers, 'Hanson-land: where the "little-battler" feels good', *Australian*, 17 September 1997.

42 Complaints on the coverage of demonstrations were enunciated in *ANNOD* — for the lack of focus on 'goons': 22 July 1997; for the omission of 'disgusting actions': 3 May 1997; for never airing violence: 12 April 1997. Hanson's claims concerning elite sponsorship of violence are reported in 'They're out to get me: Hanson', *Australian Financial Review*, 6 May 1997; 'Hanson accuses PM of inciting violence', *Sunday Age*, 11 May 1997.

43 The importance of the Web to ONP has been noted by McKenzie Wark, *Celebrities, Culture and Cyberspace: The Light on the Hill in a Postmodern World*, Pluto Press, Sydney, 1999, p. 30; Dennis Shanahan, 'Hanson aims to hold State power balance', *Weekend Australian*, 2–3 May, 1998. The claim concerning *ANNOD*'s circulation is made in the 3 September 1997 issue. The claims concerning the One Nation Party's website are made in *ANNOD*, 2 November 1998 and *ANNOD*, 9 September 1998. For website coverage of party meetings, see *ANNOD*, 5 April 1997 and 3 November 1997. For policy launches, see the launch of the One Nation firearms policy, *ANNOD*, 18 May 1998 and its tax policy, *ANNOD*, 25 August 1998. Movement publications such as *Pauline Hanson: The Truth* and *Pauline: the Hanson Phenomenon* were publicised and their sales reported in *ANNOD*, 3 May 1997; *ANNOD*, 17 November 1997 and *ANNOD*, 21 December 1997. The promotion of future media appearances happened, for example, in *ANNOD*, 15 April 1997. The opinion polls are critiqued in *ANNOD*, 14 November 1997. For critiques of media coverage, see *ANNOD*, 14 April 1997; *ANNOD*, 26 April 1997; *ANNOD*, 25 May 1997; *ANNOD*, 28 July 1997; *ANNOD*, 11 August 1998.

44 For first-person accounts of One Nation meetings, see *ANNOD*, 5 May 1997; *ANNOD*, 7 May 1997; *ANNOD*, 10 May 1997; *ANNOD*, 25 July 1997. The sound of the protest at the One Nation Party launch is reproduced in 'The protesters' at www.gwb.com.au/gwb/news/onenation/onenational1.html. For photos and personal profiles of influential protesters, see: 'Prosper Australia, Brisbane 4th October 1997' at www.gwb.com.au/gwb/news/bne. It was claimed that images posted on the Internet led to the arrest of three protesters for assault in *ANNOD*, 15 July 1997.

45 The direct quotation is from 'Making the News', Part 2, 'The left-wing extremist protesters — *Beazely's bovver boys* — Left Link:' is at gwb.com.au/gwb/news/four/2html viewed July 1998. For Balson's analysis of the Newcastle rally, see *ANNOD*, 31 May 1997. For the critique of the Liberal Party and the ALP concerning Dandenong, see *ANNOD*, 9 July 1997.

46 The Balson claim is discussed in Matthew Franklin, 'Vanstone hits out at Hanson', *Courier-Mail*, 11 July 1997, p. 2. Balson's frustration is expressed in 'Making the News', Part 2, 'The Dandenong incident, 8th July 1997: at gwb.com.au/gwb/news/four/2html viewed July 1998.

47 The direct quote is from 'Making the News' introductory section, to be found on One Nation's site gwb.com.au/gwb/news/onenation/newsint.html July 1998. For Balson's views on the ability of the Internet to involve the end of 'the mass media' and the rise of alternative interpretations, see *ANNOD*, 7 May 1998.

48 For the petition on timed local calls, *ANNOD*, 11 April 1997. For a discussion on the Hanson movement's opposition to the Multilateral Agreement on Investment, and a discussion of the contribution of the Internet, see *ANNOD*, 30 April 1998. The phone-in campaign concerning Telstra was publicised by Ray Platt, 'Message from the editor of "The Strategy"', *ANNOD*, 14 July 1998. On the Liberal Party petition, *ANNOD*, 2 November 1997 and 3 November 1997. On the exclusion of the ONP from websites, *ANNOD*, 4 August 1997; *ANNOD*, 30 August 1997.

49 The Lateline response is reported in Leonie Lamont, 'Farmers say Asia markets put at risk', *SMH*, 10 May 1997, p. 6. On the jamming of the Channel Nine switchboard, *ANNOD*, 5 July 1998. For the listing of the 'The Australia/Israel Review', see *ANNOD*, 10 July 1998. Mark Leibler's details were supplied in 'Who are these extremist zionists at the Australia/Israel Review?', *ANNOD*, 14 July 1998. For instructions to contact the Australian Press Council, *ANNOD*, 3 July 1998. For the 'call to arms' against *Sixty Minutes* see *ANNOD*, 7 June 1998, *ANNOD*, 8 June 1998; *ANNOD*, 17 June 1998.

50 For the boycott of Jet Set, *ANNOD*, 12 July 1998. For the boycott of Qantas, *ANNOD*, 10 July 1998. For the boycott of Toyota, *ANNOD*, 8 June 1998.

51 Margo Kingston, 'Release of Hanson itinerary may be a matter of tactics', *SMH*, 31 August 1998, p. 9. Of course, the ability of the itinerary to act as a magnet for protests was seriously eroded in practice by One Nation's failure to adhere to it. The organisational lapses and neglect of itineraries are noted in Kingston's interesting book *Off the Rails: The Pauline Hanson Trip*, Allen & Unwin, Sydney, 1999, esp. p. 23.

52 For the photographs of apparent calls to violence see 'Brian Webb, protest organiser, reveals the violence behind the Brisbane Anti-Racism Committee', at www.gwb.com.au/gwb/news/bne/six.html. The leaked 'conspiracy' is 'Transcript of an Intelligence report received 15th July 1997 by One Nation', at www.gwb.com.au/gwb/news/onenation/scoop1.html. The account of the 'conspiracy' is in Part 3 of 'Making the News', 'Getting media to pick up the stories', at www.gwb.com.au/gwb.news/four/3.html, viewed July 1998. The take-up of the story by Sattler and by others is reflected on in *ANNOD*, 17 July 1997.

53 Editorial, 'Hansonitis', *SMH*, 27 November 1997, p. 22. The story of the video is narrated in: Tony Wright and Greg Roberts, 'MPs pour scorn on Hanson video', *SMH*, 26 November 1997, p. 10.

54 The activist quoted is Melba Marginson, in: Ben Hutchings, 'One Nation never far away', *Australian* 15 July 1997. For advance publicity: Jacqui McArthur, 'Manly braces for Hanson Brawl', *Sun-Herald*, 18 May 1997; Carolyn Jones, 'One Student, Divided Nation', *Age*, 24 June 1998. For positive reporting: Carolyn Collins, 'Race Debate Splits Hanson City', *Australian*, 3 March 1997; Richard Guilliatt, 'Clans Claim the Corso in Hanson Protest', *SMH*, 19 May 1997.

55 For example, this was the case for rallies held in Geelong, Adelaide and Newcastle — Belinda Parsons, 'Geelong host to rival rallies with Hansonites the losers', *Age*, 20 May 1997; Andrew Ramsay and Matthew Abraham, 'Fists fly as Hanson spreads doctrine', *Australian*, 12 June 1997; Nathan Vass and Julie Delvecchio, '1200 supporters, 4000 protesters and 350 police. Is this One Nation?', *SMH*, 31 May 1997.

56 For Werribee: 'Three held for assault on Hanson supporter', *Australian*, 15 July 1997; for Newcastle: Brian Woodley, 'Thousands turn out to praise or heckle Hanson', *Australian*, 31 May–1 June 1997; for Adelaide: Andrew Ramsay and Matthew Abraham, 'Fists fly as Hanson spreads doctrine', *Australian*, 12 June 1997.
57 Edward Johnstone, 'Meeting discusses how to beat Hanson', *Green-Left Weekly*, 1 July 1998.
58 The range and flavour of actions is captured in Jo Williams and Reuben Endean, 'Victorian secondary students strike against Hanson', *Green-Left Weekly*, 1 July 1998; Keara Courtney and Becky Fairall Lea, 'High-School students arrested at anti-Hanson rally', *Green-Left Weekly*, 8 July 1998; Sean Healy, '"We will not go way [*sic*] until racism does!"', *Green-Left Weekly*, 7 November 1998.
59 The direct quote is Reuben Endean, cited in Lisa Macdonald, 'Not too young to fight racism', *Green-Left Weekly*, 22 July 1998. The opposition of headmasters in Canberra is noted in: Jordie Collins, 'Canberra high-school walkout against One Nation', *Green-Left Weekly*, 8 July 1997. The support of a private school is sympathetically assayed in Carolyn Jones, 'It's this school's principle to take a uniform stand against racism', *Age*, 1 August 1998. Examples of commentary and analysis include Belinda Parsons, 'Young and Angry', *Age*, 29 June 1998; Janet McCalman, 'Schools lead the war on racism', *Age*, 5 August 1998; Stephanie Peatling, 'PolitiKids', *SMH*, 10 August 1998; PP McGuinness, 'Youth and naivety an attractive front', *SMH*, 9 July 1998; Murray Hogarth, 'Young, organised, and out there', *SMH*, 11 July 1998; Piers Akerman, 'David's Over the Hill', *Sunday Telegraph*, 9 August 1998. The 'conscience of the nation' quote is from Sue Williams, 'Future in safe hands', *Sun-Herald*, 5 July 1998. The estimates of support and the specific reference to the Deputy-Lord Mayor is found in John Percy, 'Youth in Revolt: The '60s and Today', *Green-Left Weekly*, 19 August 1998.
60 This account of Pantsdown is drawn from McKenzie Wark, *Celebrities, Culture and Cyberspace*, pp. 249–50; Helen Basili, 'Appeal rejected in battle of the Paulines', *Green-Left Weekly*, 7 October 1998, p. 6; James Smith, 'Pantsdown: political protest through satire', *Green-Left Weekly*, 30 September 1998, p. 27. The direct quote from Hunt is from the latter. David Marr's appraisal is in his 'Little Johnny's little helper', *SMH*, 7 August 2000, p. 15.
61 Albie Thoms, 'The Videosphere', *Tharunka*, 3 August 1971, p. 12.
62 Craig Calhoun, 'Community without Propinquity Revisited: Communications Technology and the Transformation of the Urban Public Sphere', *Sociological Inquiry*, 68, 3, 1998, pp. 373–74. On the ability of the already powerful to constrain the political impact of the Internet, see Tim Jordan, *Cyberpower: The Culture and Politics of Cyberspace and the Internet*, Routledge, London and New York, 1999, p. 167. On corporate penetration, see Jay Kinney, 'Is There a New Political Paradigm Lurking in Cyberspace?', in Ziauddin Sardar and Jerome R Ravetz (eds), *Cyberfutures: Culture and Politics on the Information Superhighway*, New York University Press, 1996, pp. 149, 152. On the promise of cyberdemocracy for the development of new identities, see SP Wilbur, 'An Archaeology of Cyberspaces: virtuality, community, identity', in David Porter (ed.), *Internet Culture*, Routledge, New York and London, 1997, p. 12; for decentralised dialogue and the challenging of hierarchies: Mark Poster, 'Cyberdemocracy: Internet and the Public Sphere', in Porter, *Internet Culture*, pp. 210–13.
63 Recent work in cultural geography has emphasised the coexistence of the 'virtual' and the 'real' in a spatial sense, and has even questioned the notion that an

'authentic' reality exists in contradistinction to the 'virtual' at all. See Marcus A Doel and David B Clarke, 'Virtual Worlds: Simulation, Suppletion, S(ed)uction and Simulacra', in Mike Crang, Phil Crang and Jon May (eds), *Virtual Geographies: Bodies, Space and Relations*, Routledge, London and New York, 1999, pp. 261–83. For an analogous questioning of whether 'real' space can be contrasted with 'virtual' or 'electronic' space, see also Mike Crang, 'Public Space, Urban Space and Electronic Space: Would the Real City Please Stand Up?', *Urban Studies*, 37, 2, 2000, pp. 301–17. On the coexistence of 'old' and 'new' movement activity, see Calhoun, 'Community without Propinquity Revisited', p. 382.

64 See a fascinating study recently published: Manuel Castells, Shujiro Yazawa and Emma Kiselyara, 'Insurgents Against the Global Order: A Comparative Analysis of the Zapatistas in Mexico, the American Militia and Japan's AUM Shinrikyo', *Berkeley Journal of Sociology*, 40, 1995–96. Balson's claims on the cyberbattle were discussed earlier in this chapter.

65 The word 'mediatisation' is derived from Gianpietro Mazzoleni and Winfred Schulz, '"Mediatization" of Politics: A challenge for democracy?', *Political Communication*, 16, 3, 1999, pp. 247–62.

66 For an insistence on non-violence, see the article by Vanessa Walker, Ben Mitchell and Guy Healy, 'The www.protest survival guide', *Australian*, 30 August 2000, p. 5. For letters, see David Roser, James Slezak and Tim Roxburgh in *SMH*, 30 August 2000, p. 17 and Phil Davey, Jenny Ryde and David Ash, *SMH*, 6 September 2000, p. 17. The S11 website is www.s11.org. The Melbourne indyBulletin is at www.melbourne.indymedia.org. For the non-violence of Seattle, see *indyBulletin*, 28 August 2000, p. 1. For the rights of protesters, *indyBulletin*, 4 September 2000, p. 3.

67 On the Nike hacking, 'Hackers Strike At Nike', *Herald-Sun*, 26 June 2000, p. 9; Rebecca Payne and Cecilia Leung, 'Fight Back', in *SMH*, E)MAG, September 2000, pp. 18–22. The reference to the Melbourne Festival website is in Vaughan Palz, 'Front Row', *Herald-Sun*, 15 August 2000, p. 67.

68 For the threat of legal action: Kathleen Cuthbertson, 'Farnham acts on protesters', *Herald-Sun*, 24 August 2000, p. 2. For the S11 refusal to comply: 'The Voice Stays On-Line', *Daily Telegraph*, 25 August 2000, p. 18. On Wheatley's fears: Mark Dunn and Kathleen Cuthbertson, 'Radicals Lure Kids', *Herald-Sun*, 25 August 2000, p. 1. The flood of letters and discussion is under 'John Farnham tries to sue S11' at the indymedia site. The S11 defence of the song as the 'people's anthem' is cited in Toni O'Loughlin, 'Whispering Jack speaks out as radicals try to hijack his Voice', *SMH*, 25 August 2000, p. 3. For the Ross Wilson offer, Ben Mitchell, 'Daddy Cool Sings Praises of Protest', *Australian*, 31 August 2000, p. 5. For the claim of inadvertent public attention, see 'Divisions in s11 over anthem', *indyBulletin*, 28 August 2000, p. 2. The claims concerning the sites popularity are sourced to the *Australian Financial Review*, 16 September 2000, and reproduced at: www.s11.org. Reported hit rates for websites are unverifiable.

69 For an account of media coverage at the time, see Peter Wilmoth, 'Violence has media seeing blood', *Age*, 13 September 2000. The details of media coverage of the protest, and protester counter-tactics are discussed in Kurt Iveson and Sean Scalmer, 'Contesting the Inevitable: Notes on S11', *Overland*, 161, 2000, pp. 4–12. Video footage of apparent police harassment is in *Channel Seven News*, Sydney late edition, 12 September 2000. A picture by Tandy Cameron of the protester hit by a car accompanies the article by Michael Bachelard, 'Three days of anger end under wheels of justice', *Australian*, 14 September 2000, p. 1. The

direct account of the protest by S11 activist 'Rob' is in *indyBulletin*, 12 September 2000, p. 2. For evidence on violence against protesters, see 'Lawyers gather evidence over baton charges', at www.melbourne.indymedia.org. The announcement of an inquiry by the Ombudsman is in Peter Mickelburough and Mark Dunn, 'Police Protest Probe', *Herald-Sun*, 15 September 2000, p. 17. For the partial retreat of the Victorian Premier, and a decision to cancel a barbeque of thanks for police, see '"Spineless" Bracks Calls Off Barbie', *Canberra Times*, 23 September 2000, p. 3. For an example of positive treatment of later, more moderate protests concerning globalisation, see Malcolm Brown, 'Protesters seek fair play for the world's poor', *SMH*, 19 September 2000, p. 4. In June 2001, the Ombudsman found that in most cases the police acted rightly.

INDEX

Aarons, Brian 51
Abbott, Tony 152
Aboriginal activists
   criticism of Aboriginal organisations 88–9
   and the Left 130, 131–2
   methods 19–20
   mobilisation 27, 81–2, 91–2
   at the Moratorium marches 86
   and Whitlam dismissal protests 138
   see also Black Moratorium, land rights
Aboriginal Tent Embassy 98–9
abortion 92–3
activism, sites of 57–62 see also specific sites
Adelaide University
   Miss Fresher contest protest 32, 87
Age 152
Aid to National Liberation Front Committee 51–2
Aldermaston marches 12
Althusser, Louis 110, 122
Altman, Dennis 71, 92, 93, 95, 131
Americans, Baby 66–7
Aminzade, Ronald 63
Amos, Leonard 84
AMR: Quantum Harris 152
anti-disciplinary politics 34
anti-Hanson movement

   autonomous gatherings 166–8
   comparison with Moratorium marches 143, 176
   contestational gatherings 154–5
   and Far Left parties 158–9
   media coverage of 156–60, 161, 168
   mobilisation of 153–4
   multiculturalism 166–7
   racism, opposition to 155, 158
   sites of protest 154–5
   student protests 167–8
   use of parody 169–70
   violent nature of 156–60, 165
   see also Hanson, Pauline; One Nation Party
Anzac Day protests 93–4
apartheid protests see South African sporting tours protests
Arena
   Communist Party of Australia 128, 129, 135
   contemporary international theory 117–8, 121–3
   cultural studies 131–2, 133
   labour movement 125, 128
   Marxism 112–20, 122, 127, 128, 133, 134–5
   as a small enterprise 133
   social movements 123–5

social theory 112, 118, 134–5
student activism 120, 123–5
Arena thesis 125–34 *see also* intellectuals
arrest, as a tactic 51, 53, 71
Askin, Bob 47, 48, 59, 146
Association for Love and Freedom 33, 34
Australia/Israel Review 163–4
Australian 147, 164, 173
Australian Council of Salaried and Professional Associations 17
Australian Council of Trade Unions 89–90, 145
Australian Labor Party
  1966 electoral defeat 50
  student opposition to 51
  website linked to Far Left groups 162
  see also Whitlam Government
Australian Landfall 3, 4
Australian National News of the Day
  linking the ALP to Far Left sites 162
  on One Nation Party meetings 161
  public opinion campaigns 163–5
  size of readership 161
  on violence of anti-Hanson protesters 165
  see also Balson, Scott
Australian National University
  Miss ANU Competition 87
  teach-ins 44
Australian New Left 128
Australian Student Christian Movement 19
Australian Union of Students
  oppression within 84
  racism within 88
  support for Whitlam Government 137–8
autonomous actions
  anti-Hanson movement 166–8
  prevalence 56–7
  tactics and strategy 61
Bacon, Wendy 84
Bailey, Harry, Dr. 96
Baker, JS 17
Baldwin, James 19
Balson, Scott 161–3, 165, 170–1
Bandler, Faith 82, 97
Barker, Greg 4, 6
Bassett, Jan 144–5
beauty contests 32, 77, 87
Bell, Terry 96
Bertha Blither's Adventures in Czechoslovakia 2
Bishop, Julie 138

Black Guards 33–4
Black Moratorium 77–8
Black Muslims 33
Black Power 88–9
Blainey, Geoffrey 143
Blake, Jack 129
Bonsall-Boone, Peter 95
Bottomley, Bill 50
Bracks, Steve 173
Brisbane Anti-Racism Campaign 165
Brooks, Deborah 149
Bryant, Gordon 99
Builders Labourers' Federation 100, 138
Bulletin 152–3
Cairns, Jim 143
Calhoun, Craig 170
Cameron, Jim 95
Campaign Against Moral Persecution 95
Campaign for Nuclear Disarmament 12, 13, 51
cannabis legislation protests 32
Carley, Kathleen 113
CBS News 18
censorship protests 63
Certeau, Michel de 61–2
Chabot, Sean 12
Chalk, David 152
Channel, Ian 33–5
Channel Seven 151–2
civil disobedience 12, 46, 51, 52–3
civil rights movement 14–18, 28
class
  analysis 119, 124, 127, 136
  and new social movements 131–2, 135
  oppression 83
Cloward, Richard 63
Coe, Paul 86
Cold War 42–3, 73
Collingburn, Neil 58
Committee of 100 12
Communist Party of Australia
  authority of Marxism 116
  criticism of 129, 135
  denial of right to protest 73
  interpretation of Paris 1968 129, 135
  and marches 43
  role of women within 88
Conference-Ville 89
Congress Against War and Fascism 1, 2
Congress for International Co-operation and Disarmament 50
content analysis 113
contentious politics 2
contestational actions

anti-Hanson movement 154–5
and democratic norms 55–6, 62
prevalence 56–7, 65
student movement 50, 54, 55
tactics and strategy 61–2
Cook, Gary 68
Counihan, Terry 109–10, 122
Cresswell, Tim 63
Crux 19
culture
and class analysis 131–2
sociological analysis of 111
Cutler, Roden, Sir 73
cyberbattle 10, 163, 170–1, 177 *see also*
Internet
cycle of protest 39–40
Czechoslovakian protesters 64
Daily Mirror 138–40
Dalton, Dorothy 43
death penalty demonstrations 13, 48
Della Porta, Donatella 54
democracy
effects of protests on 42, 62, 72–4
impact of the internet on 170
Democracy and Disorder 39
Deutsche, Rosalyn 73
dilemmas of the activist 41, 71–2,
140–1, 156–7, 171, 176
disruptive actions
anti-Hanson movement 156–60
definitions of 63–5
effectiveness 69
prevalence of 65–6
Dodd, Helen 150, 151
draft resisters 52–3, 59, 62–3, 67–9
draft card burning 4, 5, 6, 7, 11, 12,
29, 46, 92, 147
see also Vietnam War movement
Embassy for Aboriginal people *see*
Aboriginal Tent Embassy
Endean, Reuben 168
Eunuchwarbler, Glorfindal 79
Eureka miners' strike 6
Eureka Youth League 5
Exam Resister's Movement 76
Eyerman, Ron 133
Fairlea Five 83
Farnham, John 172
Fear of Freedom 33
Federal Council For the Advancement of
Aborigines and Torres Strait
Islanders 82, 97
feminism *see* women's movement
Feminist Action Front 93
Fire Next Time 19

flag burning 46, 50
Ford, Bill 22
Fraser, Malcolm 137
Fraser, Nancy 35
Freedom Ride
impact 25–7, 81–2
influences 14, 21–3, 29 39, 171
land rights 23–4
media coverage 22–3, 24–5, 26
violent reactions to 43–4
see also Student Action For Aborigines
French social theory 122–3
Freney, Denis 61, 86
Fromm, Eric 33
Gay and Lesbian Mardi Gras 96–7
gay and lesbian movement
influences 78
and the Left 130–2
and May Day marches 77, 87
mobilisation 91, 95–7
and the student movement 87–8
Gay Pride 96
gender segregation 94–5
Gandhi, Mahatma 51
Gerster, Robin 144–5
Giffney, Patricia 78–9
Gitlin, Todd 72
globalisation protests *see* S11 Alliance;
World Trade Organisation protests
Goffman, Erving 35, 50
Golding, Phil 68
Goodall, Heather 97
Gordon Institute of Technology 77
Gorton, John 52–3
Gould, Bob 45, 46
Gramsci, Antonio 110, 117, 122
Grass, Silas 67, 79–80
Gray, Colin 96
guerrilla theatre 33
Gulf War protests 143, 144, 176
Habermas, Jurgen 133
Hamel-Green, Michael 51, 67
Handelman, Don 36
Hanford, Bruce 141
Hanson, Pauline
debate with Charles Perkins 152
debate with Pauline Pantsdown 169
maiden parliamentary speech 149–53,
164
opinion of opposition to 161
support for 150–3
see also anti-Hanson movement; One
Nation Party
Harrison, Gillian 19
Harvest of Fear 146

Hawke, Bob 89
Haylen Wayne 4, 6, 7
Herald-Sun 143
Hiroshima Commemoration walk for peace 13
Holt, Harold 43, 45
homophobia 84, 88
Honi Soit
    Commemoration Day protests 16–17, 18
    racial discrimination 19
    sexism of 87
    student movement 12
    Women's Studies 79
Horne, Donald 144
Howard, John 153, 168
Howells, AF 2, 3
Hughes, Tom 59, 95–6
Hunt, Simon 169
I Don't Like It 169
I'm a Backdoor Man 169
industrial action 36, 37
Industrial Workers of the World 9
indyBulletin 171–2, 173
indymedia group *see indyBulletin*
innovation 45, 66, 80, 176
intellectuals
    and labour movement 127
    as social actors 111, 123, 125
    support for *Arena* thesis 129–30
    theorisation of 119, 126, 133, 135
    and Vietnam War movement 127
    see also Arena thesis
International Homosexual Day 96
Internet
    impact on democracy 170
    impact on political action 8, 9–10, 135
    impact on the mass media 163
    use by Pauline Hanson supporters 161–6
    use by S11 Alliance 171–2, 173
    see also cyberbattle
Intervention 133
Jennings, Kate 85, 86
Jensen, Nadine 31
Johnson, Lyndon 46–8, 50
Jorgensen, Justus 59
Jorgensen, Sebastian 59
Jones, Alan 151, 152
Kensell, Harry 140
Kerr, John 137
Kertzer, David 36, 55, 69
King, Martin Luther, Jr 22, 24, 25, 28, 51
Kingston, Margo 165

Kirsner, Douglas 109–10
Kisch, Egon Erwin 1–4, 5–6, 11
Kitney, Geoff 152
Koestler, Arthur 117
labour movement 81, 87–8, 125, 127
    see also trade unions
land rights 23–4, 32, 60, 97–100
Langer, Albert 33, 52
Langley, David 46
Langley, John 46
Langton, Marcia 32, 98
Leibler, Mark 164
Leyden, Mike 12
Liberation Red Cross *see* National Liberation Front
Life 18
living theatre 33, 34
Lonely Crowd 33–4
Mao, Zedong 33, 72
map analysis 113, 134
Marchant, John 5
Marcuse, Herbert 33, 56, 117, 122
Marr, David 169
Marxism
    and *Arena* 112–20, 122, 127, 128, 133
    and the Communist Party of Australia 116
    decline of 111, 115–8, 134–5
Matta, Roberto da 63–4
May Day marches 77, 87
McAdam, Doug 12, 24–5
McClelland, James 138
McDonald, Bob 12, 15
McLean, Jean 74
McLuhan, Marshall 33, 34
McMahon, William 59, 68, 98
McQueen, Humphrey 49, 124–5
media coverage 41–3, 45
    of anti-Hanson protests 157–60, 168
    bias of 140, 164, 173–4 *see also* News Limited
    of draft card burning 5
    effect on political activity 8, 67, 72
    of Freedom Ride 22–3, 24–5, 26
    of Kisch action 2, 3
    of Lyndon Johnson protests 47
    of nuclear testing protests 143–4, 147, 149
    of Palm Sunday rallies 144, 147, 149
    of Pauline Hanson 150–3
    of S11 protests 173
    of reconciliation marches 144, 147–8
    use of by activists 4, 7, 33–4
    of Vietnam War protests 48–9, 142–4
    see also dilemmas of the activist

mediatised politics 8, 171, 174–7
Mejane 87
Melbourne Rising 173
Melrose, Robin 5
Menzies, Robert Gordon 1, 2, 3
Midday Show 151
Middleton, Peter 49
Mill, John Stuart 72
Mohideen, Reihana 155
Monash University 33, 68
  Labor Club 50
  teach-ins 44
Moorhouse, Frank 47, 66–7, 89
Moratorium marches 37, 67, 70, 84, 85
  achievements of 146
  aims of 145–6
  comparisons with other protests 142–6, 176
  media representation of 142, 145
  methods adopted by other movements 77–8
  myth-making 144–6
  reaction to 145–6
  reported size of 143–4
  see also Vietnam War movement
Morgan, Patrick 78, 79
Morison, Lin 19
Morrison, Ian 56
Movement Against War and Fascism 3
Mullen, Geoff 67
Murdoch press *see* News Limited
Murphy, John 146
My Lai massacre 67
National Aborigines Day *see* Black Moratorium
National Liberation Front 51–2, 54, 124–5
National Tribal Council 89
National U 78, 84, 87–8 109
New Left Review 122
News Limited
  coverage of Whitlam government dismissal 139, 140
  protests against 138–42, 171
No Soul 172
Noonuccal, Oodgeroo 20
nuclear testing rallies 146–9
O'Shea, Chris 76
O'Shea, Clarrie 124
occupation of university buildings 68
Oldfield, David 169
On Dit 70
One Nation Party
  formation of 153
  media coverage of 159, 160

public meetings 156–9, 161, 164–5
support for 154, 159
website 150, 161
see also anti-Hanson movement; Hanson, Pauline
opinion polls 151–3
Osmond, Warren 56, 124, 128
Owens, Ken 140
Palm Sunday rallies 144, 146–9
Pantsdown, Pauline 169–70
Paris 1968 51, 120–2, 124, 133, 134, 135
parliament buildings, protests at 57, 68
Pauline Hanson Story 150
Pauline Hanson: The Truth 150
Pauline: The Hanson Phenomenon 150
passive resistance 21–2, 23, 28
peace movement
  British 13
  coverage in *Arena* 123–5
  decline in activity 50
  internal disputes 49
  and new social movements 79, 81
  oppression within 88
  World War II 1–4
  see also Vietnam War movement
People and Place 152
People For Nuclear Disarmament 143–4
People's Liberation Army 59–60, 68
People's Walk *see* reconciliation marches
Perkins, Charles 22, 24, 25–6, 99, 152
Perry, Barry 173
Piven, Frances Fox 63
police
  conflict with protesters 41–2, 48, 54, 64, 66
  protection of protesters 44
  violence against gay activists 96
  violence during Commemoration Day protests 17
  violence during S11 protests 173
political correctness 150, 152
Practice of Everyday Life 61–2
Presentation of Self in Everyday Life 35
Pringle, Bob 138, 139
Printing and Kindred Industries Union 138, 140
private spaces, protests at 37, 59–60, 80
professional protesters 49
protests, size of 143–4, 148–9
public spaces, depoliticisation 73
Pyatt II, Charlie 18
Queensland Times 165
racial segregation 23, 25, 27 82
racism 19, 20, 91 *see also* anti-Hanson

INDEX • 217

movement
radicalesbians 95 *see also* gay and lesbian movement
radio talkback hosts 150–3, 165
rape 92–4
reconciliation marches 144, 146–9
repressive tolerance 56
revolutionary action, cult of 66
Revolutionary Kidney Punch 47
Richardson, Graham 152
Riesman, David 33
right to protest 48, 73–4, 141
road safety demonstrations 13
Robinson, Barry 4, 5, 6, 7
Robinson, Harry 47
Romeril, John 33
role-playing 35
Rothenbuhler, Eric 36
Rowley, Kelvin 109–10, 122
Russell, Bertrand 12, 13
S11 Alliance
   aims 171
   comparison with Vietnam Moratorium Movement 143, 176
   media coverage of 173–4
   protest anthem 172
   violence of protests 173
   website 171–2, 173
Santamaria, BA 152
Sattler, Howard 165
Save Our Sons 5, 74, 82–3
Savo, Mario 117
Seattle 1999 *see* World Trade Organisation protests
Seeger, Peter 14, 15
Sewell, WH, Jr. 121
sex education 9–3
sexism 79, 87–8, 89–91
sexual violence *see* rape
Sharp, Geoff 126, 127, 129–30, 131, 132
Sharp, Nonie 129
Shearston, Gary 19
Short, Penny 95
Sharpeville massacre demonstrations 13
Shnookal, Deb 93
sin-ins 63
sit-ins 20, 27–8, 29, 36, 52–3, 62
Situationist International 9
Sixty Minutes 164
Slessor, Kenneth 2
Snedden, Billy 67, 145
social interaction 35
social theory
   Australian 134

transformation of 111
within *Arena* 112, 117–8, 121–3
socialist society 130
Socialist Youth Alliance 84
sociological analysis of culture 111
sociology of knowledge 111, 134
South African sporting tours, protests 59
   cricket team tours 13, 69
   Springbok Rugby tours 69, 71, 78
   swimming 31
Spigelman, Jim 21, 22, 23, 72
sports stadiums, protests at 58
Springbok Rugby tours *see under* South African sporting tours, protests
Starrs, Frank 70
Stephens, Julie 34
Stock Exchange protests 60–1, 138
Strathaird 1
street theatre 9, 33
Student Action For Aborigines 21–7, 43–4, 82, 97, 99–100
student movement
   anti-Hanson activists 167–8
   comparisons with Vietnam War movement 142–3
   conservative nature of 142
   coverage in *Arena* 120, 123–5
   diffusion of causes 79, 81
   homophobia of 88
   influences 12–13, 14, 19–25, 51
   internal disputes 49
   oppression within 84–5, 88
   radical activists 50–1, 56, 67–9, 72, 74
   relations with police 54, 64
   support for Aboriginal rights 19–20 *see also* Freedom Ride; Student Action for Aborigines
   theoretical analysis within 109–10
   Vietnam War protests 45, 168
Students for Democratic Action 48
Students for a Democratic Society 12, 33, 109–10
Student Non-Violent Co-ordinating Committee 21
suffragettes 9
Sunday Mirror 138–40
Sunday Telegraph 138–40
Sydney Gay Liberation 77
Sydney Morning Herald
   Aboriginal workers' strike 81
   anti-conscription protests 53
   contestational actions 72
   Freedom Ride 44
   Kisch demonstrations 3

Pauline Hanson 152, 165
reconciliation marches 148
Springboks Rugby tour protests 78
women activists 83
Sydney Sun 78–9
tactical innovation 39–40, 41, 51, 65
Tarrow, Sidney 12, 39, 63, 80
teach-ins 44, 54
television 33, 34
Tharunka 49, 67
Thesis Eleven 134
theorisation 110
theoretical change 111
theory production 111, 133
This Day Tonight 67
Thoms, Albie 170
Tilly, Charles 37, 57
trade unions
  reaction to Moratorium marches 145
  reaction to News Limited protests 140
  and student movement 76–7
  sexism of 88–90
  see also labour movement
tram drivers 76
transformative events 121
Tree Liberation 77
Understanding Media 33
United Front 65
University of Melbourne
  Draft Resistance siege 67
  Exam Resisters Movement 76
University of New England
  Greek military dictatorship protests 32
University of New South Wales
  Black Guards 33–4
  university wizard 34
University of Sydney
  Commemoration Day protests 15–17, 29, 81
  teach-ins 44
  Women's Studies 78–9, 84–5
Uren, Tom 138
US Civil Rights Bill 15
Victorian State Government 171, 173
video
  impact on democracy 170
  use by Pauline Hanson 165
  use by S11 protesters 173
Vietnam Action Committee 45
Vietnam War movement 31–2, 43, 45–9
  and Aboriginal activists 86
  anti-conscription protests 4–7, 45, 52–3
  decline in activity 50
  denial of right to protest 73–4

disruptive actions 45–6, 67–9
intellectuals involvement in 127
methods adopted by others 76–9
protests against private companies 60
protests at private residences 58–9
teach-ins 44
workers' involvement in 125
and women 82–3, 85
see also draft resisters; Moratorium marches; peace movement
violence
  of anti-Hanson protests 156–60
  in protests 49, 50, 141–2
  of S11 protests 173
  see also police
Walker, Kath *see* Noonuccal, Oodgeroo
Warburton, Keith 157
Watson, Len 89
Wentworth, John 69
wharf labourers 45
Wheatley, Glenn 172
White, Doug 52, 120, 126, 129
White, William 47
Whitlam, Gough 48, 139
Whitlam Government 132
  dismissal, protests against 137–8
  media coverage of dismissal 139, 140
Wilenski, Peter 12–13
Willett, Graham 96
Willmott, Deirdre 142
Wilson, Ross 172
Wizard of Christchurch 34
Women's International League for Peace and Freedom 43, 82
women's movement
  and the Left 83–9, 130–2
  methods 32, 78–9, 81, 82–3
  May Day marches 77, 87
  mobilisation 91–5
Women's Studies *see under* University of Sydney
Workers' Weekly 3
Working Papers' Group 134
World Economic Forum protests *see* S11 Alliance
World Trade Organisation protests 171–2
You're the Voice 172
Youth Campaign Against Conscription 4–5
youth culture 14–15
Yu, Peter 148